Collectible

Cups & Saucers

Identification & Values

BOOK III

Jim & Susan Harran

COLLECTOR BOOKS
A Division of Schroeder Publishing Co., Inc.

On the cover:

KPM Berlin demitasse cup and saucer.
c. 1870 – 1890.

Cover design by
Beth Summers

Book design by
Allan Ramsey

COLLECTOR BOOKS
P.O. Box 3009
Paducah, Kentucky 42002-3009
www.collectorbooks.com

Copyright © 2004 Jim and Susan Harran

The current values in this book should be used only as a guide. They
are not intended to set prices, which vary from one section of the country
to another. Auction prices as well as dealer prices vary greatly and are
affected by condition as well as demand. Neither the author nor the publisher assumes responsibility for any losses that might be incurred as a
result of consulting this guide.

Searching For A Publisher?

We are always looking for people knowledgeable within their fields. If
you feel that there is a real need for a book on your collectible subject and
have a large comprehensive collection, contact Collector Books.

CONTENTS

ACKNOWLEDGMENTS

First and foremost, we'd like to thank the members of the staff of Collector Books. If it had not been for our publisher Bill Schroeder, our editor Gail Ashburn, and her assistant Amy Hopper, this book would not have been possible. The staff at Collector Books is professional, talented, and always helpful.

We would like to express our appreciation to those collectors and dealers who so generously gave of their time and knowledge to make this book a reality. We are indebted to Mia and Hans Alphenaar of the Netherlands for sharing photographs of their wonderful miniature cup and saucer collection. Mia had all her miniatures carefully researched and cataloged, and we appreciate the professional quality of Hans' photography.

A special thank you to Lisa Cilli, of Hackensack, New Jersey, who shared so many photographs of her lovely collection of all types of cups and saucers. Lisa has fond memories of sharing a cup of tea with her grandmother and mother and has collected cups and saucers since she was 15 years old. The quality of her photographs was excellent.

Many thanks again to Brenda Pardee from Bloomville, New York. Brenda also helped us with our second book and has a wonderful, eclectic collection. We also appreciate the photographs she graciously supplied us that show how she displays her collection.

Once again, we would like to thank Dick Gidman of Dainty Blue Antiques, North Truro, Massachusetts, who also sent us many photographs for book II. He has an exceptional collection of Shelley and Titian Ware.

We deeply appreciate the help Gary Baldwin of Baltimore, Maryland, gave us. If not for his lovely Moser photographs, we wouldn't have been able to do a chapter on glass cups and saucers. Gary is a respected dealer in fine quality glassware and has written two books, *Moser — Artistry in Glass 1857 – 1938* (co-authored with Lee Carno) and *Moser Artistic Glass Edition 2.*

Special thanks to Karen Piper of Martinez, California, for sending us some wonderful photographs of cabinet cups and saucers, especially the rare Shelley Blue Swallow boxed demitasse set. Karen has over 350 sets from many different makers.

We are grateful to Mary Davis of San Diego, California, for sending us photographs of her lovely collection of English and European cobalt blue trios. We appreciate the professional quality of her photographs.

We thank Terri Truax of Fowlerville, New York, for sending us photographs of Japanese cups and saucers. This started us off on our search for many fascinating cups and saucers from Japan.

Special thanks to Valerie Smollan of Capetown, South Africa, for sending us photographs of two special miniatures. We appreciate Joyce L. Geeser of Rockford, Illinois, for sending us a photograph of a rare Chelsea tea bowl. Thanks again to Richard Rendall for helping us find some of our beautiful cabinet cups and saucers. We always appreciate his help and photographs. Thanks again to Frances Pryor of Greenfield, Indiana. Our appreciation is extended to Jerry Taylor and Bob Hill of Last Chance Antiques, Palm Beach Gardens, Florida for allowing us to photograph some of their glass cups and saucers.

We would like to express our sincere appreciation to our friends at Lenox, Inc., Pomona, New Jersey, for giving us such a wonderful tour of their facility. We are grateful that they also allowed us to take photographs during our visit.

Lastly, we again thank Todd Robertson, owner of Sure Service Photo in Neptune City, New Jersey, and the members of his staff, Barbara and Marie, for their support in our challenging task. They were never too busy to process our films in a professional manner.

DEDICATION

To our beloved grandchildren: Michelle, Alyssa, Adam,
Emily, Sophie, Ryan, and Michael

ABOUT THE AUTHORS

Susan and Jim Harran, antique dealers of A Moment In Time, specialize in English and continental porcelains and antique cups and saucers. The Harrans have authored three books, entitled *Collectible Cups and Saucers Book I* and *Book II* and *Dresden Porcelain Studios*. They write feature articles for various antique publications and have a monthly column in *AntiqueWeek*, entitled "The World of Ceramics." They are contributors to *Schroeder's Antiques Price Guide* and *Maloney's Antiques & Collectibles Resource Directory*. Susan is a member of the Antique Appraisal Association of America, Inc. The Harrans display their antiques at some of the top antique shows in the country. They also do business on the Internet. Their website is www.tias.com/stores/amit. The Harrans enjoy traveling around the country to keep abreast of trends in the antiques marketplace. They reside in Neptune, New Jersey.

PREFACE

As antique dealers and collectors for 22 years, we are still actively buying and selling cups and saucers. We see a continued interest in them at antique shows and on the Internet. On Ebay alone, over 1,500 individual cups and saucers are listed daily.

We have received numerous letters and emails from collectors and dealers who have read our first two books, and we deeply appreciate all the favorable comments and offers of help. Because there is such an infinite variety of cups and saucers in the marketplace, we decided to write a third book. Again, our purpose has been to concentrate on actual cups and saucers that are readily available rather than in museums. We have tried to give our readers fresh new information and have included over 1,000 photographs.

This book includes an introduction with some interesting facts about tea, coffee, and chocolate. It was due to the popularity of these three beverages that cups and saucers evolved into such important, useful items. Tea is especially linked with china, and many times we've heard someone say, "Tea tastes better in a china cup."

We were very fortunate to have the opportunity to visit the Lenox manufacturing facility in Pomona, New Jersey to watch a cup and saucer being made first hand. We were taken through all the steps — from raw materials to the finished product — and are happy to share this enlightening trip with our readers.

In this volume we have expanded the section on cabinet cups and saucers. Advanced collectors enjoy acquiring the best decorated examples of the various manufacturers that they can find, and many of our readers asked us to include more information and photographs of these magnificent sets. We believe that a beautifully decorated cabinet cup and saucer is a work of art that will be treasured for generations.

The second category of cups and saucers, late-nineteenth and twentieth-century European and American dinnerware, is still the foundation of most collections. We have included tea, coffee, demitasse, mustache and chocolate cups and saucers, trios, snack sets, and popular pot de crème cups from many companies in Europe and the United States. We've also included some useful information about the grading systems that some companies use.

The third group remains popular with collectors and consists of the attractive twentieth-century English bone china and earthenware cups and saucers. These cups and saucers are not only enjoyed for their beauty, they are used as well. Cups with butterfly or flower handles and fortune telling cups and saucers are discussed.

Our fourth group is a brand new category, Japanese cups and saucers. We briefly discuss the importance of tea in Japan and the development of Japanese ceramics. We discuss the fascinating Japanese tea ceremony that plays such an important role in the artistic and spiritual life of the Japanese people. Finally, we discuss some representative makers of Japanese cups and saucers. Unfortunately, it has been very difficult to find information about many of the Japanese companies that were in business before World War II.

The fifth category is miniatures, the collection of which is one of the world's leading hobbies. We were most fortunate to have been able to interview Mia Alphenaar, a miniature collector from the Netherlands, as well as share photographs from her spectacular collection.

In our brand new sixth category, we discuss the beautiful art glass cups and saucers made by the leading glass factories in Europe and the United States. Art glass cups and saucers were not produced in large quantities and are, therefore, not easily found in the marketplace. The hunt is exciting, and the rewards are great when that elusive glass cup and saucer is found.

We've included our popular marks section and an index. Once again, we've included useful information for the collector and dealer. This time we have shared some helpful observations and advice from some of our collector friends.

Many publications and sources on the Internet have supplied helpful information, and these are acknowledged in the bibliography. We hope this book will make it easier for the novice or advanced collector, or the dealer or appraiser to identify and price cups and saucers. We realize that in a book of this nature and scope, some degree of error is unavoidable, and we apologize in advance.

We always enjoy hearing your comments, and our address is below. If you would like a reply, please include a self-addressed, stamped envelope.

Susan and Jim Harran
208 Hemlock Drive
Neptune, NJ 07753

Miniature coffee cup and saucer. Coalport, c. 1881 – 1890. Can with ring handle, 1"w x 1¼"h, saucer 2⅓"; lovely hand-painted castle scenes on gold ground, gilt wear on saucer well. $450.00 – 500.00.

INTERESTING FACTS ABOUT TEA

"It's glamorous, good for you and cheap. In this troubled world, more and more people are taking time out to indulge in a bit of genteel pleasure. That is, they're taking tea."
("Tea Time," by Frappa Stout. *USA Weekend Lifestyle*, March 15 – 17, 2002.)

Much like the recent popularity of coffee houses in the 1990s, today tea salons are the craze. "We're not just talking tea bags," Stout explains. "Discerning drinkers are partaking in the ritual of the tea ceremony by brewing, straining, and steeping their own cups from loose leaves. Casual drinkers become connoisseurs and share their passion with others."

"Won't you join me in a cup of tea?" postcard, USA.

Trendy tea shops are popping up all over the country, such as Tea in Sympathy in Manhattan and Lovejoy's Antiques and Tea Room in San Francisco. Often, attractive cups and saucers decorate the shops and are available for sale. The latest rage among young 20-year-olds is bubble tea, or pearl tea. A cold, milky tea with tapioca balls, it originated in Taiwan. It is sipped through a wide straw to accommodate the big chewy lumps.

New research shows that regular consumption of tea has been linked to a lower risk of both heart disease and cancer. John A. Weisburger, PhD of the American Health Foundation in Valhalla, New York, says, "It seems more and more that drinking tea is something like drinking a vegetable. And it sure beats drinking brewed spinach leaves."

DEVELOPMENT OF TEA IN AMERICA

Tea was introduced to America in 1650 by Peter Stuyvesant, who brought tea to the colonists in the Dutch settlement of New Amsterdam (later renamed New York by the English). Settlers there became confirmed tea drinkers, and it caught on all across the colonies. Tea Gardens were first opened in New York City in the late 1600s.

Although feelings about tea changed in 1773, when the Boston tea party occurred, tea drinking remained popular among the wealthy and the rising middle classes. "Tea" was the designation of the customary evening meal in many American families for about two centuries.

Beginning in the late 1880s, fine hotels in big cities began to offer tea services in tea rooms and tea courts. Served in the late afternoon, gracious ladies and their gentlemen friends could meet for tea and conversation over dainty sandwiches and fine porcelain cups and saucers. Many of these tea services became the hallmark of the elegance of the hotel, such as the tea services at the Ritz Hotel in Boston or the Plaza Hotel in New York.

"Tea Time" postcard, © Reinthal & Newman, NY.

During the beginning of the twentieth century, two major American contributions to the tea industry occurred. Iced tea was created at the St. Louis World's Fair in 1904. An English exhibitor and tea plantation owner, Richard Blechynde, planned to give away free samples of hot tea to visitors at the fair. Unfortunately, St. Louis was in the middle of a heat wave, and no one was interested in hot tea. To save his investment of time and travel, Blechynde dumped a load of ice into the brewed tea. He tasted it, and it was quite good, so he served it to the visitors. It was an immediate success. Iced tea is still a popular summer beverage, especially in the South. About 50 billion glasses of iced tea are served in the United States each year.

The other contribution occurred four years later. Thomas Sullivan, a tea importer from New York City, developed the first tea bag. To economize on his operating expenses, he began to send samples of tea in little silk bags to his customers. He immediately received orders from all his customers and sent them boxes of tea. To his surprise, they weren't interested in the loose tea; they wanted tea in the silk bags. Silk was too expensive for bagging, so he invented tea bags made of gauze. Today, tea bags are made from strained paper.

During the 1950s, "teacup showers" were given for brides-to-be in England, Canada, and the United States. Each guest brought a different cup and matching saucer, selecting a pattern, style and color that would appeal to the bride-to-be. These teacup collections were meant to be used for entertaining. In her article "Loving Cups," in the April 2000 issue of *Savvy Education*, Mary Gottschalk says, "Cups and saucers appeared at dessert time, creating an instant visual display of beauty."

Today, tea drinking is more popular than ever in the United States. "Tea sipping can not only delight the senses, but it just might be good for your health as well," (*Prevention*, May 1996).

"A Persian Tea Party," Raphael Tuck & Sons postcard, series 8175.

THE RUSSIAN TEA TRADITION

Russia's interest in tea began as early as 1618, when the Chinese Ambassador in Moscow presented several chests of tea to Czar Alexis. By 1796, tea prices had dropped, and tea drinking spread throughout Russian society. Tea was ideally suited to Russian life, as it was hearty, warm, and sustaining.

The samovar, adopted from the Tibetan "hot pot," is both a teapot and a bubbling hot water heater. Placed in the center of the table in a Russian home, it could run all day and serve up to 40 cups of tea at a time. Guests sipped their tea from glasses in silver holders, very similar to Turkish coffee cups. After the Imperial Porcelain Factory began operation in the late 1700s, beautiful porcelain teacups were used.

The Russians have always preferred strong tea highly sweetened with sugar, honey, or jam. Tea (along with vodka) is the national drink of Russia today.

"5 o'clock Tea" postcard printed in England.

THE WELSH TEA PARTY

Tea was introduced to Great Britain in the 1650s, and tea drinking quickly caught on all over the country. In Wales, one of the most popular customs was the Welsh tea party. Women dressed in Welsh costume sat at a table with elaborate tea services. In the late 1800s, it was how some Welsh women choose to have themselves photographed.

The Welsh tea party became a national icon focused around the respectable activity of drinking tea, as opposed to the non-respectable activity of drinking beer. The collection of china fit for display and use at a tea party became interwoven with Welsh feminine identity.

"Welsh Women," "Valesque" postcard, © Dundee and London, published by Valentine & Sons, LTD.

THE POPULARITY OF COFFEE

Coffee is the most traded commodity in the world after oil. Brazil, Columbia, Indonesia, Vietnam, and Mexico are the largest exporters, and the United States is the largest importer. Eighty percent of adult Americans are regular or occasional coffee drinkers, and the average consumption is 3.3 cups a day.

Coffee is popular in Europe as well, especially in France, Italy, and Spain. The French family consumes a couple of pounds a week. They make it strong, using little water. In his article "In My Cups," in the *National Review* (June 23, 1993), Digby Anderson explains, "They use proper cups with saucers and without slogans."

Anderson goes on to lay down some basic ground rules for Americans. "Coffee is drunk at meals, off tables and sitting down…The coffee is served in china cups and saucers, white or dark green and gold. Each cup will have no more than a twentieth of a part of water. If you are thirsty, drink a glass of water but do not ruin coffee with it."

Levering's Coffee trade card, E. Levering & Co.

Coffee beans were originally taken as a food and not as a beverage. East African tribes ground the coffee beans together, mixing it into a paste with animal fat. The mixture was then rolled into little balls. African warriors believed it gave them much needed energy for battle. During the eleventh century, coffee was first developed into a beverage.

Wild coffee plants were taken from Ethiopia to the Yemen Province of Arabia in the fifteenth century. About 1650, a Moslem pilgrim from India named Baba Buda was the first to sneak some seeds out of Arabia. The Dutch carried the descendants of these seeds to Java, where coffee growing was established on a regular basis.

The Don Juan of coffee production was Francisco de Mello Palheta of Brazil. He was sent to French Guana in 1727 by the Emperor of Brazil, who wanted to get his country involved in the lucrative coffee market. Even though Palheta was handsome and persuasive, he had a difficult time getting seeds for his country. Fortunately for coffee drinkers all over the world, he so successfully charmed the French governor's wife that she sent him, buried in a bouquet of flowers, all the seeds and shoots he needed to start the billion-dollar coffee industry of Brazil.

CHOCOLATE – THE DIVINE DRINK

Chocolate has been consumed for at least 28 centuries. The word cocoa was translated from the hieroglyphic word kaka, which was found on pottery jars in Mayan tombs around 500 B.C. These jars were used as chocolate pots. The Mayan people would pour the contents of one pot into another to produce a frothy head of foam. The drink was known as cacahuatl, or "cocoa water."

The Mayans and Aztecs worshipped cacahuatl and included it in many of their religious ceremonies. They sometimes mixed it with a red powder so that it resembled blood. Its consumption was restricted to men, because chocolate was thought too invigorating a drink for women.

Cocoa drinking reached new heights with the rise of the Aztec empire. It was believed to be an aphrodisiac, and the Aztec ruler, Montezuma, reportedly drank 50 or more bowls of it daily.

When the Spanish arrived in 1517, they were repelled by the drink, which was served cold and mixed with a variety of local ingredients that included cornflower and chilies. The Spanish explorer Hernan Cortéz could see the potential, however. He described chocolatl, or chocolate water, as the divine drink which builds up resistance and fights fatigue. By the middle of the sixteenth century, the Spanish conceived of sweetening the bitter drink with cane sugar and drinking it hot.

Spain wisely began to plant cocoa trees in its overseas possessions. The processing of the beans was done in monasteries, under a clock of secrecy. They were able to keep it concealed from the rest of the world for one hundred years.

The earliest chocolate cup is the mancerina, which was a standard part of the Spanish chocolate service. Its origin is traced to the Marquis de Mancera, Viceroy of Peru from 1639 to 1648. Before that time, chocolate drinks were consumed from Indian gourds or

small clay bowls. The mancerina was a plate or saucer with a ring-like collar in the middle into which a small Chinese porcelain cup could sit without sliding. This is the origin of the French trembleuse of the eighteenth century.

The Spanish Princess Maria Theresa presented cocoa beans as an engagement gift to Louis XIV, and chocolate soon became the rage of the French royal court. By the middle of the seventeenth century, the chocolate drink had gained widespread popularity throughout Europe. An enterprising Frenchman opened the first hot chocolate shop in London. Soon they were as prominent as coffeehouses in England.

The first porcelain chocolate services date to the 1770s, when Madame de Pompadour commissioned their production at Sevres. Elaborate porcelain chocolate services were produced for the nobility throughout Europe. In the late nineteenth century, many factories in Limoges and Dresden produced lovely chocolate sets that are eagerly collected today.

In 1828, Dutch chemist Coenraad van Houten invented the process that would bring in the modern era of chocolate making. He developed a hydraulic press that would de-fat and alkalize cocoa powder so that it could become a soluble drink.

Chocolate drinking arrived in the American colonies in 1765, when the first chocolate factory opened in New England. It was known as Walter Baker & Company and is still in business today. Thomas Jefferson praised chocolate's virtues as superior for both health and nourishment.

Chocolate drinking became very fashionable in the United States during the 1880s and 1890s. It was advertised as a health drink in those days, especially for children. Chocolate sets were given as wedding and Christmas gifts.

A painting that is often seen on chocolate sets, especially those made by the Dresden decorators, is "La Belle Chocolatiere." This painting portrays a woman in apron and bonnet and carrying a tray of chocolate cups and a pot. The woman in the painting is Anna Baltauf

(1740-1825), who was the owner of a chocolate shop in Vienna. One afternoon, the Austrian Prince Ditrichlstein came into Anna's shop. He was entranced with her grace and beauty, and they fell in love. They decided to marry, against the wishes of the court. As a present to his bride, the Prince commissioned the noted portrait painter Jean Etienne Liotard (1702-1790) to paint Anna's portrait.

In 1881, the head of the Walter Baker Chocolate Company, Henry Pierce, was on a trip to Europe. He saw the painting in a gallery in Dresden, Germany, and officially adopted it as the chocolate company's trademark in 1883.

Dresden chocolate pot showing
"La Belle Chocolatiere."

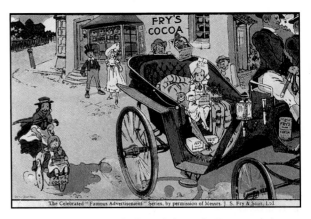

Fry's Cocoa postcard, the celebrated "Advertisement" series, J. S. Fry & Sons, LTD.

WATCHING A CUP AND SAUCER BEING MADE AT LENOX

Thanks to some wonderful people at Lenox, we were able to watch a cup and saucer being made – first-hand. We've written about the making of cups and saucers several times, but not many authors get a chance to actually see it in person. We were fortunate to visit the Lenox manufacturing facility in Pomona, New Jersey, and we'd like to share this experience with our readers.

We were able to see the process of making cups and saucers from raw materials to the finished decorated product. Gordon J. "Buzz" Cockrane took us through, step by step, and answered all of our questions. Buzz, as all of his employees call him, is Manager of Decorating Operations.

Lenox has approximately 400 employees working in Pomona. The employee with the least seniority has 20 years of service. Family relationships are common, and many sons, daughters, sisters, and brothers follow in their relative's footsteps. "We take good care of our family of workers," says Cockrane. "It's one of the many reasons our quality is so high."

Approaching Lenox by car in Pomona, New Jersey.

Lenox manufacturing plant from the outside.

RAW MATERIALS

It takes 9 to 11 days to make a cup, and the journey starts with the ingredients for making porcelain. This varies from manufacturer to manufacturer. China clay, nepheline, syenite, esva ball clay, gt kaolin, and silcosil flint are used by Lenox. These ingredients are refined and ground until they look and feel much like fine powder.

Ingredients of Lenox mixture of clay and slip.

Entrance to Lenox plant and outlet store.

Reception area; Clinton's Presidential service when he was in the White House.

The mixture for the unleaded glaze used by Lenox is proprietary. Cockrane told us it had been very difficult for the company to come up with a formula that was acceptable to them. "Leaded glaze hides a multitude of sins," he explained. "It took Lenox about five years to come up with a satisfactory unleaded glaze."

The raw materials used to be stored in bags, and impurities could get into the ingredients. Now the various materials are stored into "super sacks," which are big bags in which shakers drop down to measure out the exact amount of ingredients that is needed. When it's the right mixture for the item being made, it is pumped directly to the right station. This has cut contamination to a minimum and makes their facility extremely clean.

MOLDS

We went to the mold storage area, where we were introduced to James D. Bower, Department Manager. He showed us a computer system that could tell him what every piece of equipment was doing at any given time. We asked Bower how many molds it took to make a cup. "It could be as many as three, or it could be just one," he told us, and showed us Lenox's special cup mold that includes a handle. "In producing some cups, the handle and foot are cast manually and put on with slip," he explained.

Master molds are made from plaster of

Unleaded glaze ingredients.

Paris. These are kept indefinitely, and many production molds are made from them.

CASTING AND JIGGERING

In the casting department, a common gas pump nozzle fills the molds with smooth slip and they spin around, keeping the mixture at the consistent texture. Dry molds absorb moisture from the slip, leaving a coat of clay. When this has become the right thickness, excess slip is poured off. This process is called casting.

Clay being mixed.

Cup with handle mold.

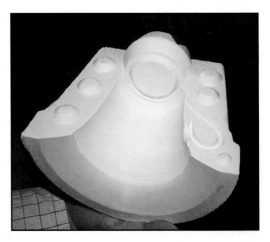
Close-up of a mold.

Cups are formed in the jiggering department. After they are formed, they are removed from the mold. Then the cups are shaped on the inside, and the excess slip is removed.

Taking a cup out of mold.

Shaping inside of cup.

Saucers are formed in the jiggering department, where they are cast first, then shaped on a modern version of the ancient potter's wheel.

This is accomplished working in three-man

Plates being shaped in modern potter's wheel.

teams, including a jiggerman, a cup take-out operator, and a mold runner. The team produces 1,400 good cups a day. After they are taken out of the mold they are cut, deseamed, and sponged smooth.

Cleaning up seams and excess clay.

FIRING

From the casting and jiggering department, the greenware is placed in giant kilns (furnaces) for the first day-long firing at 2100°F, a heat so intense it would melt many metals. During the first firing, the pieces become completely vitrified. The ware is now called biscuit ware. This biscuit ware is next thoroughly smoothed in a bath of specially formed aluminum oxide pebbles.

Biscuit ware cups in a bath of aluminum oxide pebbles to smooth.

GLAZING

The biscuit ware is then glazed. As items come out of the kiln and enter a glazing bath, they are constantly spinning to insure the glaze is distributed uniformly.

The glaze mixture comes from the hoses of a spraying machine. The pieces go into a drying unit at 500°F, where they turn pink in color. The pieces are then placed into a glost kiln at 1960°F, to fuse the biscuit ware and the glaze. They will remain in the kiln for over a day. The items are always moving in the kiln. When they come out of the kiln, they have turned ivory in color.

Drying operation.

INSPECTION

Before decorating, the pieces go through a complete inspection. All employees are quality control conscious and are involved in the quality every step of the way. The average rejection rate is 4-5%. Lenox has two grades of quality. First is marked A, and second quality is marked 9; these second quality wares are sold as seconds at reduced prices. Anything less is tossed into the dumpster. It is Lenox's meticulous attention to quality control that makes it the leading United States producer of fine quality porcelain dinnerware.

Quality control inspection.

DECORATING

Cockrane showed us the decal storage room and explained, "It is very important for this room to be temperature and humidity controlled. Lenox spends about 4.5 million dollars a year on decals." Cockrane advised us that the decals are stored end on end so the pages won't stick together.

Before a piece is to be decorated, an experienced employee sketches a line to show where the decal goes; this is done with a simple compass and a marker. Using this method, a person can do up to 4,000 saucers a day.

Several employees were busy at work in the

Lining saucers for decal placement.

decorating rooms. These rooms are open five days a week for 24 hours a day. The decorators average 382 pieces a day.

Decals are soaked in water so the designs will slide off easily. They are patted with a sponge to get out excess air and moisture.

Applying decal decoration.

We saw several liners hard at work. "Liners like to keep their brushes as long as they can, sometimes two years," says Cockrane. "The bristles are made from camel, squirrel, or mink hairs."

After the item is decorated, gold or platinum is applied and the item is put into kilns at 1485°F for two hours, in which time the decoration is permanently fused with the body.

After the gold is fired, it is ready for a final hand process of burnishing. This was demonstrated by our host, Cockrane. He took a bowl and burnished, or polished, it using a nylon wheel. It then looked like bright shiny gold. "This is Westchester, our most expensive pattern," explained Cockrane. "The gold used for this is 24kt."

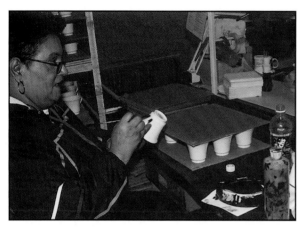

Decorating handle and foot of cup.

Buzz Cochran showing us
how gold decoration is burnished.

Lining cup.

The authors wish to thank Peter Cobuzzi, Vice President of Brand Development, and Bethany Bullard, Brand Development Associate, for setting up this visit for us. Thanks to Buddy Holt, Regional Director, who allowed us to visit the manufacturing facility. A special thank you to Buzz Cockrane for taking us on the two and a half hour tour. We noticed that not only did he know every operator, but he knew everyone by first name. Also thanks to James D. Bower, who answered many questions for us. A big thank-you to the many workers of all categories who did not seem to mind our looking over their shoulders. It was a wonderful experience for us and one that we'll remember for a long time.

Removing excess water and air from decal.

CABINET CUPS AND SAUCERS

Cabinet coffee and tea services were first produced in the 1700s. The development of this richly decorated ware owes much to royal patronage, such as Augustus II of Poland, Madame de Pompadour of France, Charles Bourbon of Naples, and Catherine II of Russia.

Porcelain or white gold was a prestigious status symbol in the 1700s. Porcelain was commissioned as gifts for family members of royalty and for foreign monarchs. The porcelain produced was richly decorated in multicolored overglaze painting and delicately modeled details.

Cabinet ware continued to be produced in the 1800s, particularly the 1870 – 1900 period. Advanced cup and saucer collectors enjoy acquiring the best decorated examples of the various manufacturers that they can find. A beautifully decorated cabinet cup and saucer is a work of art that will be treasured for generations.

Trade card of lovely cabinet cup and saucer,
Chase & Sanborn's "Seal Brand" coffee, W. E. Brewster.

DECORATION

HAND PAINTING

The palette of colors used for painting porcelain increased in variety in the nineteenth century. The painters' skills mixing these colors and modifying them by numerous firings became even greater. Exact copies of oil paintings were transferred to porcelain at Vienna, Meissen, and Berlin.

Many porcelain paintings had to go into the kiln several times, because delicate tones, such as skin, could not be achieved in just one firing. Even the final firing could jeopardize the entire work. A portrait cup may have taken months to complete, and that explains why these cups are so expensive and rare today.

GLAZES

Porcelain manufacturers experimented with different glazes during the late nineteenth century. The most unusual glaze was a deep red or oxblood glaze first achieved by Berlin in 1881, and by other factories thereafter. Crystalline glazes were discovered at Sevres, and Royal Copenhagen developed crystalline glazes that are among the most beautiful of the Art Nouveau techniques.

Further experiments were conducted with the oxblood copper oxide glaze. Air was introduced at the reduction stage of firing to produce blue, violet, and green flamed glazes. These are sometimes referred to as Tiffany luster glazes and are found on Vienna and Dresden cabinet ware.

GILDING

Gold ornamentation has been used to enhance fine porcelain since the early Oriental tea wares were imported into Europe in the seventeenth century. In their comprehensive book, entitled *Porcelain of the 19th Century*, Fäy-Hallé and Mundt emphasize the importance of gilding. "The quality of a factory's product is dependent on the quality of its gilded decoration, which gives the pieces their character."

The pieces with the large areas of gilding so popular in the early nineteenth century, when the outsides and insides of cabinet ware were gilded all over, were very expensive because of the quantity of the metal required and the laborious process of polishing. Examples of all gold KPM cups and saucers can be found in the marketplace today.

PÂTE-SUR-PÂTE

Pâte-sur-pâte (paste on paste) decoration was inspired by Chinese porcelain. Sevres made it famous in the nineteenth century. Then Marc-Louis Salon took it to the Minton Company in England. Pâte-sur-pâte is a very difficult and time consuming process. An artist traces the outline of a design on an unfired piece of porcelain. He gradually builds up the desired number of layers of slip, allowing one layer to dry before applying the next. Then the piece is fired. The Vienna Augarten Factory produced a set of cobalt cabinet demitasse cups, with pâte-sur-pâte portraits of famous rulers, in the 1920s.

SILVER OVERLAY

With the advent of the Art Nouveau movement in the late nineteenth century, many silversmiths were trying to figure out ways to increase their business and stay competitive with foreign companies. Glass and ceramic makers realized they too must create new demands for their products. Glass makers started asking silversmiths if it were possible for them to make cases for large objects such as vases and cologne bottles.

Oscar Pierre Erard of Birmingham, England, had developed an effective method of electroplating silver on glass and porcelain in 1889. Although beautiful on the outside, the reverse side of the silver design, the side next to the glass, would tarnish and turn dark.

In 1893, John H. Scharling of New Jersey patented a successful method of silver overlay. Scharling soon became famous worldwide. Of particular importance was the reverse outline of the design. Instead of the ugly black color, it was white. It is thought that the chemical contents in the flux may have helped make his results superior.

The procedures for silver overlay are basically all the same. A mix of chemicals, called flux, is applied to the object in the desired form. The object is then put in a vat which contains silver particles. An electrical charge is applied, and the silver particles adhere to the flux. The longer the object remains in the vat, the more silver is applied.

There are subtle difference in the manufacturing process for silver overlay and silver deposit. Overlay is always thick and appears raised, whereas deposit is usually thin. The delicate fruit, flowers, and abstract designs of the silver overlay patterns were also enhanced with engraving, etching, or oxidation, and some were executed in relief, such as a grape design. Items with silver overlay are almost always more expensive and desirable that those decorated with silver deposit.

Scharling shared his new process with companies in the United States and in Europe. Many Austrian and Italian glass makers, and European porcelain companies such as Royal Doulton, Rosenthal, Hutschenreuther, and factories in Limoges, France, began producing sterling deposit and overlay pieces. Not to be outdone, United States makers began producing it as fast as they could. The Lenox Company made a number of beautiful tea and coffee sets in silver overlay that are eagerly collected today.

A variety of items were decorated with silver overlay. Chocolate, tea, and coffee sets are highly collectible. Pitchers, jam jars, vases, cologne bottles, and inkwells were overlaid with sterling silver tracery. Some items had a cartouche of silver on the piece, designed for an initial or monogram. Many overlay designs featured floral and fruit forms, including roses, lilies, and thistles, or grapes and leafage.

Postcard showing silver overlay tea cups and saucers accompanied by delicious tea pastries.

MAKERS

MEISSEN

The first European porcelain company, Meissen, produced beautiful cabinet ware sets as early as the 1700s. One of the most elaborate early sets was the Swan Service ordered by Count Bruhl in 1737. The entire surface of each piece was modeled in low relief, with animals and water plants. In the 1790s, covered cylindrical porcelain cups were produced with portrait miniature decoration. The cylindrical cup shape became very important and was used by other manufacturers.

Meissen artists began to transfer the paintings in the famous Semper Gallery in Dresden, Germany, onto porcelain around 1800. Paintings by Angelica Kauffman, Giovanni Antonio Canaletto, and other favorite Dutch and Italian artists were copied onto porcelain. Nineteenth century cobalt blue quatrefoil cups and saucers done with courting scenes, and floral medallions done with wonderful hand gilding, are popular today.

Canaletto (1697 – 1768) was an Italian painter known for his sparkling views of Venice, Dresden, and other cities in Europe and England. Topographical cups with city views are highly desirable.

Another favorite Meissen cabinet cup and saucer is completely covered with applied flowers. Each piece has six feet, and the cup has a twisted stem handle. Meissen used a number of interesting handles on its cups and pots, such as a snake, a twisted feather, and its famous swan.

KPM

Frederick the Great, whose passion was white gold, gave KPM (Kings Porcelain Manufactory) its name and trademark, the royal blue scepter, in 1763. Cabinet cups and saucers commemorated historical and current events, such as the death of the popular Queen Louise. Frederick presented a cup and saucer to Emperor Joseph II on his coronation. The saucer has an equestrian portrait, and the cup has Joseph's initials and the crowns of Austria, Bohemia, and Hungary on a velvet cushion.

KPM began using mosaic decoration after 1802 to imitate Florentine type stone work. Some early cups can be found with lids, and these are treasured by collectors. KPM used biscuit relief on handles and as cameo decoration in the nineteenth century. Early cups often had a heavy gold band inside. During the mid-nineteenth century, all gold sets were made for special patrons; these were quite costly to produce.

KPM is famous for its realistic floral paintings. Each flower is meticulously painted by hand, and most works are personally initialed by the painter. Many have heavy gold paste embellishments surrounding the floral cartouche.

There have been many imitations of KPM's scepter mark. The Kranichfeld Company, c. 1903, had what looks like a scepter with a flame and .KPM. as their trademark. Paul Muller of Selb, Germany, used a scepter with an S, in 1890. The most common mark confused with Berlin today is KPM with a vertical line on top. This mark has been used by Krister Porcelain, Waldenburg, Germany, in various forms since 1885.

NYMPHENBURG

Prince Elector Max Joseph II, of Bavaria's ruling Wittelsbach family, was envious of August the Strong's Meissen factory. In 1747, he established a royal porcelain manufactory in an unused hunting lodge at Au, a town close to Munich. The factory became profitable and soon outgrew the hunting lodge. It was moved to Nymphenburg, where it remains today.

The company produced some lovely cabinet ware, such as the Perl table service used by the Bavarian court in 1795. The cups and saucers were 12-sided, elaborately gilded, and decorated with landscape scenes. Raised white jewels, or a "string of pearls," were placed around the edges of each cup and saucer. Cups with portrait miniatures of members of the royal families were quite popular.

Today many Nymphenburg cabinet sets can be found with realistic hand-painted flowers on pristine white grounds. In 1997, the company celebrated their 250th anniversary and reissued some prized early works. Their Modern cup and saucer sells for $390. The cup takes the form of a flower's petals, and the saucer a leaf. The set

is decorated with two poppies with protruding buds. The most expensive set is in the Biedermeier style and is called *Fleurs en Terrasse*. The cup has a scrolled handle that extends above the edge of the cup. The set is decorated with hand-painted flowers from an 1812 pattern book and retails for $1,700.

DRESDEN

The city of Dresden became a leading cultural center in the seventeenth century, and in the eighteenth century, it became known as the "Florence on the Elbe," because of its magnificent baroque architecture and its outstanding museums. Artists, poets, musicians, philosophers, and porcelain artists took up residence in Dresden.

Between 1855 and 1944, more than 200 painting studios existed in the city. The studios bought porcelain whiteware from manufacturers such as Meissen and Rosenthal for decorating, marketing, and reselling throughout the world. The largest included Donath & Co., Franziska Hirsch, Richard Klemm, Ambrosius Lamm, Carl Thieme, and Helena Wolfsohn.

Many of the Dresden studios produced cabinet cups and saucers in imitation of Meissen and Royal Vienna. Flower paintings enhanced with burnished gold, courting couples, landscapes, and cupids were used as decorative motifs. Sometimes the artwork equaled or even surpassed that of the Meissen factory.

Ambrosius Lamm produced cabinet cups and saucers that would enhance the most sophisticated collection. A set of six flared cups with scrolled handles, hand-painted with French court beauties such as Mme. Lebrun, are valued at $3,000 to 4,500. Other desirable cabinet cups, Rosenthal blanks, can be found decorated with a gilt star or flower cut-out. Well-painted portraits of men and women in period dress and heavy gold paste work decorate the outside of the cup and saucer. Lamm often used rich cobalt blue and luster glazes for his ground colors. Favorite decorative techniques used were jeweling and beading.

Franziska Hirsch produced a few museum quality cabinet cups and saucers as well. Some examples include a gorgeous Coalport type demitasse, with turquoise jeweling on a gold ground, and portrait sets with a burgundy luster or Tiffany glaze, with heavy gold paste work.

A number of trembleuses were made by the Dresden decorators, and the Carl Thieme Manufactory is the only company that still produces a swan cabinet cup and saucer. It retails for $495.

ROYAL VIENNA

The Vienna Porcelain Factory was founded by Claudius du Paquier in 1717. It was second to Meissen in producing hard paste porcelain. The company began producing cabinet ware derived from silver shapes decorated with Chinese motifs and exotic flowers.

Financial difficulties forced du Paquier to sell his factory to the state in 1744. At that time the Vienna mark, a shield incised or in underglaze blue, was first introduced. Exquisite cabinet ware with portrait and landscape medallions on colored grounds with gold decoration was produced for members of royalty and their families. Cups had magnificent forms, such as full swan or twisted snake handles and claw feet. In 1864, the imperial factory closed because of industrialization and rapidly growing competition.

Royal Vienna became a style in the late nineteenth century. Porcelain decorating studios in Berlin, Vienna, and Dresden copied the early Vienna style and produced some exceptional cabinet ware. Many German and Austrian porcelain manufacturers copied the "beehive" mark and produced copies, with transfers of mythological scenes or portraits, around the turn of the twentieth century. These sets are often of mediocre or poor quality and should not be confused with hand-painted sets with rich background work.

The firm reopened in 1923, when it was moved to the Augarten Castle in Vienna. The opening coincided with the Art Deco movement. The Melons mocha (demitasse) service was designed by famous designer Josef Hoffman in 1929. During the 1920s, the company experimented with pâte-sur-pâte. A wonderful cabinet demitasse service was produced in cobalt blue with white pâte-sur-pâte portraits of historical figures.

SEVRES

Sevres benefited early on from preferential royal treatment, which included the crown's 20-year monopoly on porcelain production, beginning in 1745. In 1759, Louis XV assumed control of its operations. Yearly, he conducted a sale in his private apartments at Versailles. Members of the Court were "strongly encouraged" to purchase goods.

Sevres retained royal influence throughout the nineteenth century. Tastes ran to extravagant decoration. Any number of political events called for the commission of another ornate Sevres piece. Well-known artists worked at Sevres; the company's focus on premium production and prices enabled them to attract only the best artists.

Marie Antoinette had considerable influence in the Sevres Factory. For her, decorating a table was a passion, and she only accepted the finest examples.

When Napoleon came to power in 1804, he inherited a series of royal residences and proceeded to furnish them as elegantly as possible. He became a welcome patron of the decorative arts and purchased lavish services from Sevres which often bore the symbols suggestive of the Empire, including classical and laurel leaf motifs. A boxed nineteenth-century Sevres cabinet tea service recently sold for $10,925 at a Skinner's auction. It included a tray with Napoleon's portrait, a teapot with a painting of Josephine, and 12 cups and saucers. The cups were painted with portrait busts of members of the Imperial Court.

During the nineteenth century, France became the leader in the art of cuisine that was celebrated throughout the world. As new foods came onto the French tables, along with new ways to serve them, different styles and shapes of containers were required. Elaborate tea sets and dessert services were produced; luncheon was a new, post-Revolutionary invention; and *dejeuners* were created. Ice cream or pot-de-crème cups were produced to celebrate the new popular confection.

Many pieces of undecorated wares were sold at Sevres during the 1800s, often of inferior quality. These were decorated by companies and hausmalers (free-lance painters) in France and abroad, sometimes with an intent to deceive the purchaser. Buyers should be aware that many items with Sevres marks were really decorated outside the company.

PARIS PORCELAIN

Paris porcelains were made from hard paste and were made or decorated in the city of Paris or environs from 1770s until the fall of Napoleon III's Second Empire in 1870. The name Old Paris (vieux Paris) is a term coined by antique dealers in the United States in the late nineteenth century. It reflects the location of many of the Paris porcelain factories in the northeast, or old part of the city, which was a well-known artisans' quarter.

Right from the beginning, the Paris manufacturers were highly regarded by members of royalty. Emperor Napoleon I subsidized several companies and awarded them important commissions. His favorites were Jean Nast (1754 – 1817) and Pierre-Louis Dagoty (1771 – 1840).

Dagoty supplied porcelain to Empress Josephine. He produced biscuit tea ware, with glazed interiors, in the form of swimming swans. Josephine loved swans and kept a flock of them at her Chateau de Malmaison outside of Paris. Dagoty also made lovely solitaire services with a matte black ground, often with classical figures and gilt decoration.

Some exquisite cabinet items were produced in Paris, partly due to the emergence of trade fairs in England and Europe. Paris porcelain achieved international recognition at the 1851 London Crystal Palace Exhibition, one of the greatest nineteenth-century international fairs.

Interesting examples of Paris cabinet ware can be found in the marketplace today. Covered trembleuses are available with classical figures or flower paintings. Portrait cups depicting eighteenth and nineteenth-century rulers and aristocratic ladies are quite popular. A wide variety of topographical cups and saucers were produced with well painted reserves of Parisian buildings, such as the Louvre or Notre Dame Cathedral. Italian landscapes became the rage with Paris decorators.

An interesting collector piece would be a "bread and milk" cup and saucer. These large cups and saucers were used in France for the breakfast dipping of slightly stale bread or pastry (which was too expensive to discard) in warm milk. The cup measures about 4" x 3⅝", and the saucer 6".

CAPODIMONTE STYLE

In the latter part of the nineteenth century, Ginori, in Italy, and Ernst Boehm, in Rudolstadt, Germany, created exquisite tea ware in the Capodimonte style. The trademark used was a blue or black underglaze crown over an N, the old Capodimonte mark. Delicate cups were hand-painted with mythological figures, cupids, or family scenes, with landscapes in relief and with dainty twisted branch or figural handles. The saucers often didn't match the cups exactly, and were decorated with garlands of flowers, cavorting Cupids, or armorial crests. Grounds are white or all gold with white cloud formations. Covered one-handled cups or two-handled chocolate cups can be found. Lids have an applied Cupid, pineapple, or acorn finial.

RUSSIAN PORCELAIN
The Imperial Factory

Russian porcelain had a disastrous beginning, but eventually porcelain of fine quality was produced. Peter the Great's daughter, Empress Elizabeth, contracted with German vagrant C. K. Hunger in 1744 to invent porcelain at a factory in St. Petersburg. Unfortunately, Hunger was an adventurer and a con man who constantly made excuses for his failure to make satisfactory porcelain. During a span of three years, he barely turned out a dozen cups, and they were crooked and discolored. Finally, a Russian Priest's son, Dmitri Venogrador, was ordered to learn from Hunger all the secrets of porcelain.

The Imperial Factory came into its own during the reign of Catherine II, 1762 – 1792. Catherine had a passion for building and for filling what she built with beautiful objects. She personally inspected the factory in 1763 and ordered highly skilled artisans to be hired from Germany, Austria, and France, regardless of the expense. One of her first orders was a topographical tea service for Count Bezborodko, one of her court favorites. The set had oval medallions in the center that portrayed Italian architectural scenes, and garlands of hand-painted flowers and gilt.

The art of porcelain making at the Imperial Factory reached its highest point in the first half of the nineteenth century under Alexander I and Nicholas I. Tea ware was decorated with lovely miniature paintings on grounds of rich malachite green, lapis lazuli blue, and deep maroon. The first mark of the Imperial Factory during the reigns of Elizabeth and Peter III was a black or impressed double-headed eagle. From the time of Catherine II through that of all subsequent rulers, the mark consisted of the reigning sovereign's initials painted under the glaze. Except for those marked during the reign of Catherine, these initials are surmounted by the Imperial Crown. Imperial porcelain is highly collectible today, and prices are quite high.

After the Revolution, the Imperial Factory became the State Porcelain Works. Later, it was renamed Lomonosov in honor of the founder of the Russian Academy of Science. The most famous dinnerware pattern is Cobalt Net, a dramatic diamond-shaped design in deep cobalt blue and gold. The Lomonosov Porcelain Company is still active today, but many collectors prefer pieces with the earlier mark, "Made in USSR," rather than the current mark, "Made in Russia."

Gardner

Francis Gardner, a British entrepreneur, was allowed to produce porcelain in a town outside of Moscow in 1766. In 1777, Catherine the Great commissioned three dinner services from Gardner. The company copied the styles of Meissen and KPM, and also produced tea ware with Russian peasant scenes and views of Russian villages. The company was successfully carried on by Gardner's descendants until 1891, when it was sold to the giant Kuznetsov Porcelain Factory.

Kuznetsov

The M. Kuznetsov Company is a huge family porcelain business that had its beginning in 1842. At the beginning of the twentieth century, it eliminated so many competitors that it was responsible for about two-thirds of the total quantity of pottery and porcelain throughout the Russian Empire. It is still in business today.

Popov

Popov Porcelain, an important factory near Moscow, was started by Karl Milli and taken over by A. Popov until the 1850s. It produced many porcelain services for country inns.

Popov porcelain is highly valued by collectors, especially the elaborate tea sets and plates featuring flowers or fruit in high relief.

Karnilov

The Karnilov family established a porcelain company in 1835, and produced such a high quality product that they won a gold medal at the 1839 Moscow Exhibition. Their tea ware had rich ground colors and gilding. In the last decades of the nineteenth century, the company started mass producing less expensive wares for export.

ROYAL COPENHAGEN

Royal Copenhagen's Flora Danica is one of the most prestigious dinner services in production today. It is also one of the oldest — the first piece was taken out of the kiln in 1790. Thanks to the careful attention to the age-old craft, a piece of Flora Danica produced today will be just as perfect as one made 200 years ago.

In Denmark, the chemist Frantz Henrich Müller received the backing of the royal family and spent years trying to make porcelain. He finally succeeded in producing hard paste porcelain in 1775, and the Royal Copenhagen Porcelain Manufactory was established. It was financially supported by the royal family, and Queen Julianne Marie took special interest in its production. It was her idea to have three blue wavy lines, symbolizing the three Danish waterways, as the company's trademark.

In 1761, George Christian Oeder, who was director of the new botanical gardens in Copenhagen, decided to publish an encyclopedia of the national flora of Denmark. He got official support, and engaged the engraver Michael Rössler and his son Martin to undertake this huge project. The publication was called Flora Danica, and it took over 100 years to complete. It included 3,000 hand-colored copperplate prints depicting every wild plant of the nation, including mosses, fungi, ferns, and flowers.

Crown Prince Frederick, later King Frederick VI, was pleased with the progress of this new folio and decided to commission a dinner service decorated with flora from the new publication. He needed a gift for Czarina Catherine II of Russia and thought a beautiful dinner set depicting the nation's flora would be a worthy gift for a member of royalty. The monumental task of transferring the flora from the folio on to a dinner service was given to Johann Christoph Boyer, one of the most talented and sensitive artists of the late eighteenth century.

The Flora Danica dinner service was to be Boyer's life work. It ultimately deprived him of all his strength, and destroyed his eyesight as he had to work in poor light during the long dark winter months in Denmark. He did almost all the hand painted floral decoration on the 1,802 individual pieces himself. When his eyesight became very poor in 1799, he was assisted by Christian Nicolai Faxöc, who painted, gilded, and ornamented 158 pieces. The applied flowers were modeled by Soren Preus from 1784 to 1801. The project finally came to an end in 1802, when Bayer could no longer work. By this time Catherine had died, and it was decided that the Flora Danica service would remain in Denmark as the heritage of the Danish Kings.

No other Flora Danica services were produced for sixty years. In 1863, the Danish Princess Alexandra was betrothed to the Prince of Wales, who was later to become King Edward VII of England. A group of Danish women decided to have a Flora Danica service made as a wedding gift, to express their affection for the queen-to-be. The service depicted more than 700 wild plants. It was well received by the royal couple, and is kept today at Windsor Castle. Since that time, Royal Copenhagen has continued to make the exquisite Flora Danica dinner services. They have been used on many royal occasions, and selected pieces are still used on the royal table of Queen Margrethe II on state occasions at Amalienborg Palace, the residence of the Danish royal family.

The Royal Danish Family and the Danish government still present pieces of Flora Danica as official gifts on special occasions.

This pattern is considered to be one of the most original and exquisite creations of European decorative art.

Collectors are amazed at the outstanding modeling of the pieces and the power of the painting. The late Princess Grace of Monaco wrote in her book on flowers, "One of the most delicate and beautiful porcelain patterns is the famous Flora Danica from Denmark."

While relatively few people can afford to collect an entire dinner set, most collectors are content with having a few select pieces to grace their home. "One never tires of contemporary

Flora Danica. Each and every piece is a delicate observation of the natural world portrayed on porcelain, complete with flower, leaves, stem, root and fruit, and faithful to its botanical origin." (*Flora Danica* by Royal Copenhagen Ltd., December 1989)

ENGLISH COMPANIES

Between the 1860s and the 1890s, a number of English companies looked to the Far East for inspiration. Many interesting examples of English cabinet ware are based on Japanese, Indian, and Persian styles.

Royal Worcester

Of all the porcelain factories established in England in the mid-eighteenth century, Worcester alone has survived in continual production. In his article in the November 2000 *The Australian*, Michael Reid says, "Despite the ravages of time, Royal Worcester porcelain defies the trend and continues to fetch ever higher prices at auctions."

Hand painting became Royal Worcester's specialty in the late nineteenth and early twentieth centuries, and artist signed pieces are eagerly sought by collectors. Famous artists were Austin (birds and flowers), Harry Davis (landscapes), Ernest Phillips (flowers), William Powell (birds), and the Stinton brothers (cattle and game birds). A Royal Worcester cup and saucer painted with Highland cattle in a landscape by Harry Stinton and dated 1923 would bring over $1,000 at auction.

Royal Worcester was influenced by the Japanese style, and many cups and saucers have storks, bamboo plants, or prunus blossoms in raised gold. An example is a wonderful tea set with a square shape, with embossed sprays and storks with bronze lizard handles.

The ground colors from 1880 through 1900 ranged from stained ivory to more daring color effects, the latter increasing as the years passed. These effects can be found in coral ware, which is a beautiful blush.

Grainger Company

The Grainger Company was founded by Thomas Grainger in 1801, in Worcester, England. The company was a competitor of Worcester, and it made direct copies of Worcester porcelain. It also produced some exquisite double wall reticulated cups and saucers, as well as delicate ware with fine ribbing that gives the appearance of accordion pleating. The company was taken over by Royal Worcester in 1889.

Royal Crown Derby

Perhaps more than any other English company, Royal Crown Derby was inspired by the Far East in its designs, and developed a great number of Imari and Persian style patterns. This company used rich, jewel colored grounds of mazarine, cobalt blue, coral, and jade green, ornamented with heavily raised chased gold. The designs were inspired by the birds, flowers, insects, and traditional motifs seen on priceless carpets and embroideries.

Its raised gilding was achieved by using a paste made from glass frits, ground enamel color, and a small amount of flux, bound with turpentine. The paste was applied to the hand drawn designs using a fine sable brush, after which it was fired in the kiln.

In the late nineteenth century, Royal Crown Derby introduced the eggshell body, a body so thin and translucent that the decoration can clearly be seen from the inside. This ware was mainly used for coffee sets, and each cup and saucer is a miniature masterpiece that was executed by the finest artisans. The decoration usually covers the entire surface, combining raised and flat gilding, gold shading, and jeweling, often augmented with miniature portrait medallions. Famous artists were James Platts (figures), James Rouse (flowers), J. Brownswood (flowers) and E. Trowell (landscapes).

Minton

Many Minton cabinet cups and saucers were decorated in the Aesthetic style with raised gilt and platinum or silver birds, butterflies, and foliage. One of Minton's most important painters during the last quarter of the nineteenth century was Marc-Louis Salon (1835 – 1913). He was born at Montaubon, France, and worked at Sevres between 1851 and 1871. He brought the pâte-sur-pâte technique to Minton. A Minton cabinet cup and saucer with pâte-sur-pâte decoration would be a rare treasure today.

Copeland Spode

During the 1860s and through the 1890s, Copeland produced some important jeweled cabinet ware. It also had a number of talented painters, including David Evans and Charles Hürten (flowers), Daniel Lucas (landscapes), and Samuel Alcock (figures).

Postcard of lady drinking tea from a beautiful cup while her maid stands by.

Coalport

Coalport cabinet cups and saucers are highly regarded today. One of its most famous patterns is the Eastern inspired Japanese Grove pattern, which included birds and bamboo in underglaze blue. Gold was applied to the ground around and between the individual elements of the design. The shapes to which the pattern was applied were quite fanciful.

During the nineteenth century, popular ground colors were celadon, rose-du-barry, pale yellow, ivory, turquoise, and cobalt blue. Turquoise was used with a number of patterns based upon Far Eastern styles. The turquoise was sometimes overlaid with gold decoration that might include a stylized Japanese peony or a raised water lily. Cobalt blue was often used because of the great richness and depth of color that it suggested.

Some of the most desirable Coalport cabinet cup and saucers feature gold and enamel jewels on gold ground. Until the year 1896, these jewels, or enamel droplets, were applied by hand. In his helpful book *Coalport*, Michael Messenger praises the jeweling. "The regularity of the rows and uniform size is a source of some amazement and a tribute to the skill of the decorator." In addition to the fine jeweled decoration, some of the rarest of these cabinet pieces also have hand-painted cartouches with landscapes, birds, or flowers.

Royal Doulton

The early Doulton Burslem cups and saucers had lovely naturalistic shapes with Spanish ware painting. In the 1930s, Royal Doulton came out with their famous Reynard the Fox beverage sets designed by Henry Simeon. The pieces were decorated with expressive relief paintings of the fox in different poses, with a whip as a handle.

The tales of Reynard the Fox have entertained European children for centuries. The legends began in the twelfth century and were so popular that for centuries they were the widest known tales throughout all of Europe. They were handed down mainly by word of mouth. Reynard is the embodiment of cunning and discrete valor, while his great enemy Isegrim the Wolf represents brute strength. From the beginning of this set of fables, there was satirical observation of men and their weaknesses.

Lady having a cup of coffee, German postcard.

Demitasse cup and saucer.

Dresden, Donath & Co.,
c. 1893 – 1916.

Flared cup with scalloped foot; cup with portrait of lady, hand-painted flowers and heavy gilt decoration, turquoise and cream. (See mark #34.)

$350.00 – 400.00.

Close-up of portrait.

Demitasse cup and saucer.

Dresden, Carl Thieme,
c. 1901 – present.

Six-footed slightly fluted cup with twig handle; applied forget-me-nots. (See mark #40.)

$250.00 – 300.00.

Covered demitasse cup and saucer.

Dresden, unrecognizable mark, c. 1870s.

Cup with zigzag handle, 2"w x 1½"h, saucer 4¼", finial on lid has applied pink bow; Watteau paintings alternating with hand-painted flowers on aqua.

$300.00 – 350.00.

Trembleuse cup and saucer.

Dresden, R. Klemm, c. 1900 – 1916.

Scalloped cup with gilt cone-type bottom, saucer has reticulated rail, 5"; medallions of hand-painted courting scenes and gilt cross hatching on apple green.

$400.00 – 450.00.

Trembleuse cup and saucer.

Dresden, R. Klemm, c. 1900 – 1916.

Scalloped cup with gilt cone-type bottom, saucer has reticulated rail, 5"; medallions of hand-painted courting scenes and flowers on gilt.

$400.00 – 450.00.

Demitasse cup and saucer.

Dresden, R. Klemm,
c. 1888 – 1916.

Footed cup with unusual handle, 2⅛"w x 2"h, portrait medallion of lady with pearls, saucer 4¼"; lovely peach ground with heavy gold beads and paste decoration, pearl jeweling on rims.

$400.00 – 450.00.

Demitasse cup and saucer.

Dresden, Ambrosius Lamm,
c. 1891 – 1914.

Bute cup with angular handle, 2"w x 2"h, saucer 4"; cobalt medallion with gold silhouette of a man and woman, with gold beading and cross-hatching.

$175.00 – 200.00.

Teacup and saucer.

Dresden, Ambrosius Lamm,
c. 1900s, Rosenthal blank.

Shallow cup, paper thin with gold enameled flowers inside, 4"w x 1½"h, saucer 5⅔"; two medallions of hand-painted courting scenes, network of gold lines and dots.

$375.00 – 450.00.

Demitasse cup and saucer.

Dresden, Ambrosius Lamm, c. 1891 – 1914.

Cup with gilt interior and unusual handle, 2¼"w x 2¼"h, saucer 5"; covered with bold hand-painted flowers, band of gold and beading on rim. (See mark #39.)

$300.00 – 350.00.

Demitasse cup and saucer.

Dresden, Ambrosius Lamm, c. 1890s.

Bute cup with gilt decoration and loop handle, 2¼"w x 2"h, saucer 4½"; four hand-painted portraits of men and women in period dress on cup.

$375.00 – 400.00.

Demitasse cup and saucer.

Dresden, Heufel & Co., c. 1900 – 1940.

Slightly tapered cup with fat loop handle, 2⅛"w x 2"h, saucer 4⅓"; gold border with beading and gold paste flowers, hand-painted lady with a fan on one side on cup, man on the other. (See mark #36.)

$250.00 – 275.00.

Demitasse cup and saucer.

Dresden, Heufel & Co.,
c. 1900 – 1920.

Small quatrefoil shaped cup
with ring handle, 2"w x 1¾"h,
saucer 3½"; hand-painted
flowers, pearl jeweling and
gold cross-hatching on pink.

$150.00 – 175.00.

Trembleuse chocolate cup and saucer.

Dresden, unidentified mark,
c. 1870 – 1890.

Scalloped cup with two ornate handles, 2⅞"w x 3"h, saucer with reticulated rail, 5¼", lid with rose bud finial
with leaf extensions; ornately hand-
painted with flowers and cartouches
of sailing scenes, Kutani colors.

$350.00 – 375.00.

Close-up of sailing cartouche.

Demitasse cup and saucer.

Dresden, A. Hamann,
c. 1883 – 1893.

Cup with high curled bird handle, 2¼"w x 2¼"h, saucer 4⅓"; center cartouche with a hand-painted man and woman on cup, elegant gold decoration on yellow ground.(See mark #35.)

$150.00 – 175.00.

Another view showing handle.

Demitasse cup and saucer.

Dresden, Franziska Hirsch, 1900s.

Pedestal cup with gilt interior, unusual handle, 2⅛"w x 1¾"h, saucer 4⅓"; all gold with cream border, covered with turquoise jeweling and gold beads.

$475.00 – 500.00.

Close-up of jeweling.

Demitasse cup and saucer.

Dresden, Franziska Hirsch, 1890s.

Quatrefoil cup, 3" x 2½" x 1½", saucer 4½" x 4⅞"; medallions of courting scenes and flowers on a rich cobalt blue and gilt.

$225.00 – 275.00.

Teacup, saucer, and dessert plate.

Dresden, Helena Wolfsohn, c. 1930s.

Footed cup with unusual handle, 3¾"w x 2½"h, saucer 5½", dessert plate 7⅔"; beautiful border of gilt scrolls, beads and cross-hatching on cream.

$250.00 – 300.00.

Swan cup and saucer.

Dresden, Carl Thieme, new.

Cup in form of swan, cup 4½"w x 3¼"h, saucer 5⅞" x 4⅞"; gilt swan with white bisque feathers.

$475.00 – 500.00.

Trembleuse cup and saucer.

Dresden, Lamm, c. 1890s.

Flared scalloped cup, saucer with reticulated rail, gilt rose finial on lid; gold cobblestone decoration on pink with gilt.

$350.00 – 400.00.

Demitasse cup and saucer.

Fraureuth, c. 1898 – 1935.

Six-paneled cup with angular handle; silver overlay on white.(See mark #45.)

$100.00 – 125.00.

Demitasse cup and saucer.

Freiberg Porcelain Factory, c. 1926 – 1945.

Cup 2½"w x 1¾"h, saucer 4⅔"; heavy silver overlay on blue.

$145.00 – 175.00.

Demitasse cup and saucer.

Johann Haviland, c. 1939 – 1950s.

Cup with loop handle; silver overlay on red. (See mark #54.)

$100.00 – 125.00.

Demitasse cup and saucer.

Hutschenreuther, C. M., c. 1918 – 1945, made for H. C. Hahn, Berlin.

Cup has gilt interior with unusual handle, 2½"w x 1½"h, saucer 4½"; decorated with bands of gold and garlands of flowers. (See mark #57.)

$150.00 – 200.00.

Coffee cup and saucer.

Hutschenreuther, L.,
c. 1920 – 1967.

Pedestal cup with gold interior, 3"w x 2¼"h, saucer 4¾"; ornate white decoration on green with gilt decoration. (See mark #60.)

$125.00 – 150.00.

Demitasse cup and saucer.

Hutschenreuther, c. 1950s.

Footed cup with ornate silver handle, 2¾"w x 1¾"h, saucer 4½"; heavy silver overlay on turquoise ground.

$125.00 – 150.00.

Close-up showing silver overlay on saucer.

Demitasse cup and saucer.

Hutschenreuther,
c. 1950 – 1963.

Puffy shaped cup 2¼"w x 2¼"h,
saucer 4¾"; heavy silver overlay on rich cobalt blue ground.

$175.00 – 200.00.

Demitasse cup and saucer.

Hutschenreuther,
c. 1950 – 1963.

Cup with silver foot and handle, 2¾" x 1¼", saucer 4¼";
cobalt blue with silver overlay
decoration. (See mark #58.)

$125.00 – 150.00.

Covered coffee cup and saucer.

KPM Berlin, c. 1849 – 1870.

Cup with ornate handle,
3½"w x 3¼"h, lid has unusual
gilt finial, saucer 6¾";
turquoise leaf or petal design
with gilt scrolls. (See mark
#69.)

$350.00 – 400.00.

Coffee cup and saucer.

KPM Berlin, c. 1890s.

Scalloped cup with four curved feet, all gold inside, 3¼"w x 2½"h, saucer 5⅓"; gold ground with alternating panels of hand-painted flowers and maroon cartouches with gold scrolls, chip on one edge of foot.

$300.00 – 350.00.

Close-up of painting on saucer.

Demitasse cup and saucer.

KPM Berlin, c. 1870 – 1890.

Gilt scrolled band inside cup, 2½"w x 2"h, saucer 4⅓"; hand-painted flowers and heavy gilt. (See mark #70.)

$300.00 – 350.00.

Demitasse cup and saucer.

KPM Berlin, c. 1900.

Quatrefoil cup, 2¾"w x 2"h, saucer 4¾"; hand-painted courting scenes in monochrome reddish orange, with gilt decoration on rims and inside cup.

$250.00 – 275.00.

Coffee cup and saucer.

KPM Berlin, c. 1837 – 1844.

Cup with 1" gold band inside, 4⅛"w x 2½"h, saucer 6⅓"; hand-painted flower cartouches on a deep pink and gilt ground. (See mark #68.)

$200.00 – 225.00.

Demitasse cup and saucer.

KPM Berlin, c. 1900 – 1920.

Bute cup with gilt scrolled band inside cup; magnificent hand-painted scenes of Cupids at play; heavy gold decoration.

$500.00 – 600.00.

Close-up of Cupid decoration.

Demitasse cup and saucer.

Krister Porcelain,
c. 1904 – 1927.

Cup with loop handle, gold interior with black rose inside; black rose transfer on white. (See mark #72.)

$50.00 – 75.00.

Coffee cup, saucer, and dessert plate.

Meissen, c. 1924 – 1934.

Footed cup with loop handle, 4"w x 2½"h, saucer 5¾", dessert plate 7¼"; heavy gold leaves on white. (See mark #100.)

$350.00 – 400.00.

Demitasse cup and saucer.

Meissen, c. 1850 – 1900.

Quatrefoil cup, 3¼"w x 1¾"h, saucer 5⅛" x 5½"; gilt flowers and scrolls inside and outside, rich cobalt ground with medallions of flowers on saucer and courting scene on cup.

$600.00 – 700.00.

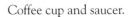

Coffee cup and saucer.

Meissen, c. 1850 – 1870.

Cup with snake handle with scales and with gilded foot, 2¾"w x 3"h, saucer with ⅓" gold band, 5⅞"; unusual nine-petal design with hand-painted bow at each point and a wreath with flowers. (See mark #99.)

$900.00 – 950.00.

Close-up of snake handle.

Coffee cup and saucer.

Meissen, c. 1870 – 1900.

Can cup with square handle, 2½"w x 2½"h, saucer 5"; gorgeous hand gilt work, rich cobalt blue ground with medallion of hand-painted flowers.

$700.00 – 750.00.

Close-up of floral cartouche.

Demitasse cup and saucer.

Meissen, c. 1930s.

Cup with twisted handle with blue ribbon and six feet; applied and hand-painted flowers and gilt.

$500.00 – 600.00.

Demitasse cup and saucer.

Meissen, c. 1850 – 1924.

Cup with swan handle; exquisite painting of exotic birds, swans, and butterflies, with gilt clover on border.

$500.00 – 550.00.

Trembleuse cup and saucer.

Meissen, c. 1850 – 1924.

Cup with two broken loop handles, saucer with reticulated rail, rose finial on lid; Purple Indian pattern.

$500.00 – 600.00.

Demitasse cup and saucer.

Nymphenburg, c. 1890s.

Can cup with loop handle; Art Nouveau style with stylized orchids on shades of pink, gilt.

$175.00 – 200.00.

Demitasse cup and saucer.

Prov Saxe, E.S. Germany, c. 1902 – 1938.

Pedestal cup with unusual ornate handle, raised well on saucer; turquoise jeweling and gold beads, some missing jewels and beads. (See mark #120.)

$100.00 – 125.00.

Coffee cup and saucer.

Rosenthal, c. 1910.

Footed cup with gilt eagle handle, 3¼"w x 4½"h, saucer 5¼"; hand-painted flowers, cobalt border with gilt rim. (See mark #126.)

$175.00 – 200.00.

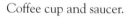

Demitasse cup and saucer.

Rosenthal, c. 1938.

Octagon-shaped cup gilt inside with loop handle, 2¼"w x 1¼"h, saucer 4"; alternate panels of purple rose on black with gold vermicelli decoration on white. (See mark #129.)

$100.00 – 125.00.

Demitasse cup and saucer.

Rosenthal, c. 1930.

Pompadour shape, gold interior of cup; gold and white flowers on royal blue. (See mark #128.)

$125.00 – 150.00.

Demitasse cup and saucer.

Rosenthal, c. 1949 – 1954.

Pompadour shape, gold interior of cup; gold and white roses on red. (See mark #132.)

$125.00 – 150.00.

Demitasse cup and saucer.

Rosenthal, U. S. Zone, c. 1945 – 1949.

Footed cup with fat loop handle, 3¼"w x 1¾"h, saucer 4¾"; silver overlay grape clusters on dark burgundy color. (See mark #130.)

$125.00 – 150.00.

Demitasse cup and saucer.

Rosenthal, c. 1923.

Cup with gold interior, squarish handle, 2½"w x 1½"h, saucer 4⅛"; medallion of flowers enhanced by gilt spokes and scrolls.

$100.00 – 125.00.

Teacup, saucer, and dessert plate.

Rosenthal, c. 1946, silver decorated by Pluderhausen Silver Co.

Footed cup 3½"w x 2½"h, saucer 6¼", plate 7¾"; silver overlay flowers on bright yellow. (See mark #131.)

$275.00 – 300.00.

Demitasse cup and saucer.

Rosenthal, c. 1960s.

Pompadour shape cup with gilt interior; black ground with roses and gilt. (See mark #133.)

$135.00 – 150.00.

Demitasse cup and saucer.

Rosenthal, c. 1901 – 1933.

Pedestal cup 3"w x 2"h, gilt interior and gilt snake handle, saucer 4¾"; gilt filigree eagles, stars on cobalt border.

$150.00 – 175.00.

Demitasse cup and saucer.

Rosenthal, c. 1929.

Cup with gold interior, 1¾"w x 2"h, saucer 4"; panel of hand-painted cathedral in Vienna, "Karls Kirche Wien," violet ground with gold leaves and beads.

$400.00 – 450.00.

Close-up of cathedral.

Demitasse cup and saucer.

Rosenthal, c. 1940s.

Cup with reinforced loop handle, 3"w x 1½"h, saucer 4½"; heavy floral overlay decoration on deep pink ground.

$175.00 – 200.00.

Demitasse cup and saucer.

Rosenthal, c. 1927.

Cup 2⅓"w x 1¼"h, saucer 4"; heavy sterling silver overlay decoration on an orange ground, wear on saucer well.

$75.00 – 100.00.

Demitasse cup and saucer.

Rosenthal, c. 1926.

Cup with gilt interior, Donatello shape; cobalt with gold fern-like decoration. (See mark #127.)

$95.00 – 125.00.

Demitasse cup and saucer.

Rosenthal, c. 1930s.

Low cup with angular handle; heavy silver overlay flowers on green.

$125.00 – 150.00.

Same set in red.

Coffee cup and saucer.

Schoenau Bros., Thuringer, c. 1887 – 1920.

Slightly tapered cup with loop handle; white leaf design on cobalt and gilt.

$125.00 – 150.00.

Demitasse cup and saucer.

Zeh, Scherzer & Co., Bavaria, c. 1880 – 1900.

Puffy effect on bottom of cup with unusual handle; turquoise jeweling on gilt and gold wavy effect on maroon. (See mark #175.)

$175.00 – 225.00.

Cabaret set.

Unmarked, numbered, probably made in Germany.

Set includes demitasse pot, covered sugar, creamer, and two cups and saucers; heavy silver overlay decoration on hot pink.

$500.00 – 600.00.

Demitasse cup and saucer.

Aich Karlsbad, c. 1920s.

Puffed-out cup with four curved gilt feet, unusual handle; three-leaf clover, panel of hand-painted scenes.

$250.00 – 300.00.

Demitasse cup and saucer.

Kuba, Joseph Carlsbad,
c. 1947 – present.

Can cup with gold interior,
four curled feet and high
curled handle, 1¾"w x 2"h,
saucer 4¾"; wide gold etched
border, cobalt and gilt decoration.

$90.00 – 125.00.

Demitasse cup and saucer.

Teplitz, Ernst Wahliss,
c. 1899 – 1918.

Pedestal cup with unusual
handle, gold interior 2½"w x
1½"h, saucer 4½"; cobalt blue
with turquoise jeweling.

$200.00 – 250.00.

Demitasse cup and saucer.

Thomas, c. 1908 – 1953.

Cup with square handle, gold
interior; paisley style flowers,
band of gilt on rim. (See mark
#159.)

$100.00 – 125.00.

Demitasse cup and saucer.

Royal Vienna type, beehive mark, c. 1890s.

Cup 2"w x 2¼"h, with square gilt handle, saucer 4½"; medallions of courting scenes on cobalt with gilt. (See mark #162.)

$150.00 – 175.00.

Demitasse cup and saucer.

Royal Vienna type, overglaze beehive mark, c. 1920s.

Can cup, 1¼"w x 2"h, deep saucer 3¾"; hand-painted panel of maiden and cupid framed with gold beading.

$175.00 – 200.00.

Coffee cup and saucer.

Royal Vienna, underglaze beehive, c. 1860s.

Cup with three paw feet and ornate swan handle, 2½"w x 3"h, deep saucer 5¼": all gold with scalloped cartouches of hand-painted roses and flowers.

$500.00 – 600.00.

Close-up of flower painting.

Demitasse cup and saucer.

Royal Vienna type, c. 1890s, artist signed, marked "der schlafende amor" on bottom, blue beehive mark.

Cup with high curved gilt handle with bird, 2¼"w x 2¼"h, saucer 4"; portrait medallion of lovers with Cupid in foreground, rich cobalt blue with gold beading and flowers.

$300.00 – 350.00.

Coffee cup and saucer.

Royal Vienna, c. 1850 – 1860.

Cup with entwined snake handle and three paw feet; medallion with a hand-painted scene of man and woman on cup; superb hand-painted white and gold leafy decoration on purple and heavy gold.

$600.00 – 650.00.

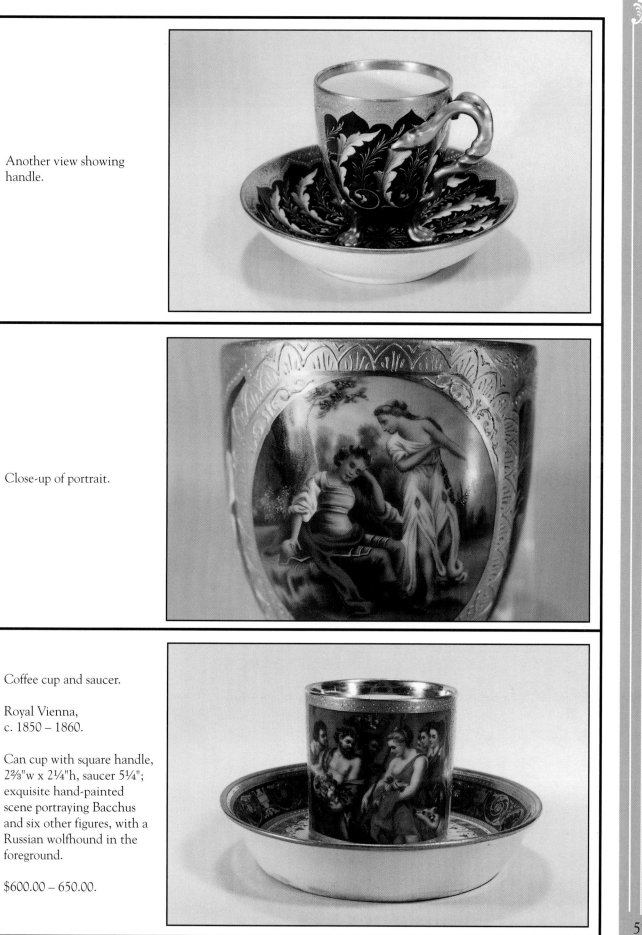

Another view showing handle.

Close-up of portrait.

Coffee cup and saucer.

Royal Vienna,
c. 1850 – 1860.

Can cup with square handle,
2⅔"w x 2¼"h, saucer 5¼";
exquisite hand-painted
scene portraying Bacchus
and six other figures, with a
Russian wolfhound in the
foreground.

$600.00 – 650.00.

Another view.

Cabaret set.

Royal Vienna, blue underglaze beehive mark, c. 1810 – 1840.

Set includes gorgeous tray with receptacles for pieces to fit, demitasse pot, covered sugar, milk jug, two cups and saucers; creamy white with exquisite applied foliate decoration and twisted leaf handles, rare set.

$1,200.00 – 1,500.00+.

Coffee cup and saucer.

Royal Vienna, c. 1850 – 1860s.

Can cup with high handle, gold interior; all gold cup and saucer with ribbing, Greek Key white design.

$250.00 – 300.00.

Demitasse cup and saucer.

Augarten, Vienna, c. 1920s.

Can cup with square snake handle, gilt interior; rare pâte-sur-pâte portrait of Greek man, cobalt and heavy gold paste.

$300.00 – 350.00.

Demitasse cup and saucer.

Pirkenhammer, c. 1918 – 1939.

Can cup with gilt interior, 2"w x 1½"h, saucer 4"; Art Nouveau design with a jeweled and enameled stained glass effect.

$175.00 – 225.00.

Breakfast cup and saucer.

Pirkenhammer, c. 1875 – 1887.

Unusually shaped cup with whimsical handle, 3⅓"w x 2"h, saucer 6"; gold and black flowers in relief with three applied black flowers.

$250.00 – 300.00.

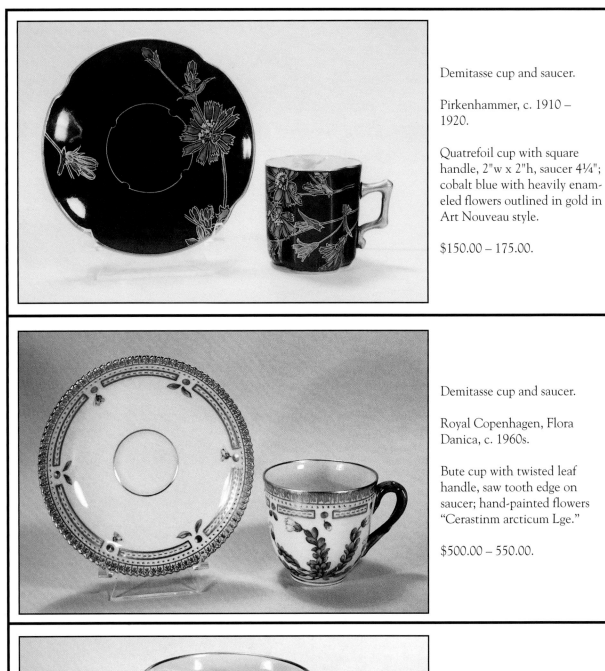

Demitasse cup and saucer.

Pirkenhammer, c. 1910 – 1920.

Quatrefoil cup with square handle, 2"w x 2"h, saucer 4¼"; cobalt blue with heavily enameled flowers outlined in gold in Art Nouveau style.

$150.00 – 175.00.

Demitasse cup and saucer.

Royal Copenhagen, Flora Danica, c. 1960s.

Bute cup with twisted leaf handle, saw tooth edge on saucer; hand-painted flowers "Cerastinm arcticum Lge."

$500.00 – 550.00.

Coffee cup and saucer.

Royal Copenhagen, Flora Danica, c. 1960s.

Bute cup with twisted leaf handle, saw tooth edge on saucer; hand-painted flowers, "Dsiyaensia lapponica L."

$500.00 – 550.00.

Close-up of flower painting.

Demitasse cup and saucer.

Capodimonte type, c. 1890s.

Cup 2¼"w x 2¼"h, twisted branch handle, saucer 4⅓"; hand-painted mythological figures in high relief with coat-of-arms on center of saucer, trimmed in gilt.

$200.00 – 250.00.

Covered coffee cup and saucer.

Capodimonte type, c. 1890s.

Cup with divided branch handle with grape extensions, 2¾"w x 3"h, saucer with high well, 5¾", lid with gold ribbing, gilt grape finial; mythological figures and cupids in relief. (See mark #7.)

$400.00 – 450.00.

Demitasse cup and saucer.

Capodimonte, c. 1890s.

Cup with red twig handle, 2¼"w x 1½"h, saucer 4¼"; hand-painted mythological scenes in relief on cup, flower draperies in relief on saucer. (See mark #8)

$175.00 – 200.00.

Close-up of relief painting.

Covered chocolate cup and saucer.

Capodimonte, c. 1870s.

Cup with two branch handles, 3"w x 3"h, saucer 5⅞", cupid finial on lid; relief scenes of Cupids busy at work and play.

$500.00 – 600.00.

Demitasse cup and saucer.

Capodimonte, c. 1890s.

Cup with twisted feather handle, 2¼"w x 2¼"h, saucer 4⅞"; mythological figures in relief, bathing scene, flowers on saucer.

$200.00 – 250.00.

Demitasse cup and saucer.

Ginori, Firenze, c. 1900 – 1920, artist signed.

Pedestal cup with gold foot and ornate handle, 2⅛"w x 2⅞"h, saucer with gold saucer well, 4⅞"; hand-painted pink and purple flowers. (See mark #47.)

$150.00 – 175.00.

Teacup and saucer.

Ginori, Firenze, c. 1900 – 1920, artist signed.

Cup with loop handle and gilt saucer well; hand-painted flowers and gilt.

$150.00 – 175.00.

Demitasse cup and saucer.

Ginori, c. 1920 – 1930s.

Footed cup with high gilt handle, ornate gold decoration on rich royal blue. (See mark #48.)

$125.00 – 150.00.

Demitasse cup and saucer.

Kuznetsov, Russia, c. 1890s.

Swirled cup, 1¾", saucer 3¾"; hand-painted blue flowers on cranberry pink shaded to white, gilt.

$100.00 – 125.00.

Demitasse cup and saucer.

Gardner Porcelain Factory, Moscow, Russia, c. 1840 – 1850.

Slightly waisted cup, gold band inside, saucer 4"; hand-painted flowers and wonderful hand gilded cross hatching, swirls, and leaves.

$250.00 – 300.00.

Coffee cup and saucer.

Imperial Russia, St. Petersburg, c. 1855 – 1881.

Cup with feathered handle, 3⅔"w x 3⅓"h, saucer 6½"; gold decoration, cup with hand-painted crown and royal monogram. (See mark #61.)

$500.00 – 550.00.

Close-up of crown and monogram.

Teacup and saucer.

Soviet period marks, Leningrad Petersburg Jewelry Factory, Russia, c. 1970s.

Tapered cup, gold interior; silver gilt and enamel.

$250.00 – 300.00.

Teacup and saucer.

Terchovys & Kiselyov, Russia, c. 1820 – 1850.

Slightly flared cup, gold interior; enameled roses on cobalt and gilt.

$300.00 – 350.00.

Demitasse cup and saucer.

Limoges, Pouyat, c. 1876 – 1890.

Cup with four curved gold feet and wonderful handle, 2⅔"w x 2½"h, unusually shaped saucer is 4½" x 5¼"; cobalt blue ground. (See mark #95.)

$300.00 – 350.00.

Coffee cup and saucer.

Limoges, GDM, c. 1882 – 1900.

Naturalistic cup, 2⅔"w x 2"h, saucer 4½"; satiny glaze with flowers decorated in the Spanish Ware technique. (See mark #85.)

$150.00 – 175.00.

Demitasse cup and saucer.

Limoges, Legrand, c. 1920s.

Can cup with gilt interior, 1⅞"w x 1⅞"h, saucer 4¼"; cobalt blue with beautiful gold paste work. (See mark #91.)

$235.00 – 275.00.

Demitasse cup and saucer.

Limoges, R. Laporte, c. 1891 – 1897.

Swirled cup with ornate handle and gold interior, 2⅓"w x 1¾"h, saucer 4¼"; rich cobalt blue with heavy gold paste roses. (See mark #92.)

$250.00 – 275.00.

Covered trembleuse chocolate cup and saucer.

Limoges, Touze, Lemartre & Blancher, c. 1920 – 1930s.

Cup with ornate handles, 3½"w x 4"h, deep saucer 6¼", lid 3¾"; heavy gold with pink flowers in an Art Nouveau motif.

$325.00 – 375.00.

Demitasse cup and saucer.

Limoges, decorated by Paris Studio, c. 1890s, made for Maple & Co., London.

Swirled and fluted cup with gilt interior, 2¼"w x 2"h, saucer 4¼"w; heavily decorated with gilt roses and beads.

$225.00 – 250.00.

Coffee cup and saucer.

Limoges, Le Tallec, Paris, c. 1950s.

Cup in Fragonhard shape with high coiled handle; heavy gold decoration on cobalt blue. (See mark #97.)

$250.00 – 300.00.

Demitasse cup and saucer.

Limoges, Bawo & Dotter, c. 1896 – 1900.

Six-sided cup with unusual handle, 1¾"w x 2¼"h, saucer 4¼"; light blue ground with hand-painted flowers, two heavy bands of gilt. (See mark #82.)

$125.00 – 150.00.

Demitasse cup and saucer.

Limoges, J. Pouyat,
c. 1862 – 1900.

Square cup with ornate foot
and wonderful handle, 2"w x
2½"h, square saucer 4";
hand-painted birds in natural
settings, gilt.

$150.00 – 175.00.

Close-up of painting on saucer.

Demitasse cup and saucer.

Limoges, Klingenburg,
c. 1890s.

Four-paneled cup; Japanese-
style heavy gold flowering
branch on pink and yellow.

$100.00 – 125.00.

Coffee cup and saucer.

Limoges, Unidentified maker, c. 1900 – 1920.

Fluted shape with question-mark handle; gold ribs on foot and saucer well; pink roses with dark green trim.

$150.00 – 175.00.

Demitasse cup and saucer.

Limoges, Unknown maker, c. 1900 – 1920.

Tapered cup with rustic gilt handle, gold interior; lovely floral design on gold.

$150.00 – 175.00.

Demitasse cup and saucer.

Unmarked, Paris decorator, c. 1890s.

Tapered cup with gilt interior; two hand-painted floral panels, gold molded leaves, aqua and white.

$125.00 – 150.00.

Demitasse cup and saucer.

Unmarked, Paris decorator, c. 1920s.

Fluted cup with unusual handle; beautiful hand-painted flowers and heavy gilt paste.

$175.00 – 200.00.

Coffee cup and saucer.

Paris, M. E. Bloch, c. 1868 – 1887.

Footed cup 3"w x 2½"h, unusual handle, saucer 5"; mixed decoration with bands of flowers and gilt. (See mark #4.)

$150.00 – 175.00.

Coffee cup and saucer.

Paris, c. 1840 – 1850s.

Cup with scalloped foot and ornate handle, gilt band inside rim, 3¼"w x 2¾"h, saucer 5¾"; exquisite flower painting and gold decoration.

$200.00 – 250.00.

Covered chocolate trembleuse cup and saucer.

Paris, marked BV in gold script, c. 1870 – 1890s.

Hand-painted coat-of-arms and garlands of roses on the border with gilt dots.

$400.00 – 450.00.

Demitasse cup and saucer.

Sevres blank, outside decoration, c. 1920s.

Straight-sided cup with loop handle, band of hand gilded decoration inside cup, 2½", saucer 4¾"; man and woman on horseback attired in regal hunting costumes riding after a fox and dog on cup, fox and dog on saucer, gilt.

$250.00 – 300.00.

Coffee cup and saucer.

Sevres, c. 1840.

Cup has cipher of Louis Phillipe; cobalt blue ground with medallion of two cupids, border of hand gilded leaves. (See mark #153.)

$200.00 – 250.00.

Coffee cup and saucer.

Sevres type, c. 1870s.

Cup with ring handle; intricate decoration with four Grecian medallions. (See mark #154.)

$200.00 – 225.00.

Coffee cup and saucer.

Sevres, First Empire, c. 1804 – 1909.

Empire-shaped cup with high ring handle with unusual carved white bisque piece in part of the hole, 2¾" x 4", saucer 5¼"; center medallion on cup with hand-painted portrait of lovely lady, signed Obrun, blue ground. (See mark #152.)

$350.00 – 400.00.

Close-up of handle.

Demitasse cup and saucer.

Sevres type, c. 1890s.

Translucent porcelain, cup 2¾"w x 2¼"h, saucer 4¾"; medallion with hand-painted courting scene on cup; floral medallions on saucer.

$275.00 – 300.00.

Demitasse cup and saucer.

Sevres, c. 1890s.

Cup with ring handle, 2¼"w x 2"h, saucer 4"; portrait of lady with scarf on her head, silver overlay decoration.

$350.00 – 400.00.

Coffee cup and saucer.

Sevres, c. 1860 – 1880.

Can cup, 3¼"w x 2"h, deep saucer 5¼"; medallion of hand-painted courting scene, artist signed, cobalt blue ground with lovely silver over-lay decoration.

$400.00 – 450.00.

Demitasse cup and saucer.

Sevres, c. 1860 – 1880.

Cup 2½"w x 2½"h, saucer 4⅞"; dark cobalt blue with silver overlay, hand-painted portrait of M. de Garaliers.

$400.00 – 450.00.

Close-up of portrait.

Coffee cup and saucer.

Sevres type, c. 1877.

Cup with ring handle; hand-painted bird, butterfly, and flowers.

$200.00 – 250.00.

Coffee cup and saucer.

Sevres type, probably decorated in Paris, c. 1890s.

Cup 2⅔"w x 2½"h, saucer 4⅞"; magnificent portrait of Louis XIV on cup, framed by a gold leafy decoration that is also on the saucer.

$235.00 – 265.00.

Teacup and saucer.

Aynsley, c. 1930s.

Footed cup, handle with thumb rest; white flowers and green leaves on gold luster; red and blue butterflies. (See mark #2.)

$125.00 – 150.00.

Teacup, saucer, and dessert plate.

Aynsley, c. 1891 – 1901.

Fluted cup with gold flower inside, 3½"w x 2½"h, saucer 5⅜"; cobalt blue with gold floral decoration. (See mark #1.)

$125.00 – 150.00.

Teacup and saucer.

Brownfield, c. 1880s.

Figural cup with branch handle extending to form handle and feet; wonderful naturalistic flower form.

$250.00 – 300.00.

Demitasse cup and saucer.

Carlton Ware (Wiltshaw & Robinson), c. 1920s.

Quatrefoil cup with gold interior, 2½"w x 2½"h, saucer 4¼"; pale peach with turquoise jewels.

$125.00 – 150.00.

Demitasse cup and saucer.

Carlton Ware, c. 1920s.

Quatrefoil shaped cup with gold interior, ear handle, 2½"w x 2½"h, saucer 4¼"; burgundy luster with jewels.

$125.00 – 150.00.

Demitasse cup and saucer.

Carlton Ware, c. 1925.

Can cup with gold interior, 2"w x 2¼"h, saucer 4⅛"; hand enameled flying ducks and pussy willows.

$150.00 – 175.00.

Demitasse cup and saucer.

Carlton Ware, c. 1925.

Quatrefoil cup with gold interior, ear handle, 2½"w x 2½"h, saucer 4¼"; cobalt blue luster with Oriental scene, ornate gold border.

$150.00 – 175.00.

Demitasse cup and saucer.

Carlton Ware, c. 1925+.

Quatrefoil cup, 2½"w x 2¼"h, saucer 4¼"; cobalt blue luster with gilt decoration and orange jeweling. (See mark #10.)

$150.00 – 175 .00.

Demitasse cup and saucer.

Carlton Ware, c. 1920s.

Quatrefoil cup with gold interior, 2½"w x 2¼"h, saucer 4¼"; green luster with gold leaves and pink enameled berries.

$125.00 – 150.00.

Demitasse cup and saucer.

Carlton Ware, c. 1920 – 1925.

Footed cup with gold interior, 2¼", saucer 4¼"; mustard yellow with black and gold border on rims. (See mark #9.)

$115.00 – 125.00.

Demitasse cup and saucer.

Cauldon, c. 1905 – 1920, artist signed A. Boullemier.

Can cup; hand-painted medallion of a lady feeding three baby chicks, heavy gold paste floral decoration.

$300.00 – 350.00.

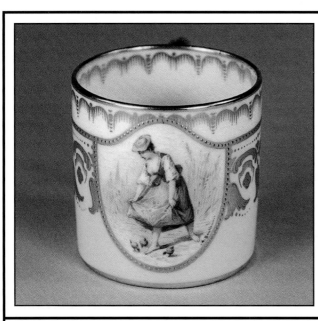

Close-up of portrait.

Teacup and saucer.

Brown-Westhead, Cauldon, c. 1891.

Cup with loop handle; gold spoke decoration, floral border. (See mark #6.)

$125.00 – 150.00.

Teacup and saucer.

Cauldon, c. 1905 – 1920, made for Ovington Bros.

Low cup with loop handle; magnificent gilt work on pink ground.

$175.00 – 200.00.

Teacup and saucer.

Cauldon, c. 1920s, made for Henry Morgan & Co., Colonial House, Montreal.

Cup with scalloped foot; cobalt blue with heavy gold flower and heart design. (See mark #12.)

$150.00 – 175.00.

Demitasse cup and saucer.

Cauldon, c. 1905 – 1920, made for C. A. Selzer, Cleveland.

Bute cup with loop handle, 2⅛"w x 2"h, saucer 4¼"; stained-glass-type decoration on turquoise, gilt.

$100.00 – 125.00.

Teacup and saucer.

Cauldon, c. 1920s, made for Davis Collamore & Co., New York, c. 1920s.

Cup with high curved handle, 2¾"w x 3"h, saucer 5⅛"; luscious gilt and roses.

$100.00 – 125.00.

Demitasse cup and saucer.

Cauldon, c. 1905 – 1920.

Bute cup with fat loop handle; cobalt and etched gold.

$115.00 – 125.00.

Tea bowl.

Chelsea, red anchor mark, c. 1755.

Rare tea bowl; hand-painted birds.

$700.00 – 800.00+.

Demitasse cup and saucer.

Coalport, c. 1881 – 1890, made for Davis Collamore & Co., New York.

Eight-fluted cup with gold interior, 1¾"w x 1¾"h, unusual white and gold twisted rope handle, saucer 3¾"; gilt beading and pearl jeweling on pink, some wear on saucer and some crazing on bottom of cup. (See mark #13.)

$350.00 – 400.00.

Demitasse cup and saucer.

Coalport, c. 1891 – 1920.

Quatrefoil cup with gold interior, gold ring handle, 2¼"w x 1"h, saucer 3⅛"; exquisite turquoise jeweling on gold, minor crazing on base of cup. (See mark #14.)

$550.00 – 650.00.

Demitasse cup and saucer.

Coalport, c. 1920s.

Shell figural cup with branch handle and four claw feet; all white with gilt rims, handle, and feet.

$100.00 – 125.00.

Boxed set of demitasse cups and saucers with sterling silver spoons.

Coalport, c. 1920s, made for Dimmer & Sons Ltd., Liverpool, England.

Cup with gold interior, 2"w x 2"h, saucer 3¾"; yellow ground with gold beads and floral decoration.

$1,500.00 – 1,700.00.

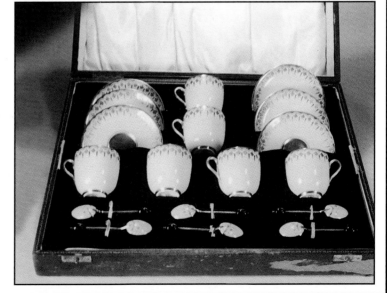

Demitasse cup and saucer.

Coalport, c. 1890, made for W. W. Wattles, Pittsburgh.

Crimped rim on cup, swirled at bottom, 1¾"w x 2"h, saucer 4¼"; coral shading to cream, with gilt.

$75.00 – 100.00.

Demitasse cup and saucer.

Coalport, c. 1891 – 1920.

Eight-paneled cup with gold interior, 2¼"w x 1¾"h, saucer 2¼"; turquoise jeweling and gold beading on gold ground. Some crazing.

$550.00 – 650.00.

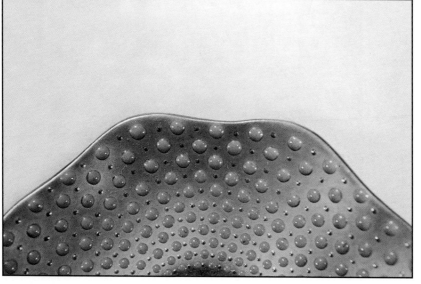

Close-up of jeweling.

Demitasse cup and saucer.

Coalport, c. 1891 – 1920.

Cup with gold interior, 2⅛"w x 2"h, saucer 4½"; embossed gold, with green medallions and turquoise jeweling and gold beads.

$475.00 – 500.00.

Demitasse cup and saucer.

Coalport, c. 1891 – 1920.

Cup with gold interior, 2¼"w x 2¼"h, saucer 4½"; medallions of flowers on lavender ground with lavish gilt.

$200.00 – 250.00.

Demitasse cup and saucer.

Coalport, c. 1891 – 1920.

Quatrefoil cup, 2¼"w x 1½"h, saucer 3⅛"; pink with gold decoration and beading.

$300.00 – 350.00.

Demitasse cup and saucer.

Coalport, c. 1891 – 1920.

Bute cup with gold interior, 1¾"w x 3¾"h; Imari-type decoration.

$300.00 – 325.00.

Demitasse cup and saucer.

Coalport, c. 1891 – 1920.

Bute cup with loop handle, 2¼"w x 2"h, saucer 4⅔"; dark red ground with heavy gold paste decoration.

$200.00 – 225.00.

Teacup and saucer.

Coalport, c. 1891 – 1920, made for Raphael Weil & Co., San Francisco.

Cup with gilt interior, 3⅓"w x 2"h, saucer 5⅓"; Japanese Grove pattern.

$235.00 – 260.00.

Demitasse cup and saucer.

Coalport, c. 1891 – 1920.

Bute cup with gilt interior and loop handle, 1⅞"w x 2"h, saucer 3¾"; all gold, with cobalt and white flowers painted under the glaze.

$300.00 – 350.00.

Close-up of floral painting.

Demitasse cup and saucer.

Coalport, c. 1891 – 1920.

Fluted cup with gold interior and ring handle, 2"w x 1¼"h, saucer 3⅓"; green leaves, gilt.

$275.00 – 300.00.

Coffee cup and saucer.

Coalport, c. 1881, made for Gilman Collamore, New York.

Quatrefoil cup, 2⅔"w x 2½"h, twisted stem handle, saucer 5¼"; beautiful pink flowers with lily-pad-type leaves in relief.

$175.00 – 200.00.

Demitasse cup and saucer.

Coalport, c. 1891 – 1920.

Quatrefoil cup with gold interior and ring handle, 2¼"w x 1½"h, saucer 3¼"; border of gold beaded flowers on pink.

$250.00 – 300.00.

Demitasse cup and saucer.

Coalport, c. 1891 – 1920.

Quatrefoil cup with ring handle, pink inside cup; magnificent example of jeweling, two turquoise on gold panels alternating with cabochon jewels on cream.

$700.00 – 900.00.

Close-up of saucer.

Demitasse cup and saucer.

Coalport, c. 1881 – 1890.

Can with loop handle; Japanese Grove pattern.

$225.00 – 250.00.

Demitasse cup and saucer.

Coalport, c. 1891 – 1920.

Quatrefoil cup with ring handle; gilt medallions with turquoise jewels, gold beads on pink.

$300.00 – 350.00.

Teacup and saucer.

Coalport, c. 1891 – 1920, made for Ovington Bros., New York.

Cup with loop handle; white medallions with fancy florals, cobalt with gilt flowers and scrolls.

$200.00 – 250.00.

Demitasse cup and saucer.

Copeland Spode, c. 1891 – 1900, made for Wigmore Daniell, London.

Puffy-shaped cup, 1½"w x 1¼"h, saucer 3¾"; gold swirls, beads and turquoise jeweling on green. (See mark #18.)

$225.00 – 250.00.

Close-up of jeweling on saucer.

Demitasse cup and saucer.

Copeland Spode, c. 1891 – 1920s, made for Davis Collamore & Co., New York.

Bute cup with loop handle, sponged gold on red, hand-painted florals. (See mark #19.)

$75.00 – 100.00.

Demitasse cup and saucer.

Copeland Spode, c. 1920s.

Can in repoussé sterling silver holder; yellow ground, with gilt decoration on border.

$75.00 – 100.00.

Demitasse cup and saucer.

Crown Devon (S. Fielding), c. 1930s.

Cup with gilt interior and unusual handle, 2½"w x 2¼"h, saucer 4¾"; cobalt ground, with gold on border and heavily enameled flowers. (See mark #24.)

$150.00 – 175.00.

Demitasse cup and saucer.

Crown Ducal, c. 1915 – 1925.

Can with loop handle; Spectria Flambé. (See mark #26.)

$100.00 – 125.00.

Demitasse cup and saucer.

Royal Crown Derby, c. 1888, made for Gilman & Collamore.

Quatrefoil cup with gold interior, 2¼"w x 2"h, saucer 4¼"; hand decorated, with gold flowers on pink.

$250.00 – 275.00.

Demitasse cup and saucer.

Royal Crown Derby, c. 1891.

Quatrefoil cup, 2¼"w x 2"h, saucer 4¼"; aqua with gilt flowers.

$275.00 – 300.00.

Demitasse cup and saucer.

Crown Staffordshire, c. 1930s, made for Tiffany & Co., New York.

Tapered cup with loop handle; heavily etched gold border.

$100.00 – 125.00.

Teacup and saucer.

Crown Staffordshire, c. 1906 – 1920s.

Footed cup with decorated loop handle; cobalt panels with gilt that alternate with flowers on white. (See mark #28.)

$100.00 – 125.00.

Teacup and saucer.

Davenport, c. 1860 – 1870.

Cup with ring handle; cobalt and gilt spokes.

$175.00 – 100.00.

Demitasse cup and saucer.

Doulton Burslem,
c. 1891 – 1902.

Quatrefoil cup, 2¼"w x 2"h,
saucer 4½"; Art Nouveau
style, gilt stylized trees on
cobalt blue.

$200.00 – 250.00.

Demitasse cup and saucer.

Royal Doulton, c. 1930s.

Gilded interior on cup; green
with hand gilding and beads.
(See mark #33.)

$250.00 – 275.00.

Demitasse cup and saucer.

Doulton Burslem,
c. 1882 – 1890.

Cup with ring handle, 2¼"w x
2½"h, saucer 4½"; decorated
with Spanish Ware technique
of hand-painted flowers outlined in gilt. (See mark #31.)

$150.00 – 175.00.

Demitasse cup and saucer.

Doulton Burslem,
c. 1891 – 1902.

Scalloped cup, loop floral
handle; hand-painted flowers,
yellow border.

$150.00 – 175.00.

Demitasse cup and saucer.

Royal Doulton,
c. 1920 – 1930s, signed
by Henry Simeon.

Cup with whip handle, 2"w x
2¾"h, saucer 4½"; relief
painting of Reynard the Fox.

$200.00 – 225.00.

Close-up of fox.

Demitasse cup and saucer.

Doulton, Burslem,
c. 1891 – 1902.

Ribbed cup with loop handle;
lovely blue floral transfer and
gilt. (See mark #32.)

$115.00 – 125.00.

Demitasse cup and saucer.

Doulton, Burslem,
c. 1891 – 1902.

Flower petal molded cup with
stem handle, 1½"w x 1¾"h,
saucer 4"; pale pink with aqua
and pink flowers.

$150.00 – 175.00.

Chocolate cup and saucer.

Doulton, Burslem,
c. 1881 – 1890.

Fluted cup, deep saucer; heavy
gold paste flowering branches.

$150.00 – 175.00.

Demitasse cup and saucer.

Hammersley, c. 1887 – 1912, made for Davis Collamore & Co., New York.

Slightly quatrefoil-shaped cup with bamboo handle, 2½"w x 2"h, saucer 4½"; Aesthetic style decoration, with heavy gold paste butterflies and flowering branches in gold and bronze coloration. (See mark #51.)

$100.00 – 125.00.

Teacup and saucer.

Hammersley, c. 1903.

Footed scalloped cup with broken loop handle; pink and blue flowers with heavy overlay of gilt flowers.

$125.00 – 150.00.

Demitasse cup and saucer.

Hammersley, c. 1887 – 1912, Ovington Bros., New York.

Footed cup with gilt interior; white ruffled design on foot and around saucer well; cobalt border with turquoise jewels and heavy gold paste.

$350.00 – 400.00.

Close-up of saucer.

Demitasse cup and saucer.

Minton, c. 1891 – 1902.

Cup with loop handle, 2"w x 2"h, saucer 4"; elaborate raised gilt decoration and beading on blush pink and white.

$275.00 – 300.00.

Demitasse cup and saucer.

Minton, c. 1891 – 1902.

Cup with loop handle, 2"w x 2"h, saucer 4"; Aesthetic style, with raised gilt and platinum birds, insects, trees, and foliage on blush pink. (See mark #106.)

$300.00 – 325.00.

Teacup and saucer.

Minton, c. 1912 – 1920.

Rich turquoise with white center, heavy gold decoration.

$250.00 – 275.00.

Demitasse cup and saucer.

Minton insert, Tiffany sterling holder and saucer, c. 1891 – 1901.

All gold insert, with beads on outside and heavily enameling with gold flowers with turquoise centers on inside; repoussé floral design on holder, band of leaves on saucer.

$350.00 – 400.00.

Demitasse cup and saucer.

Moorcroft, c. 1928 – 1948.

Cup 2⅓"w x 2⅓"h, saucer 4"; Leaf & Berry pattern on green ground.

$450.00 – 500.00.

Demitasse cups and saucers.

Shelley, c. 1925, holders by Elkington & Co.

Six cups in sterling silver holders in leather, satin, and velvet case; Blue Swallow pattern.

$1,000.00 – 1,500.00.

One cup and saucer from above set.

Demitasse cup and saucer.

Wedgwood, c. 1910 – 1920.

Can cup, 2⅓"w x 2¼"h, saucer with deep well, 4¾"; mottled magenta ground with turquoise, emerald, and coral jeweling with gilt decoration. (See mark #165.)

$150.00 – 175.00.

Demitasse cup and saucer.

Royal Worcester, c. 1898.

Straight-sided cup with gilt interior, 2"w x 2"h, saucer 3¾"; black ground with pearl jeweling, lavish gilding. (See mark #169.)

$300.00 – 350.00.

Demitasse cup and saucer.

Grainger Worcester, c. 1889.

Footed cup with unusual gold ring handle, 2¾"w x 2"h, saucer 4¼"; accordion pleating with turquoise jewels and gold beads. (See mark #173.)

$450.00 – 500.00.

Demitasse cup and saucer.

Royal Worcester, c. 1934, made special for Asprey's, London.

Pedestal cup with unusual handle, gilt inside; lavender compartments on pale green, with gold flowers and beads.

$275.00 – 300.00.

Demitasse cup and saucer.

Royal Worcester, c. 1912.

Cup with gold interior, 2"w x 1¾"h, saucer 3¾"; border of pearl jeweling and gold beads on cobalt ground.

$225.00 – 250.00.

Demitasse cup and saucer.

Royal Worcester, c. 1924.

Cup with loop handle, 2"w x 2"h, saucer 3¾"; emerald jeweling, Persian-type floral design.

$200.00 – 225.00.

Trembleuse cup and saucer.

Royal Worcester, c. 1870 – 1890s, made for Goode & Co., London.

Tapered cup with square handle, rim area 2⅔"w x 2½"h, deep indentation on 5½" saucer; cream with band of pink and turquoise jeweling and gold decoration, hairline on cup (See mark #167.)

$75.00 – 100.00.

Demitasse cup and saucer.

Worcester Grainger, c. 1901.

Cup with flowers inside, 3"w x 2"h, saucer 4¾"; satiny matte glaze with colorful flowers, gilt rim. (See mark #174.)

$230.00 – 260.00.

Teacup, saucer, plate.

Royal Worcester, 1909 – 1910.

Cup 3⅛"w x 2"h, saucer 4¾", plate 6"; hand-painted yellow, pink, and white roses, trimmed with gilt, attributed to Worcester flower artist Mabel Lander.

$225.00 – 250.00.

Demitasse cup and saucer.

Royal Worcester, c. 1925, made for Hardy Bros. Ltd.

Can cup with gilt interior, 2", saucer 4¼"; cobalt blue with gilt decoration and pearl and emerald jeweling. (See mark #170.)

$225.00 – 250.00.

Demitasse cup and saucer.

Royal Worcester, c. 1887.

Partially ribbed tapered cup with bamboo handle, 2"w x 2"h, saucer 4", hand-painted flowers outlined in gilt. (See mark #168.)

$175.00 – 200.00.

Teacup and saucer.

Royal Worcester, c. 1940.

Pink ground with heavy gold paste decoration, etched gold border on rims. (See mark #171.)

$200.00 – 225.00.

Teacup and saucer.

Royal Worcester, c. 1876, marked IP, probably made for Paris Exhibition.

Cup 2⅞"w x 2⅞"h, saucer 5⅓"; pearl jeweling and gold beads on the rim, fabulous bird painting attributed to Worcester bird painter James Hopewell.

$400.00 – 450.00.

Close-up of bird painting.

Teacup and saucer.

Royal Worcester, c. 1865 – 1880.

Cup with branch handle; naturalistic leaf motif.

$175.00 – 225.00.

Demitasse cup and saucer.

Royal Worcester, c. 1915.

Cup 2¼"w x 1½"h, saucer 3¾"; hand-painted fruit painting inside cup is signed Phillips, matching saucer is signed Ricketts.

$500.00 – 550.00.

Demitasse cup and saucer.

Grainger Worcester,
c. 1870 – 1889.

Double-wall reticulated cup
and saucer with bamboo handle, gilt. (See mark #172.)

$500.00 – 600.00.

Close-up of saucer.

Teacup and saucer.

Coxon Belleek, Wooster,
Ohio, c. 1926 – 1930.

Flared cup with fat loop handle; hand-painted flowers, gilt
rims and handle.

$125.00 – 150.00.

Teacup and saucer.

Lotus Ware, Knowles, Taylor & Knowles, c. 1891 – 1898.

Round cup with feathered handle; ribbed star motif, heavy gold flowering branches.

$175.00 – 200.00.

Demitasse cup and saucer.

Lenox insert, Tiffany sterling holder and saucer, c. 1920 – 1930s.

Plain cream insert; repoussé floral design on holder, band of leaves on saucer.

$125.00 – 150.00.

Demitasse cup and saucer.

Pickard, c. 1895 – 1898.

Cup with three curved feet; heavy gold paste flowers and drapes on a blush pink ground.

$300.00 – 350.00.

Demitasse cup and saucer.

Pickard, c. 1925 – 1930, Thomas blank.

Footed cup with gold interior, 2⅔"w x 2"h, saucer 4½"; etched gold with a black band with hand-painted flowers. (See mark #117.)

$200.00 – 225.00.

DINNERWARE SERVICES

Cups and saucers from the elegant dinnerware services of the late nineteenth and the twentieth centuries provide much variety and offer good value to collectors.

Two kittens gazing at a French snack set and croissant, early postcard.

EUROPEAN MAKERS

CHARLES AHRENFELDT

Charles Ahrenfeldt had a porcelain manufactory in Limoges, France, and a decorating shop in Altrohlau, Bohemia (now Stara Rale, Czechoslovakia), from 1886 to 1910. He decorated unmarked porcelain blanks from local factories near Karlsbad and applied his own marks. The company also imported porcelain from the von Schierholz Company in Plaue, Germany. Ahrenfeldt decorated hand-painted reticulated plates and tea wares in the Dresden style.

DRESDEN

A large group of Dresden porcelains were made to satisfy the middle-class market for dinnerware. Many services were decorated with the famous flower and gilt painting so typical of Dresden's style. These Deutsche Blumen (German flowers) have remained popular among collectors and are still a favorite of porcelain painters. In this style, flowers are realistically represented but have fanciful colors. They may be strewn across a porcelain surface as though scattered by a breeze, painted in an S-shaped

bouquet, or draped in garlands. The Dresden decorator Franziska Hirsch painted many lovely dinnerware sets with flowers and gilt.

Another Dresden design popular with collectors is that of courting scenes alternating with floral cartouches. Helen Wolfsohn decorated many cups and saucers in this style, in the quatrefoil shape. Some collectors try to find examples in different ground colors.

Some Dresden cups and saucers are eggshell thin and so translucent you can see your hand through them. Many intricate molds, such as a basketweave or shell motif, were used, and some saucers were further enhanced with reticulation.

Kitten looking into a lovely hand-painted cup and saucer, early die-cut card.

JOHANN HAVILAND

Johann Haviland formed a porcelain company in 1907, in Waldershof, Germany. Everyday china, hotel china, and high quality porcelain were made. In 1924, the company was sold to Richard Ginori, and the name of the firm was called Waldershof Factory. Rosenthal bought it in 1937, and began producing fine china for export to the United States. Popular patterns were Moss Rose and Blue Garland. A variety of lovely cobalt and gold demitasse sets were made. In the 1970s and 1980s, many patterns were sold in grocery stores as premiums.

HUTSCHENREUTHER

Carl Magnus Hutschenreuther began the first industrial production of porcelain in Bavaria in 1814. He established his company in Hohneberg. His son Lorenz set up his own company in Selb in 1857. In 1969, the two companies merged to become Hutschenreuther AG in Selb. The company produced many lovely dinner sets for export to the United States. Famous patterns are Richelieu, Belrose, Mirabelle, and Blue Onion. Highly desirable are the cobalt blue cups and saucers with a gold lace pattern. Both demitasse and full-size coffee cups and saucers were made with this real lace decoration.

MEISSEN

The Meissen Company produced many exquisite dinner sets with hand-painted flowers. Meissen flowers are a stylized version of well-known garden flowers (Deutsche Blumen) adapted for the decoration of porcelain. During the 1930s, many dinnerware sets of Meissen's Rose pattern were exported to the United States. The demand was so great for this pattern that many sets were decorated out of the factory and have strike marks to indicate outside painting. Another popular pattern is the Full Green Vine Wreath, and cups and saucers in this design can be found in a number of interesting shapes.

The oldest Meissen tableware decorations were its East Indian patterns with stylized sectionalized paintings of Oriental animals, flowers, and landscapes. Today the painters of East Indian designs have a selection of 160 colors and many different patterns, such as Purple Indian and the popular Court Dragon. Meissen cups and saucers are always top quality and are prized by collectors.

ROSENTHAL

Philip Rosenthal operated a porcelain factory in Selb, Germany, in 1879, producing fine dinnerware, decorative items, and figures. The high quality workmanship and simplicity of design made Rosenthal's dinnerware highly acclaimed, and much was exported to the United States. Collectors look for early patterns with hand painting and intricate molds. Rosenthal named its shapes, and some of the most popular are Pompadour, Maria, Donatello, and Coupe, a modern, streamlined shape that became popular in the 1950s.

Rosenthal made a number of lovely flower patterns in luxury lines exported to the United States from 1949 to 1954, including Vienna, Phoenix, and Florinda. These were embellished with lavish gilt. In the 1990s, Rosenthal produced an ornate pattern, Medusa, to honor the late fashion designer Versace. A new cup and saucer in this pattern retails for $160.

SCHUMANN

Heinrich Schumann founded this factory in 1881, in Arzburg, Bavaria, and the company is still in operation today. It produces decorative porcelain, dinnerware services, gift articles, and fancy coffee and tea sets which are very popular with collectors today. Its best known patterns had the "Dresden flowers" motif and were named Empress, Chateau, and Dresden Rose. In the 1930s, the company used a special mark, "Dresdner Art Germany." Schumann uses high-quality transfer decoration and lovely gilding, and many of its plates and serving pieces have reticulated borders. It has also copied Helena Wolfsohn's style of courting scenes that alternate with flowers. The difference is that Dresden tableware is hand painted, while Schumann is not.

TIRSCHENREUTH COMPANY

The Tirschenreuth Company was established in 1838, in Tirschenreuth, Bavaria. It made dinnerware services and decorative porcelain. In 1927, the company was acquired by the L. Hutschenreuther Company. Cups and saucers are available with good quality transfer decoration, many in cobalt and gilt.

HEREND

Herend is the largest hand-decorated porcelain factory in the world today. They employee 1,560 people, including 700 painters and 35 master painters. According to Herend, no other porcelain manufacturer has as many items or patterns in its inventory. Thousands of shapes are available in more than 5,000 different patterns.

One of these famous patterns was produced in 1851 for the London World Exhibition. Queen Victoria liked it so much, she commissioned a large table service for Windsor Castle. The pattern became known as Queen Victoria, and remains one of Herend's most popular patterns today.

Another well-known pattern, Rothschild Bird, was based on an old Hungarian legend. In the early nineteenth century, a princess who was traveling along the shores of Lake Balaton was accosted by robbers who took her royal jewels. While retreating, the robbers dropped a necklace on the ground. A bird was attracted to it and took it to her nest. A search party saw it dangling from a branch where the nest was and took it back to the princess. This story was the inspiration for the pattern, and the necklace is shown in the early design.

One reason collectors appreciate Herend china is the amount of hand work that goes into each piece of dinnerware. Painters earn the right to sign their names on the base of each piece they decorate, alongside the Herend logo. For collectors, such pieces are among Herend's most sought after items. A signed coffee cup and saucer in a chinoiserie pattern can cost as much as $650.00.

PIRKENHAMMER

In 1803, Frederic Höcke founded the Pirkenhammer Company in Pirkenhammer, Bohemia, which is presently Brezova, Czechoslovakia. The company produced household porcelain and pipe bowls and had many owners. Fischer & Mieg brought it to prominence c. 1857 – 1918. Many lovely tableware and decorative porcelains with hand-painted flowers and gilt were made during this period.

ROYAL COPENHAGEN

This company was founded in 1775, and soon became world famous for its underglaze blue porcelain dinnerware. Its most famous service was Blue Fluted, which was made in the Full, Half, and Plain patterns. During Royal Copenhagen's 225th anniversary in 2000, a young student from the School of Danish Design, Karen Kjaeldgard-Larsen, contacted Royal Copenhagen with her idea of a new version of the pattern. She called it Blue Fluted Mega, and it was adopted by the company.

The Blue Flower pattern was developed in 1779. As opposed to Blue Fluted, this pattern reflected the contemporary European style of naturalistic flowers. This pattern, also painted by hand, is very popular today.

LIMOGES

The porcelain industry in the Limoges area employed about 200 workers around 1807. By 1830, the number had increased to over 1,800 employees. The period of the mid-to-late 1800s was the golden age for the Limoges porcelain industry.

Production became industrialized, and new methods of manufacturing and decoration were introduced. To meet the growing demand of a large export market, new mass production techniques were introduced. Approximately 75% of the porcelain was exported, and the largest percentage of this was sent to the United States. The number of companies increased from 32 in the late 1800s to 48 in the 1920s, and entire families were employed because many jobs could be accomplished by women and children.

With the tremendous amount of porcelain produced, the market couldn't absorb all the wares. After World War I and the economic depressions of the 1920s and 1930s, many older companies were forced out of business. There was some revitalization after World War II, and today Limoges is still the center of hard paste porcelain production in France. Cups and saucers from dinnerware, demitasse, and chocolate sets from any of the companies located in and around Limoges, France, are eagerly collected because they offer a variety of shapes and decorations and are usually quite affordable.

UNITED STATES MAKERS

CASTLETON CHINA CO.

Castleton China Company, a subsidiary of Shenango China, was established in 1940 at New Castle, Pennsylvania. The head of the company, Louis E. Hellman, was an expert in European porcelains, and his goal was to produce contemporary designs in fine tableware, combining the old craftsmanship of Europe with the technical superiority of America. He hired some of the world's most outstanding artists to create new designs, and many fine tablewares were produced.

A talented designer, Eva Zeisel, created the first free form modern shape in fine china in 1946, named Museum. It was commissioned by the Museum of Modern Art and was praised throughout the world as marking a new epoch in ceramic history.

Castleton China graced the tables of the White House for Presidents Eisenhower and Johnson. Unfortunately, parent company Shenango China went through hard economic times and became the property of the Anchor Hocking Corporation in 1979. The company manufactures a fine line of hotel, restaurant, and institutional ware today.

FRANCISCAN CHINA

Gladding, McBean & Company was founded in 1875, in Lincoln, California, after an exceptional deposit of clay was found in the area. Sewer pipes were made first, followed by ceramic tiles. In 1933, dinnerware was produced, and the trade name of Franciscan Pot-

tery was chosen for the line in order to honor the monks who helped settle California. By 1939, fifteen new patterns were produced. A new line of embossed hand-painted dinnerware was created. Patterns included the Apple pattern and the Desert Rose pattern, which is the best selling American dinnerware pattern in history. Annette Honeywell, a free-lance artist, is credited with the Desert Rose design. Franciscan China is characterized by bold colors in florals and fruits and is popular with collectors. The company went thorough many changes, and it closed in 1984.

HOMER LAUGHLIN CHINA COMPANY

Homer and Shakespeare Laughlin started their company in East Liverpool, Ohio, in 1871. The company moved to Newell, West Virginia, in 1929, and is still in operation today. Dinnerware and commercial china became the main products of the company. Homer Laughlin China is best known for Fiesta, designed by Frederick Rhead in 1936. The company produced a Dresden eggshell pattern during World War II. Its eggshell was a fine, thin, semi-porcelain dinnerware with excellent decoration. Imperial Blue Dresden, a copy of Meissen's famous Blue Onion pattern, is a top seller for the company and is still being made today.

LENOX, INC.

Lenox is the major producer of fine china in the United States today. Its dinnerware is known for its uniformity of glaze, translucency, perfectly applied design, durability, and consistent color.

Lenox china has been in use at the White House since 1917, when Woodrow Wilson commissioned a 1,700-piece dinner set. It's been ordered by Presidents Roosevelt, Truman, Reagan, and Clinton. Lenox dinnerware can be found in more than half of our governor's mansions, and in United States embassies throughout the world.

Collectors enjoy looking for older cups and saucers, especially the early Belleek examples with fine hand-painted decoration. Favorite modern patterns are Autumn, Castle Garden, Fair Lady, Holiday, and Ming. Lenox's Guarantee of Satisfaction is:

"Lenox takes pride in offering works of uncompromising high standards
of quality, crafted with care and dedication by skilled artisans. Our goal,
in every case, is to meet the highest expectations of artistry and fine
workmanship. Therefore, if you are ever less than completely satisfied,
Lenox will either replace your work or refund your purchase price.

Breakage Protection Policy: If you ever break or damage a work you
own, Lenox will strive to satisfy you as well. If the edition is still open
and a replacement is available, Lenox will send it to you at only one-
half the current price of the work."

MOTTAHEDEH

In 1929, Mildred Root, a young New York interior designer, married Rafi Y. Mottahedeh, an importer and antiques dealer. The couple collected early Chinese and European porcelain and, in the mid-1940s, established the Mottahedeh Company. They worked directly with European factories to produce the high quality reproductions that are the hallmark of their company. Mildred designed pieces for the Reagan and Bush administrations. She believed that everyone should have access to the china and tableware that kings and rulers had. When Mildred died in February of 2000, at the age of 91, Mottahedeh employee Kirsten

Rohrs paid this tribute to her: "She was a legend in the tabletop industry, a porcelain expert and collector...and was the driving creative force behind the company." Today, Mottahedeh porcelain is sold in most museum shops and upscale department stores. It is now under new ownership.

Collectors look for cups and saucers in a variety of patterns, such as Chelsea Bird, based on an eighteenth-century English Chelsea plate in the Williamsburg Museum.

Imperial Blue is copied from an eighteenth-century Chinese Export pattern and has a rich underglaze blue floral design.

The most popular and expensive pattern today is Tobacco Leaf. It has 27 glaze colors and is highlighted by 22kt gold. It is based on an eighteenth-century Chinese Export piece and depicts a small phoenix perched on a flowering tobacco plant. A cup and saucer in this pattern runs about $100 – 125.

SYRACUSE CHINA

The Onondaga Pottery Company began operation in Syracuse, New York, in 1871. By 1890, they were making a vitrified china that was white, translucent, and stronger than European porcelain. In 1893, the name "Syracuse China" was introduced, and the company was awarded a medal at the Colombian Exposition in Chicago. In 1896, it created its "rolled edge" china, which became a standard body form. Syracuse China discontinued its line of china for home use in 1970. In 1971, it became one of the country's largest producers of hotel, restaurant, airline, and commercial tableware.

Collectors enjoy finding cups and saucers in the Bracelet pattern, which has a wide encrusted gold rim. Another favorite, the Victoria pattern, was designed by John Wigley in 1939. It has a center rose and buds on an old ivory ground and is quite striking.

Adorable little girl drinking out of a hand-painted teacup and saucer
that matches her nightgown; B.B. London, series L.

POT DE CRÈME CUPS

Pot de crème refers to a French custard dessert, as well as the small lidded pots in which this dessert is served. The French word for custard is "crème". Technically, the pot de crème is a lightly set, baked custard which is soft and best served in small pots. The traditional flavor was vanilla, but recipes can be found in many flavors.

The pots are typically made of porcelain and hold approximately three ounces of custard. Limoges companies have been making them since the early 1800s, and many European companies have made them as well. Most cups have a single small handle. The lids are normally adorned with a finial on the top, such as a piece of fruit, an acorn, a rose, or a bird. The designs vary from plain white with gilt to intricate floral patterns.

Pot de crème cups were frequently sold in sets. Sets with six cups are the most common, but sets for two and for eight have been found. Sometimes a set includes a serving tray; other sets may include small saucers. The pot de crème cups are still being made today by some porcelain companies. The average price for a set of six is $200 – 300. A single pot de crème cup made by Royal Copenhagen in their famous Flora Danica pattern is valued at $650.

GRADING SYSTEM

Some ceramic manufacturers grade their porcelain just as meat producers grade their beef. The earliest European porcelain manufacturer, Meissen, began a system of grading its wares as early as 1712.

In 1869, Meissen used four sorting grades, and two to four incisions were made across the blue crossed swords mark. Decorated first choice wares were sold without an incision. Second choice porcelain with painting was identified by two incisions across the swords, third choice by three incisions, and fourth choice by four. Today, because kilns are computer controlled, Meissen just uses one incised mark for minor defects.

Royal Copenhagen also marks seconds. Those pieces which fail the inspection procedure, but are deemed worthy of sale, are marked under the base by a scratch made by a grinding wheel, canceling the three wavy lines that are the trademark of Royal Copenhagen porcelain. In his helpful book, *Royal Copenhagen Porcelain Animals and Figurines*, Robert J. Heritage says, "It is very much a personal judgment about how much a piece may be devalued by being given second quality status, but these pieces may be quite acceptable to the collector, particularly if the items are rarely seen now."

Herend is another porcelain company who marks factory seconds. Two lines are ground across the center of the Herend trademark. It is sometimes hard to see without magnification. The Roman numeral II was sometimes used to mark a second. The name Herend, with crossed paint brushes below, marks third class items, mostly painted by student painters. Older pieces marked with TERTIA show that the item is third class, regardless of other marks. TERTIA is widely misrepresented as an artist signature. If only an impressed mark is present, without any other trademark, as a general rule the item is not first quality.

Collectors should not necessarily pass up a beautiful piece of porcelain because it has cut marks. Sometimes it is difficult to understand why a piece is not considered first quality. It might be a tiny flaw in the manufacturing, such as a black kiln spot, a glaze skip or bump, or a firing crack. Possibly the decoration is not deemed 100% up to par. An extra paint line, a paint bubble, uneven gilding, and an odd choice of marking or coloration can influence the grading decision.

The piece should be judged on its own merits. Is the porcelain itself pure white and mainly unblemished? Is the painting attractive? Is the gilding rich and even? If the piece is pleasing to you, by all means buy it. The prices of Meissen are sky rocketing, and some nice bargains can be had with seconds or thirds. Some dealers and collectors look for items having cut marks because they are much more affordable.

The important thing to remember is that you don't want to pay full price for second or third quality merchandise. In the case of Internet auctions and web sites, many sellers are not aware of merchandise grading and don't call items with cut marks. Often the incised marks don't show up in photographs, and you can be fooled. When in doubt, it is best to question the seller, "Is your item first quality or are there incised marks?" Many times the seller does not know what this means, and you can explain it to him/her.

The price you should pay for items of second or third quality is quite subjective. Two cut marks on a Meissen piece certainly doesn't indicate that it is damaged, merely that it is not quite up to Meissen's rigid standards and quality control. Perhaps a reduction of one-forth or one-third would be reasonable. It's your call.

Demitasse cup and saucer.

Ahrenfeldt, Charles, Saxe, c. 1900.

Cup with high ornate handle, 2¼"w x 2½"h, saucer 4⅓"; medallion of birds on yellow ground, with border of green leaves with red berries.

$45.00 – 55.00.

Demitasse cup and saucer.

Bareuther & Co., c. 1930 – 1950s.

Tapered cup; cobalt blue with gilt flowers.

$40.00 – 55.00.

Chocolate cup and saucer.

Dresden, Richard Klemm, c. 1888 – 1916.

Straight-sided cup, 2"w x 3"h, saucer 4¾"; hand-painted flowers and gilt.

$85.00 – 100.00.

Coffee cup and saucer.

Dresden, Richard Klemm, c. 1890s.

Fragonhard cup with bird handle; hand-painted strewn flowers and gilt.

$90.00 – 125.00.

Demitasse cup and saucer.

Dresden, Donath & Co., c. 1890s.

Cup 2½"w x 2½"h, saucer 4½"; hand-painted flowers on yellow alternating with courting scenes on saucer, sailing scenes on cup.

$100.00 – 125.00.

Demitasse cup and saucer.

Dresden, Hutschenreuther Art Studio, c. 1918 – 1945.

Footed cup with angular handle, gilt interior; gilt flowers on orange and cream.

$100.00 – 125.00.

Demitasse cup and saucer.

Dresden, Franziska Hirsch, 1901 – 1930.

Cup slightly paneled at bottom, with ornate handle, 2½"w x 2¼"h, scalloped saucer 4½"; garlands of hand-painted flowers and gilt. (See mark #37.)

$75.00 – 95.00.

Coffee cup and saucer.

Dresden, Helena Wolfsohn, c. 1890s.

Quatrefoil cup, 3¼"w x 3"h, saucer 5½"; hand-painted flowers on turquoise alternating with courting scenes.

$100.00 – 125.00.

Snack set.

Dresden, Richard Klemm.

Footed cup with decorated square handle, 2⅔"w x 2"h; saucer tray with pierced border, 6½"; hand-painted flowers and gold.

$150.00 – 200.00.

Breakfast cup and saucer.

Dresden, Richard Klemm, c. 1891 – 1914.

Footed cup with ornate handle, 3¾"w x 2"h, scalloped saucer 5¾"; vivid flowers and gilt. (See mark #38.)

$75.00 – 100.00.

Teacup, saucer, and dessert plate.

Dresden, Carl Thieme, c. 1920s.

Cup with scalloped foot, 4"w x 2"h, saucer 5⅞", plate 8½"; hand-painted yellow flowers and gilt.

$100.00 – 125.00.

Coffee cup and saucer.

Dresden, Ambrosius Lamm, c. 1887-1914.

Quatrefoil shaped cup, 2⅞"w x 3"h, saucer 5¾"; yellow band with large array of hand-painted flowers and gilt decoration.

$200.00 – 225.00.

Demitasse cup and saucer.

Dresden, Richard Klemm, c. 1900.

Eight-fluted cup with gilt floral and leaf twisted handle, 1¾", saucer 4"; hand-painted flowers and gilt.

$100.00 – 125.00.

Tea set.

Dresden, Ambrosius Lamm, c. 1887 – 1914.

Set includes teapot, covered sugar, creamer, and four cups and saucers; hand-painted pink and yellow roses and blue forget-me-nots, lavish gold.

$600.00 – 700.00.

Chocolate set.

Dresden, Carl Thieme, c. 1920 – 1930s.

Set includes pot and six cups and saucers, with reticulated borders on saucers; hand-painted flowers and gilt.

$900.00 – 1,200.00.

Chocolate cup and saucer from set.

Demitasse cup and saucer.

Dresden, Ambrosius Lamm, c. 1887 – 1914.

Can cup 1¾", saucer 3¾"; courting scene silhouette in black on cup, strewn flowers and gilt on cup and saucer.

$100.00 – 125.00.

Close-up of silhouette.

Demitasse cup and saucer.

Dresden, Franziska Hirsch, 1901 – 1930.

Footed cup with butterfly handle; hand-painted flowers and gilt.

$200.00 – 225.00.

Teacup and saucer.

Edelstein Porcelain Factory, c. 1934 – present.

Tapered molded cup with ruffled foot, unusual handle; gilt decoration on ivory. (See mark #42.)

$25.00 – 30.00.

Teacup and saucer.

Furstenberg Porcelain Manufactory, c. 1950s.

Footed cup with wide loop handle; cartouches of roses on robins egg blue. (See mark #46.)

$40.00 – 45.00.

Coffee cup and saucer.

Goebel, c. 1935 – 1937.

Straight-sided cup; Art Deco Harem motif.

$75.00 – 85.00.

Teacup and saucer.

Golden Crown, W. Germany (Ebeling & Reuss Co.), c. 1955 – 1980s.

Tapered cup with loop handle; band of cobalt with gold flowers.

$35.00 – 45.00.

Teacup and saucer.

Hertel, Jacob & Co. (Melitta Works), c. 1969 – present.

Footed cup with elongated loop handle; reproduction of Art Nouveau motif.

$50.00 – 75.00.

Teacup and saucer.

Hertel, Jacob & Co. (Melitta Works), c. 1969 – present.

Footed cup with loop handle; reproduction of Art Nouveau motif, gilt decoration on red.

$50.00 – 75.00.

Teacup, saucer, dessert plate.

Hutschenreuther, c. 1920 – 1930s, artist signed B. S. Welch.

Round cup, 3½"w x 2"h, saucer 5½", dessert plate 7½"; hand-painted cherry blossoms and forget-me-nots with gilt.

$75.00 – 100.00.

Demitasse cup and saucer.

Hutschenreuther, c. 1940s.

Footed cup with broken loop handle, 2¾"w x 1¾"h; gold lace design on cobalt.

$100.00 – 125.00.

Demitasse cup and saucer.

Hutschenreuther, Black Knight, c. 1925 – 1941.

Cup with angular gilt handle, 2"w x 2¼"h, saucer 4½"; colorful birds and bowls of fruit on a black band, with bands of etched gold.

$80.00 – 95.00.

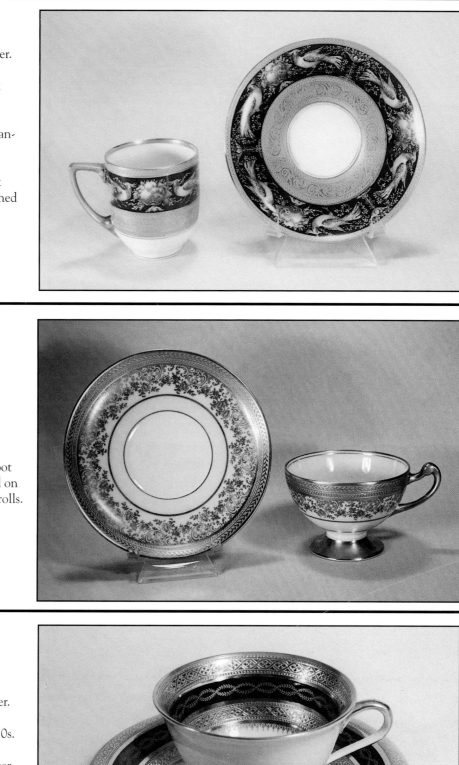

Coffee cup and saucer.

Hutschenreuther, c. 1920 – 1967.

Pedestal cup with gilt foot and band of etched gold on rim; gold flowers and scrolls.

$55.00 – 65.00.

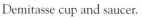

Demitasse cup and saucer.

Hutschenreuther, c. 1950s.

Cup 2¾"w x 1½"h, saucer 4¾"; gold and cobalt etched border.

$40.00 – 50.00.

Demitasse cup and saucer.

Hutschenreuther, Black Knight, c 1925 – 1941.

Quatrefoil cup with ring handle and gold interior, 2½"w x 2"h, saucer 4"; lavender ground with gilt. (See mark #59.)

$75.00 – 95.00.

Same cup and saucer with green ground.

Demitasse set.

Johann Haviland, c. 1939 – 1950s.

Set includes demitasse pot, creamer, sugar, six pedestal cups and saucers, and six dessert plates; cobalt and gilt decoration.

$500.00 – 600.00.

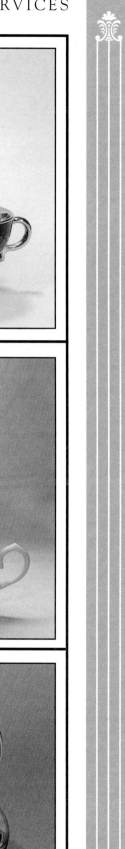

Demitasse cup and saucer.

Johann Haviland,
c. 1939 – 1950s.

Footed cup with zigzag handle, gold interior, 2¾" x 1½", saucer 4¼"; cobalt with gold flowers.

$45.00 – 60.00.

Coffee cup and saucer.

Johann Haviland,
c. 1938 – present.

Footed cup with reinforced loop handle; transfers of children.

$40.00 – 55.00.

Coffee cup and saucer.

KPM Berlin, c. 1849 – 1870.

Cup 3"w x 3"h, saucer 6¼"; gilt and cobalt decoration on white.

$125.00 – 150.00.

Demitasse cup and saucer.

KPM Berlin, c. 1920s.

Cup with wishbone handle and basketweave mold, 2", saucer 4½"; hand-painted flowers and a butterfly.

$145.00 – 175.00.

Demitasse cup and saucer.

KPM Berlin, c. 1915 – 1918.

Cup puffed out at bottom, high swan handle, 2¼", saucer 4"; red and gilt. (See mark #71.)

$125.00 – 150.00.

Demitasse cup and saucer.

KPM Berlin, c. 1900 – 1920.

Cup with high curled handle, 2¼"w x 2"h, saucer 3¾"; blue border and gold grape and leaf decoration.

$125.00 – 150.00.

Demitasse cup and saucer.

KPM Berlin, c. 1900 – 1920.

Cup in leafy mold, 2"w x 1¾"h, saucer 4¼"; hand-painted flowers and gilt.

$125.00 – 150.00.

Demitasse cup and saucer.

Krautheim & Adelberg Porcelain Factory, c. 1922 – 1945.

Tapered cup with loop handle; floral transfer.

$30.00 – 40.00.

Demitasse cup and saucer.

Lettin (Heinrich Baensch), c. 1900 – 1930.

Can cup with square handle; cobalt with green clover and enameled jewels.

$40.00 – 55.00.

Demitasse cup and saucer.

Lindner Porcelain Factory, c. 1948 – 1981.

Paneled and waisted cup with scalloped foot and broken loop handle, gold interior; panels of cobalt and etched gilt.

$75.00 – 100.00.

Teacup and saucer.

Meissen, c. 1850 – 1924.

Royal Flute cup with twisted feather handle, 3¼"w x 2¼"h, saucer 5½"; strewn flower design.

$175.00 – 200.00.

Coffee cup and saucer.

Meissen, c. 1930s.

Cup with swan handle, 3¼"w x 2¾"h, saucer 6"; Full Green Vine Wreath pattern with gilt.

$125.00 – 150.00.

Demitasse cup and saucer.

Meissen, c. 1950s.

Scalloped cup with entwined leaf handle, 2½"w x 1¾"h, saucer 4¼"; Rich Blue Onion pattern.

$175.00 – 200.00.

Demitasse cup and saucer.

Meissen, c. 1930s.

Cup in Royal Flute shape, 2½"w x 2"h, saucer 4"; yellow jonquils and blue forget-me-nots. (See mark #101.)

$200.00 – 225.00.

Teacup, saucer, and dessert plate.

Meissen, c. 1950s.

Royal Flute cup, 3½"w x 2½", saucer 5½", plate 6¾"; colorful hand-painted flowers with gilt.

$300.00 – 350.00.

Demitasse cup and saucer.

Meissen, c. 1850 – 1924.

Cup 2⅔"w x 2¼"h with snake handle, saucer 4½"; garland of small roses and gilt, with torch and scepter on cup.

$250.00 – 275.00.

Coffee cup and saucer.

Meissen, c. 1850 – 1924.

Cup in Royal Flute shape; hand-painted Court Dragon pattern.

$250.00 – 300.00.

Same in green.

Demitasse cup and saucer.

Meissen, c. 1930s, second quality.

Cup 3"w x 2"h, saucer 4⅞"; hand-painted flowers and gilt. (See mark #102.)

$125.00 – 150.00.

Coffee cup and saucer.

Meissen, c. 1930s.

Cup with swan handle, 2½"w x 2"h, saucer 5½"; beautifully painted flowers and gilt.

$200.00 – 250.00.

Demitasse cup and saucer.

Meissen, c. 1850 – 1920.

Quatrefoil cup, 2½", saucer 4½" x 5¼"; Purple Indian with Gold Dots pattern.

$250.00 – 275.00.

Demitasse cup and saucer.

Meissen, c. 1930s, second quality.

Quatrefoil cup, 3¼"w x 2"h, saucer 4⅞"; Blue Onion pattern.

$100.00 – 125.00.

Teacup and saucer.

Meissen, c. 1930s.

Cup with curled handle, gold band inside cup; molded pink and gold decoration.

$200.00 – 225.00.

Demitasse cup and saucer.

Nymphenburg, 1920s.

Round cup with loop handle; hand-painted flowers.

$75.00 – 100.00.

Teacup, saucer, and dessert plate.

Nymphenburg, c. 1961 – 1968.

Cup with decorated feather handle, 3½"w x 2"h, saucer 5", plate 6¾"; hand-painted flowers and gilt. (See mark #111.)

$125.00 – 150.00.

Demitasse cup and saucer.

Retsch & Co., Wunsiedel, c. 1953 – present.

Flared can with four gilt curved feet, high bird handle; courting scene transfers.

$45.00 – 65.00.

Demitasse cup and saucer.

Retsch & Co., Wunsiedel, c. 1953 – present.

Slightly flared cup with gilt handle with inner spur; cobalt ground with gilt roses. (See mark #124.)

$50.00 – 75.00.

Demitasse cup and saucer.

Rosenthal, c. 1898 – 1906.

Can-shaped scalloped cup with fancy handle; hand-painted pansies and gilt. (See mark #125.)

$65.00 – 85.00.

Demitasse cup and saucer.

Rosenthal, c. 1925 – 1941.

Pompadour shape; white wreath and beads on a Wedgwood blue ground.

$45.00 – 60.00.

Coffee cup and saucer.

Rosenthal, c. 1908 – 1935.

Cup with angular handle, 2¼"w x 2½"h, saucer 5"; large yellow roses on cobalt blue shading.

$60.00 – 75.00.

Teacup, saucer, and dessert plate.

Rosenthal, c. 1949 – 1955.

Cup 3¼"w x 2"h, saucer 5¾", plate 7½"; butterfly luster.

$150.00 – 175.00.

Chocolate cup and saucer.

Rosenthal, c. 1891 – 1907.

Swirled cup on deeply scalloped base, 1¾"w x 3½"h, saucer 4¾"; pink roses and gilt.

$60.00 – 75.00.

Breakfast cup and saucer.

Rosenthal, c. 1901 – 1933.

Cup with heart-shaped handle, 4½"w x 2¼"h, saucer 6½"; transfer portrait of lady sitting on the grass.

$60.00 – 75.00.

Teacup, saucer, and dessert plate.

Rosenthal, c. 1950s.

Cup 4"w x 2"h, saucer 5¾", plate 7½"; plain gilt wheat arrangement with cobalt border.

$60.00 – 75.00.

Demitasse cup and saucer.

Rosenthal, c. 1990s.

Can cup, 2½"w x 2"h, saucer 4¼"; Medusa pattern to honor the designer Versace.

$125.00 – 150.00.

Demitasse cup and saucer.

Rosenthal, c. 1948.

Cup 1¾"w x 2¼"h, saucer 4¼"; chinoiserie design, gold portrait of an Oriental woman carrying water, trees and flowers.

$75.00 – 85.00.

Demitasse cup and saucer.

Rosenthal, c. 1949 – 1954.

Cup 2½"w x 2"h, saucer 4½"; Vienna pattern.

$45.00 – 60.00.

Teacup and saucer.

Rosenthal, c. 1949 – 1955.

Red band, floral bouquet with enamel centers, luscious gold.

$50.00 – 65.00.

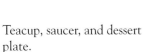

Teacup, saucer, and dessert plate.

Rosenthal, c. 1950s.

Cup 4"w x 1½"h, saucer 5¾", plate 7¾"; Vienna pattern.

$85.00 – 100.00.

Demitasse cup and saucer.

Rosenthal, c. 1925, also bee-hive mark and Austria.

Cup with partial gilt interior, 2⅓"w x 1½"h, saucer 4⅓"; decorated in Vienna style, with border of pink and yellow roses on saucer and outside of the cup; courting scene transfer inside cup and saucer well.

$80.00 – 100.00.

Cup interior.

Coffee and dessert set.

Rosenthal, c. 1901.

Set includes coffeepot, covered sugar, creamer, six cups and saucers, and six dessert plates; large hand-painted pink roses, green leaves, and luxurious gilt decoration.

$800.00 – 1000.00.

Beverage and dessert set.

Rosenthal, c. 1930s.

Set includes pot, covered sugar, creamer, ten cups and saucers, and ten dessert plates; colorful floral transfer pattern with gilt.

$500.00 – 600.00.

Demitasse cup and saucer.

Rosenthal, c. 1898 – 1906.

Can cup with ornate handle, 1¾"w x 2"h, saucer 4½"; light green on border, flowers and gilt.

$85.00 – 100.00.

Cream soup cup and saucer.

Rosenthal, c. 1949 – 1954.

Flared cup with two wing-shaped handles; floral transfer inside cup and saucer well, lavish gilt on red.

$75.00 – 100.00.

Teacup and saucer.

Rosenthal, c. 1949 – 1955.

Flared cup with angular handle; Phoenix pattern.

$40.00 – 55.00.

Teacup and saucer.

Royal Bayreuth,
c. 1916 – 1930s.

Cup 4"w x 2¼"h, saucer 5⅔"; pink with flower pots and garlands of roses, trimmed in gilt. (See mark #138.)

$40.00 – 55.00.

Demitasse cup and saucer.

R. S. Germany, c. 1904 – 1920.

Cup with gold interior, 1¾", saucer 4¼"; gold Art Nouveau decoration on cobalt blue shaded to green. (See mark #147.)

$80.00 – 100.00.

Demitasse cup and saucer.

R. S. Prussia, c. 1904 – 1938.

Footed cup with angular handle; pastel floral transfer. (See mark #148.)

$75.00 – 95.00.

Chocolate cup and saucer.

R. S. Prussia, c. 1904 – 1938.

Graceful molded cup, 2¼"w x 3"h, saucer 4½"; rose transfer decoration.

$75.00 – 95.00.

Demitasse cup and saucer.

R. S. Prussia, c. 1904 – 1938.

Footed cup with broken loop handle; floral transfer.

$75.00 – 100.00.

Teacup and saucer.

Schonwald Porcelain Factory, c. 1930s.

Low footed cup with fat loop handle; peach and yellow flowers with silver leaves.

$40.00 – 45.00.

Teacup, saucer, dessert plate.

Schumann, Carl, c. 1918.

Saucer and dessert plate have reticulated rim; floral transfer in Dresden style, gilt. (See mark #151.)

$100.00 – 125.00.

Teacup, saucer, and dessert plate.

Schumann, Carl, U. S. Zone, c. 1945 – 1949.

Dresden flowers, lavish gilding.

$100.00 – 125.00.

Demitasse set.

Schumann, Carl, U. S. Zone,
c. 1945 – 1949.

Set includes demitasse pot, covered sugar,
creamer, eight cups and saucers; Dresden
flowers pattern.

$600.00 – 700.00.

Demitasse set.

Von Schierholz, Plaue,
c. 1920 – 1930s.

Set includes demitasse pot, covered
sugar, creamer, six cups and saucers,
rose finials on lids; style of Meissen's
Red Indian pattern with gilt trim.
(See mark #150.)

$500.00 – 600.00.

Teacup and saucer.

Johann Seltman Porcelain
Factory, c. 1930s.

Footed cup with loop han-
dle; cocoa brown border
with gilt decoration and gilt
band.

$45.00 – 60.00.

Teacup and saucer.

Johann Seltmann,
c. 1901 – present.

Cup with fat loop handle; floral
transfer.

$35.00 – 40.00.

Coffee cup and saucer.

Swaine & Co., Germany,
c. 1900 – 1920.

Round cup with unusual
handle; floral cartouches on
cobalt ground with gilt stylized
flowers.

$40.00 – 55.00.

Teacup and saucer.

Tirschenreuth Porcelain Factory, c. 1969 – present.

Footed cup with oval ring
handle; band of green, floral
transfer inside cup. (See mark
#160.)

$40.00 – 45.00.

Teacup and saucer.

Tirschenreuth,
c. 1969 – present.

Footed waisted cup with
unusual loop handle; band of
gilt filigree design, flowers
inside cup.

$40.00 – 45.00.

Teacup and saucer.

Tirschenreuth,
c. 1969 – present.

Footed waisted cup, partial
ring handle with thumb rest;
floral transfer with gilt.

$35.00 – 45.00.

Demitasse cup and saucer.

Tirschenreuth,
c. 1930 – 1950s.

Slightly waisted cup, loop
handle with spurs and
thumb rest; underglaze blue
bird painting.

$40.00 – 45.00.

Teacup and saucer.

Tirschenreuth, c. 1950s.

Footed cup with gilt handle; light green ground, flowers inside cup.

$30.00 – 40.00.

Teacup and saucer.

R. Wachter, Bavaria, c. 1930s.

Cup with aqua border with gilt warriors on horseback. (See mark #164.)

$35.00 – 45.00.

Teacup and saucer.

Winterling Fine Ceramics, c. 1970 – present.

Tapered footed cup with loop handle; band of red with gilt inside cup and on saucer.

$35.00 – 45.00.

Coffee cup and saucer.

Unmarked, probably German, c. 1900.

Heart cartouches with hand-painted stylized flowers in Art Nouveau style.

$30.00 – 40.00.

Coffee cup and saucer.

Unmarked, probably German, c. 1890s.

Round cup with an unusual handle and four gold feet; five yellow medallions with gold flowers and trimmed with applied white ruffle, pink luster.

$35.00 – 40.00.

Coffee cup and saucer.

Unmarked, German, c. 1890s.

Straight cup with round loop handle; ornate four-petal gilt flower and purple jewels on pink luster.

$35.00 – 40.00.

Snack Set.

Unidentified German mark,
c. 1890 – 1920s.

Footed cup with square decorated handle;
reticulated saucer tray; white flowers on
green.

$175.00 – 200.00.

Coffee cup and saucer.

Marked Germany, c. 1930 – 1940s.

Straight-sided cup with loop handle; lion transfer.

$25.00 – 35.00.

Teacup, saucer, dessert plate.

Vienna Porcelain Factory,
Augarten, c. 1923 – 1960s.

Cup 3¼"w x 2½"h, saucer
5½", dessert plate 7½"; green
hand-painted roses on white,
gilt trim.

$150.00 – 175.00.

Close-up of rose painting.

Breakfast cup and saucer.

Vienna Porcelain Factory, Augarten, c. 1923 – 1960s.

Cup with broken loop handle, 4"w x 2¼"h, saucer 5¾"; bright hand-painted flowers with gilt. (See mark #163.)

$100.00 – 125.00.

Demitasse cup and saucer.

Vienna Porcelain Factory, Augarten, c. 1923 – 1960s.

Can cup with square handle, 1¾"w x 2"h, saucer 4⅛"; purple with medallion of hand-painted birds.

$125.00 – 150.00.

Demitasse cup and saucer.

Beehive mark, c. 1900.

Can cup, gilt interior, loop handle; Vienna-type courting scene transfer and decoration.

$50.00 – 75.00.

Demitasse cup and saucer.

Unmarked, probably Czechoslovakia, c. 1930s.

Cup with square handle; cobalt blue with gold frieze, pearl jeweling.

$50.00 – 75.00.

Teacup and saucer.

Schneider & Co., Czechoslovakia.

Footed flared cup with loop handle with spur and thumb rest; blue and gilt border, flowers inside cup and saucer well.

$40.00 – 45.00.

Demitasse cup and saucer.

Pirkenhammer, c. 1950s.

Cup 2½"w x 1½"h, saucer 4½"; decorated with lavish gold and floral transfer. (See mark #119.)

$40.00 – 50.00.

Demitasse cup and saucer.

Ginori, c. 1950s.

Cup 2½"w x 1¼"h, saucer 4¾"; band of cobalt on rim with gilt; red, green, and gold floral decoration.

$45.00 – 60.00.

Teacup and saucer.

Ginori, c. 1950s.

Footed cup with broken loop handle; silver deposit leaf pattern.

$60.00 – 75.00.

Demitasse cup and saucer.

Ginori, Firenze Ware, c. 1920s.

Slightly puffed out cup with ribbon handle; floral transfer, hand gilt decoration.

$40.00 – 55.00.

Demitasse cup and saucer.

Ginori, c. 1930s.

Can cup with angular loop handle; bands of etched gilt, leafy gold decoration.

$40.00 – 55.00.

Demitasse cup and saucer.

Unidentified, marked "Norleans, Made in Italy."

Footed and heavily molded cup with ornate broken loop handle; all white.

$40.00 – 50.00.

Pot de crème cup with saucer.

Mottahedeh, c. 1980s.

Applied flower on lid, reproduction of early Wedgwood
Queensware, cream earthenware with embossed dots and
flowers. (See mark #108.)

$100.00 – 125.00.

Three demitasse cups and
saucers.

Hackefors Co., Sweden,
c. 1929.

Art Deco ring form cup,
2½"w x 1¼"h, saucer 4½";
yellow, cobalt, and black
rings.

$35.00 – 40.00 each.

Teacup and plate.

Herend, c. 1900.

Cup 4¼"w x 2"h, plate
5¾"(saucer missing); hand-
painted flowers and butterflies. (See mark #55.)

$40.00 – 50.00.

Teacup and saucer.

Herend, c. 1930s.

Scalloped cup with curled handle; hand-painted green clovers and gilt.

$60.00 – 75.00.

Teacup and saucer.

Herend, c. 1940s, marked Tertia (third quality).

Cup with dots on handle, green rim, 3½"w x 2"h, saucer 5½"; amateur decorated pink flowers, basket weave mold on rim.

$55.00 – 65.00.

Teacup and saucer.

Herend, c. 1941.

Footed cup with wishbone handle; hand-painted magenta flowers. (See mark #56.)

$75.00 – 100.00.

Coffee cup and saucer.

Herend, c. 1900.

Scalloped cup with wishbone handle; vivid hand-painted flowers and gilt.

$100.00 – 125.00.

Pot de crème cup.

Herend, c. 1980s.

Slightly waisted cup with squarish handle, bird finial on lid; hand-painted birds and gilt.

$75.00 – 100.00.

Teacup and saucer.

Leart, Brazil, c. 1950s.

Footed cup, loop handle with spurs and thumb rest; band of cobalt with gilt flowers, rose in center of both cup and saucer. (See mark #73.)

$35.00 – 45.00.

Teacup and saucer.

Leningrad Factory, Russia,
c. 1950 – 1960s.

Slightly fluted cup, 4"w x 2"h,
saucer 5¾"; underglaze cobalt
blue exotic bird with gilt. (See
mark #75.)

$40.00 – 50.00.

Demitasse cup and saucer.

Unidentified mark, Russia.

Swirled cup with loop handle;
underglaze blue flowers with
gilt.

$75.00 – 100.00.

Demitasse cup and saucer.

Bing & Grondahl, c. 1950s.

Cup and saucer with matching
spoon holder; modern leafy
design.

$50.00 – 60.00.

Teacup and saucer.

Royal Copenhagen,
c. 1920s.

Ribbed cup with square
handle; Blue Fluted pattern.

$60.00 – 75.00.

Demitasse cup and saucer.

Royal Copenhagen,
c. 1920s.

Bute cup with ring handle;
underglaze blue and white
floral design. (See mark
#140.)

$40.00 – 60.00.

Two demitasse cups and
saucers.

Royal Copenhagen,
c. 1970s.

Slightly waisted cups with
loop handle, gold interior;
Confetti pattern.

$30.00 – 35.00 each.

Teacup and saucer.

Royal Copenhagen, c. 1920s.

Shallow cup with kicked loop handle; underglaze Blue Flowers pattern.

$40.00 – 55.00.

Chocolate cup and saucer.

Limoges, M. Redon, c. 1882-1890.

Shell mold, ornate handle, cup 2"w x 2¾"h, saucer 4¼"; orange and yellow flowers with green and brown leaves, on white ground. (See mark #96.)

$45.00 – 60.00.

Covered bouillon cup and saucer.

Limoges, William Guerin, c. 1890-1932.

Cup 3½"w x 2"h, saucer 5½"; beautifully decorated with ⅓" band of etched gold followed by ½" band of cobalt with gilt decoration on white. (See mark #86.)

$150.00 – 200.00.

Breakfast snack set.

Limoges, Haviland,
c. 1903 – 1925.

Large cup, 4¼"w x 2¼"h,
unusually shaped saucer tray;
vivid floral transfers.

$100.00 – 125.00.

Snack Set.

Limoges, Guerin,
c. 1900 – 1932.

Molded cup, kidney-shaped
saucer tray; soft coral, with pale
green leaves and gilt trim.

$125.00 – 150.00.

Demitasse cup and saucer.

Limoges, Haviland,
c. 1876 – 1880.

Cup 2⅛"w x 2¼"h, saucer
4⅔"; hand-painted geometric
design. (See mark #87.)

$30.00 – 35.00.

Demitasse cup and saucer.

Limoges, T & V,
c. 1892 – 1907.

Six-fluted cup on four leafy
feet, 2¾"w x 2"h, saucer 4";
hand-painted roses and gilt.

$80.00 – 95.00.

Same cup with blue flowers.

Teacup and saucer.

Limoges, B & H, c. 1890s.

Eight-paneled cup, 3¼"w x
2"h, octagonal saucer 5¼";
hand-painted white flowers.
(See mark #80.)

$40.00 – 50.00.

Demitasse cup and saucer.

Limoges, Haviland, c. 1904 – 1925, made for Bailey, Banks & Biddle, Philadelphia.

Slightly fluted cup with kicked loop handle, 2½"w x 2"h, saucer 4¾"; pale flowers and gilt. (See mark #89.)

$45.00 – 55.00.

Snack set.

Limoges, GDM, c. 1890, artist signed and dated.

Cup 2¼"w x 2½"h, saucer tray 7"; hand-painted violets outlined in gilt decoration.

$125.00 – 150.00.

Snack set.

Limoges, GDM, c. 1890, artist signed and dated.

Cup 2¼"w x 2½"h, saucer tray 7"; hand-painted yellow flowers.

$125.00 – 150.00.

Demitasse cup and saucer.

Limoges, blank made by Coiffe, decorated by Bawo & Dotter, c. 1891 – 1914.

Fluted cup, 2¼"w x 2"h, saucer 4¾"; shaded from white to coral, with heavy gold paste flowers.

$60.00 – 75.00.

Snack set.

Limoges, Haviland, c. 1876 – 1930.

Cup with stem handle with leaf extensions, 3¼"w x 2"h, leaf-shaped saucer tray 8¼" x 6"; floral transfer.

$100.00 – 125.00.

Demitasse cup and saucer.

Limoges, L. S. & S., c. 1890 – 1925.

Delicately fluted cup with puffy wave-like mold, 1¼"w x 2¼"h, saucer 4¼"; pink flowers.

$70.00 – 85.00.

Demitasse cup and saucer.

Limoges, Bawo & Dotter, c. 1896 – 1900.

Cup with head of dragon handle, 2"w x 1¼"h, saucer 4¼"; gold flowering branches in Japanese style.

$55.00 – 65.00.

Teacup and saucer.

Limoges, M. Redon, c. 1891 – 1896, Bazar Costa, Montevideo.

Quatrefoil cup with ornate handle, 3¼"w x 2½"h, saucer 5⅔"; medallion of figures on rich cobalt ground, flowers and gilt.

$175.00 – 200.00.

Demitasse cup and saucer.

Limoges, Klingenberg, c. 1900 – 1910.

Cup 2⅛"w x 2½"h, scalloped saucer 4⅔"; roses and heavy gilt ferns and swirls. (See mark #90.)

$75.00 – 95.00.

Demitasse cup and saucer.

Limoges, Latrille Frères, c. 1899 – 1913.

Can cup, 1¾"w x 2"h, saucer 3¾"; black ground, gold design. (See mark #93.)

$55.00 – 65.00.

Teacup and saucer.

Limoges, Guerin, c. 1925 – 1932.

Tapered cup with kicked fat loop handle; almost all gold ground, with cartouches of flowers.

$60.00 – 75.00.

Teacup and saucer.

Limoges, M. Redon, c. 1891 – 1896.

Footed cup with pinched loop handle; Art Nouveau style with red peonies and gilt.

$40.00 – 50.00.

Chocolate cup and saucer.

Limoges, L. S. & S.,
c. 1890 – 1925.

Swirled cup with twisted
stippled handle, 2"w x
2¾"h, saucer 4⅔"; heavily
enameled flowers and gold
paste on shades of pink and
white. (See mark #94.)

$60.00 – 75.00.

Chocolate cup and saucer.

Limoges, Redon, M.,
c. 1891 – 1896.

Petal-shaped cup with gold
scalloped foot and ornate
handle, 1¾"w x 2¾"h,
saucer 4⅓"; gilt decoration
on yellow ground.

$80.00 –95.00.

Snack set.

Limoges, L. S. & S., c. 1890.

Cup ribbed at bottom,
embossed with unusual
handle, 3¼"w x 2"h, kid-
ney-shaped saucer 8¼" x
6½"; gold border on rim
with green leaf decoration.

$100.00 – 125.00.

Demitasse cup and saucer.

Limoges, Haviland,
c. 1876 – 1880.

Cup with blue butterfly handle, 2⅛"w x 2½"h, saucer with deep well, 4¾"; amateur decorated with hand-painted scene of three birds in a tree.

$80.00 – 100.00.

Chocolate cup and saucer.

Limoges, T & V,
c. 1892 – 1907, artist signed.

Straight-sided cup with ornate handle; gorgeous hand-painted flowers and heavy gold band, professional decoration. (See mark #98.)

$125.00 – 150.00.

Close-up of decoration on saucer.

Chocolate set.

Limoges, Borgfeldt, George, c. 1906 – 1930.

Set includes chocolate pot and eight cups and saucers and dessert plates; vivid pink flowers with heavy gilt stems, green leaves, and green and gold decoration on rims. (See mark #83.)

$1,300.00 – 1,500.00.

Trio from above set.

Chocolate set.

Limoges, Barney, Rigoni & Langle, c. 1904 – 1906.

Set includes rare tray, chocolate pot, and six cups and saucers; intricate mold, twig handles, delicate array of violet flowers. (See mark #81.)

$900.00 – 1,000.00.

Teacup, saucer, and dessert plate.

Limoges, LaPorte, Raymond, c. 1883 – 1897.

Cup 2½"w x 2¼"h, saucer 4⅞", dessert plate 6⅔"; heavy gold paste flowers, leaves, bugs, and butterflies.

$100.00 – 125.00.

Teacup and saucer.

Limoges, Haviland, c. 1894 – 1931.

Low cup with unusual handle; Art Nouveau-style garlands of flowers, heavy etched gilt on rims. (See mark #88.)

$45.00 – 60.00.

Mustache cup and saucer.

Limoges, D & Co., c. 1894 – 1900.

Slightly flared cup with braided gilt handle; hand-painted violets, lovely shading, gilt rims. (See mark #84.)

$250.00 – 275.00.

Mustache cup and saucer.

Limoges, T & V, c. 1900.

Slightly tapered molded cup with loop handle with thumb rest; delicate purple flowers inside and outside the cup, gilt trim.

$250.00 – 275.00.

Rare Mr. And Mrs. mustache set.

Limoges, Klingenburg, c. 1880 – 1890.

Cups with large ring handles, 4"w x 2½"h, saucers 6½"; hand-painted leaves and heavy gold paste flowers.

$300.00 – 350.00+.

Mustache cup and saucer.

Limoges, B & F, imported by Levy & Strauss, c. 1890 – 1920.

Pink wavy type design on bottom of cup, twisted gilt handle; heavy gold decoration with hand-painted flowers. (See mark #79.)

$275.00 – 300.00.

Mustache cup and saucer.

Limoges, Klingenberg, c. 1890 – 1910.

Rounded cup with ring type handle; hand-painted purple roses, white enamel scrolls, shaded green and purple ground.

$250.00 – 275.00.

Coffee cup and saucer.

Limoges, Ahrenfeldt, Charles, Paris studio CRA, c. 1900s.

Empire-shaped cup; hand-painted flowers and ornate gold scrolls. (See mark #78.)

$100.00 – 125.00.

Pot de crème cup.

Paris, c. 1880s.

Footed and ribbed, 3"w x 4¼"h; hand-painted roses and forget-me-nots.

$100.00 – 125.00.

Set of pot de crème cups with tray.

Paris, c. 1920 – 1950s.

Set includes round tray and six covered pot de crème cups, measuring 2¼"w x 2¼"h; cream with gilt decoration.

$200.00 – 300.00.

Pot de crème cup with unusual holder.

Unmarked, probably Paris.

Cup with loop handle, cover, and holder; heavy gilt leafy decoration on pink.

$150.00 – 200.00.

Swan cup and saucer.

Paris, c. 1890s.

Cup 5"w x 3½"h, saucer 6¼" x 5"; stylized version of Swan cup and saucer, white with orange trim.

$100.00 – 125.00.

Demitasse cup and saucer.

Castleton China Inc., c. 1940+.

Footed cup with kicked pinched loop handle; rose transfer with gilt. (See mark #11.)

$40.00 – 45.00.

Demitasse cup and saucer.

Franciscan Ware (Gladding, McBean & Co.), c. 1938 – 1939.

Footed cup with loop handle; leaf decoration on cobalt, gilt band.

$30.00 – 35.00.

Demitasse cup and saucer.

Leneige, c. 1930s.

Quatrefoil cup and saucer; floral transfer. (See mark #74.)

$40.00 – 50.00.

Chocolate cup and saucer.

CAC Belleek,
c. 1906 – 1924, made for
Bailey, Banks & Biddle,
Philadelphia.

Straight-sided cup with
unusual handle; Art Nou-
veau decoration.

$100.00 – 125.00.

Demitasse cup and saucer.

Lenox, c. 1906 – 1924.

Six-sided and tapered cup,
2¼"w x 2½"h; Belleek body,
cream.

$45.00 – 60.00.

Demitasse cup and saucer.

Lenox, c. 1930 – 1940s,
made for Joseph Horne Co.,
Pittsburgh.

Footed cup 2¼"w x 2½"h,
saucer 4¾"; covered with
ornate etched gold, inside
the cup as well. (See mark
#77.)

$45.00 – 60.00.

Demitasse cup and saucer.

Lenox Belleek, c. 1906 – 1924.

Pedestal cup, 2⅓"w x 3¾"h, saucer 4¾"; Art Nouveau style, with hand-painted roses and gold bars. (See mark #76.)

$125.00 – 150.00.

Set of 12 demitasse cups and saucers.

Lenox, c. 1930s, silver made by M. Fred Hirsch Co., Jersey City, New Jersey.

Sterling silver liners and saucers; cream inserts.

$500.00 – 600.00.

Demitasse cup and saucer.

Pickard, c. 1912 – 1918.

Straight-sided cup with loop handle; gold band on rim, hand-painted flowers. (See mark #116.)

$75.00 – 90.00.

Demitasse cup and saucer.

Pickard, c. 1935 – 1939.

Can cup, 2¼"w x 2¼"h, saucer 4½"; aqua band with hand-painted flowers signed by E. Challinor. (See mark #118.)

$60.00 – 75.00.

Teacup and saucer.

Pickard, c. 1925 – 1938.

Scalloped and footed cup with reinforced loop handle; gilt interior, black ground.

$45.00 – 60.00.

Teacup and saucer.

Onondaga Pottery Co., Syracuse, New York, c. 1950 – 1966.

Footed cup with squarish handle; bouquets of flowers with gilt scrolls on rim.

$40.00 – 45.00.

Demitasse cup and saucer.

Stouffer, c. 1930 – 1940s.

Rounded cup with gilt handle; heavy gold rim and handle with hand-painted pink flowers with gold leaves and stems. (See mark #158.)

$60.00 – 75.00.

Demitasse cup and saucer.

Willets, c. 1879 – 1912.

Tridacna shaped, with a yellow pearlized glaze inside the cup and on the saucer. (See mark #166.)

$125.00 – 150.00.

Teacup and saucer.

Unknown maker, artist signed Alice Halth Nyberg, c. 1948.

Flared and fluted cup with molded gilt leaves at bottom, unusual handle; gilt inside cup, hand-painted roses on pale green.

$75.00 – 100.00.

Coffee cup and saucer.

Signed Dorothy C. Thorbe, California.

Tapered cup with loop handle; hand-painted floral and leaf design with gilt.

$50.00 – 75.00.

ENGLISH TABLEWARES

Bone china became the standard English porcelain body throughout the nineteenth century and remains preferred today. The light weight and translucency of bone china makes it appealing for tea ware. Bone china is made using crushed animal bone that is combined with clay, giving the mixture more stability. Some bone china is so fine you can see your hand through it when the piece is held up to light.

Many English companies have produced beautiful teacups and saucers. During the early twentieth century, lovely bone china and earthenware dinnerware with colorful transfers or hand-painted decoration were produced. It was fashionable for young brides to collect cups and saucers to use or to decorate their homes. These are still being collected and used today. At many tea and dinner parties, each guest can choose his or her own unique teacup and saucer. They are durable, washable in the dishwasher, can be used over and over, and can be mixed and matched.

UNUSUAL HANDLES

Cups and saucers with butterfly and flower handles were very much in vogue in England in the 1930s. They are highly prized by collectors today, especially in England, Australia, and the United States and command high prices.

BUTTERFLY HANDLES

From the beginning of time, butterflies have been used as an artist's motif. The Chinese and Japanese used these beautiful creatures when embroidering and painting; they used them on pottery and porcelain. The ancient Greeks believed that butterflies represented the departed souls of the dead. The butterfly represents flight, freedom, and creative thinking. It is also a symbol of spring and reflects the beauty of nature.

Some producers of butterfly handled cups were Aynsley, Minton, Paragon, Melba, and Coalport. A Coalport tea service in the Japanese Grove pattern can be found in the Shrewsbury Museum in England. The cups are quatrefoil shaped, with butterfly handles. Aynsley made a number of cups with the lovely Monarch butterfly on its handles. These are valued in the $200 – 250 range.

Buyers should be aware that some cups with butterfly handles are brand new and are appearing on Internet auctions. In some cases, sellers are trying to pass them off as antique.

FLOWER HANDLES

Flower handles have been popular since ancient times. When the Antechamber door of the Tomb of Tutankhamen was opened, the first thing seen was a beautiful wishing cup. It was of pure semi-translucent alabaster, with a lotus flower handle on each side.

Some producers of flower handled cups were Aynsley, Delphine China Company, Melba China Company, Phoenix China, Paragon, Samuel Radford, Royal Stafford China, and Royal Standard. Aynsley flower handled cups are especially popular with collectors today. A plain white flower form Aynsley cup with a pink rose handle could command as much as $200 today.

Several flower handled cups made by Paragon during the 1930s have a three-ring Art Deco shape. Some handles are designed with several flowers, and some have just a single bud. These are in the $150 – 175 price range today.

FORTUNE TELLING CUPS AND SAUCERS

Reading tea leaves became popular in the 1940 – 1950's, and many companies, particularly in England, made "Fortune Telling" teacups and saucers. The art of reading tea leaves is called Tasseography. The patterns of symbols made by tea leaves in a cup are interpreted. This is not a new science; it was developed thousands of years ago in China. It has also been associated with Eastern European Gypsies. Today, Tasseography is enjoying a resurgence as part of some New Age philosophies.

For many people, especially tea drinkers, it is just plain fun to try to read tea leaves. A variety of symbols are found on the cups and saucers. The reader interprets how the clusters of tea leaves are associated with the symbols. The International Collectors Guild Ltd. of Japan made a fortune telling cup and saucer in 1975 and included instructions. The outside of the cup says, "Perchance this cup will show it thee. Wouldn't thy fortune like to be?" Fortune telling cups are popular with collectors today.

One fortune telling cup and saucer called "Gypsy Theresa's Fortune Telling Cup" is unmarked on the bottom and dates from the 1930s. The inside of the cup and the saucer have numbered playing cards. The residual tea leaves were probably used with the cards to make a prediction.

Fortune telling cup and saucer postcard, © 1907, by Fred C. Lounsbury.

"The Tea Cup's Fortune Telling," 1909 postcard, supplement to Indianapolis Star.

All witches cups and saucers are very rare. They are available in a variety of colors, but the most common are black, green, and red. Some of the decorations include sailing ships, which represent Salem, Massachusetts, and witches' drinking vessels, snakes, skull and crossbones, and various colorful divination symbols. The decoration is usually mixed decoration, with hand-painting done over decals. Some are bone china blanks that were bought from a manufacturer and decorated by hand.

DISTRIBUTORS/RETAILERS

Certain cups and saucers, usually of top quality, were ordered by select distributors or retailers. These dealers would order items directly from the manufacturer and have the words "made exclusively for (name of company)" added to the backstamp. This does not always add to the value of the item, but it does usually mean it is a cut above regular cups and saucers. There are some cup and saucer collectors that collect these examples, such as items made for Tiffany & Company, exclusively.

A partial list of distributors and retailers is:

Gilmore & Collamore, New York
Davis, Collamore & Co., New York
Bailey, Banks & Biddle, Philadelphia
Tiffany & Co., New York
Ovington Brothers, New York
J. E. Caldwell & Co., Philadelphia
Wright, Tyndall & Von Roden, Philadelphia
Phillips & Pierce, London

MAKERS

AYNSLEY

The Aynsley Company was started by John Aynsley in 1775, in Longton, Staffordshire, England. The company produced porcelain bone china and was well known for its lovely tea ware. Today, collectors look for Aynsley fruit cups and saucers signed by D. Jones and

H. Brunt, and flower cups and saucers signed by J. A. Bailey. Some lovely cups with butterfly and flower handles were produced in the 1930s. Popular patterns are Leighton Cobalt, Pembroke, Cottage Garden, and Famille Rose.

BODLEY

Quality porcelain was produced by Bodley from 1875 to 1892. Edwin James Drew Bodley worked at Samuel Alcock's Old Hill Pottery at Burslem, which had been divided into separate china and earthenware factories in 1867. The china works (now called Crown Works) was taken over first by Bodley and Diggory, and then by Bodley & Son, until Edwin J. D. Bodley began to do business under his own name in June of 1875. Bodley produced fine quality porcelains with Oriental-style flowers. Cups and saucers in the Aesthetic style are highly regarded by collectors.

BOOTHS

Booths began operation in 1845, and had a number of different names through the years. It is currently part of the Royal Doulton Tableware Group. In the early 1920s, Booths produced its popular Fruit Bowl pattern, along with a number of Imari-style designs. In 1948, the company hired two Hungarian designers to produce a line of wares inspired by Hungarian folklore. After 1953, the Booths factory concentrated on producing a line of fine quality dinnerware in traditional patterns.

CAULDON POTTERIES

Cauldon Potteries was the successor to Cauldon (1905 – 1920), which had previously been Brown-Westhead Moore & Company in Hanley, England. Although the firm is best known for its useful wares, it also produced a number of interesting decorative lines. The company produced many cups and saucers for firms like Tiffany & Company and Davis, Collamore & Co. Two of its most popular patterns are Blue Lagoon and Oriental.

COLCLOUGH

Colclough China Company was founded in 1890, by Herbert Joseph Colclough. After a number of changes and mergers, the company became Colclough China Limited in 1937. The company specialized in producing fine quality bone china at different levels, to satisfy both the domestic and export markets. In the early 1970s, Colclough was taken into the Royal Doulton Tableware Group, but it continued using its own name and expanded some of its most popular designs of dinnerware, such as the Crinoline Lady pattern. The factory closed in 1996.

COALPORT

Coalport tableware has delighted collectors since its inception in 1750. Its Oriental patterns have always been popular with collectors. The celebrated Indian Tree pattern was introduced in 1801 and has an application of enamel colors over a printed outline. Other favorite Oriental style tea ware patterns are Broseley Dragon, Japan Green Dragon, Blue Canton, Blue Willow, and Ming tree. These are all printed patterns with some color added. Today, Coalport is part of the Wedgwood group.

COPELAND SPODE

Josiah Spode established his factory in 1784, in Stoke. At the end of the eighteenth century, Josiah Spode was responsible for the single most important development in his industry — the perfection of the formula for fine bone china. His was the whitest, most translucent, strongest, and most resonant bone china in the industry.

He also perfected the process of blue underglaze printing, and Spode's blue and white designs have become some of the most sought after in the history of ceramics. Three original patterns that are still being produced today are Tower Blue, Willow, and Blue Italian, a collectors favorite.

Spode teacup handles are considered the best, and are perfectly designed to combine comfortable function with aesthetic appeal.

Connoisseurs believe that they can recognize a Spode teacup even when unmarked, simply by the feel of the handle.

William Taylor Copeland bought the firm from Josiah III in 1833. In 1976, Spode became part of the Royal Worcester Company and together they became known as the Royal Worcester Spode Group. Today, Spode tableware is basically still being made the same way; the original bone china formula is still being used.

ROYAL CROWN DERBY

Royal Crown Derby is best known for its Japanese Imari inspired patterns, and these lovely blue, red, and gilt patterns remain popular today, as well as Derby Posies, Royal Antoinette, and Mikado. Mikado was inspired by a Far Eastern drawing on rice paper. The favorite Olde Avesbury pattern was inspired by an embroidery decorated with colorful birds of paradise and Oriental pheasants. During the 1930s and 1940s, monochrome variations of Olde Avesbury were created in a variety of shades.

CROWN STAFFORDSHIRE

Crown Staffordshire started in 1897, in Fenton, England. At the turn of the twentieth century, the company was producing a wide range of bone china products that included dinnerware, tea and coffee sets, and miniatures. In 1973, the company became part of the Wedgwood group. Crown Staffordshire cups and saucers are always of excellent quality.

DENBY CHINA

The Denby Pottery Company was in operation from 1809 to 1960, under the name Joseph Bourne & Son Ltd. The trade name Denby was used for the company, after the village of Denby, located in rural Derbyshire, England. Denby made a wide range of tableware and kitchenware. Collectors can find cups and saucers with colorful hand-painted designs.

DEVON POTTERIES

The founder of S. Fielding & Co., Simon Fielding, invested in Railway Pottery in Stoke-on-Trent, Staffordshire, England, in 1878. The company manufactured majolica and stoneware. Simon's son, Abraham, was a color maker at the Blythe Color Works, another company owned by his father. The Works supplied color to potteries in the area, and Abraham made frequent visits to his father's firm to settle accounts. On one visit in 1879, Abraham found bailiffs at the door — ready to foreclose on the debt-ridden company. Abraham decided to pay off the debts and become a pottery manufacturer himself. He was only 24 years old and had no knowledge of making pottery, so this bold step showed considerable courage.

Abraham was a hard worker, and became actively involved in all aspects of the firm. He had two primary goals. One was to improve efficiency and, therefore, increase production. The other goal was to insure the comfort and health of the work force, particularly the women. He made sure the pottery work rooms were light, airy, and ventilated well with fans. This concern for his employees resulted in both their loyalty to him and in a family spirit among the work force.

Soon the company became very successful, and by 1905 it had grown to almost five times the size it had been when Abraham had taken it over. Two significant factors in its success were the ability to attract high quality people and the creation of an atmosphere that would ensure their loyalty.

Another big reason for the success of the firm was its practice of providing good quality products at competitive prices. Abraham realized that the manufacture of fancy goods was being neglected by English potters due to an abundance of cheap foreign imports. He visited the Leipiz Fair to see first-hand what the Germans were producing. He bought some of their wares and asked his modelers to see if they could make comparable goods. As a result, a range of fancy table lines in pottery evolved which were to sell well for years to come.

Abraham made sure that different pieces were provided each year, especially for the Christmas trade. The firm used a variety of promotional activities to bring new wares to the attention of the retailers and the buying public. Their marketing strategies were so successful that the wares became better known than the name of the pottery that produced them, and the factory name was changed from Railway to Devon.

In 1932, Abraham Fielding died at the age of 77, and his only son, Arthur Ross, became the third generation of the family to head the company. Arthur's son, Reginald, succeeded him after his death in 1947. The Fielding family connection with the firm came to an end with Reginald's retirement in 1967. After personnel changes, reorganizations, and England's recession, which destroyed 20,000 jobs in the pottery industry, the firm closed its doors in 1986.

ROYAL DOULTON

Doulton was established in 1815, as a partnership between John Doulton, Martha Jones, and John Watts, and became known as Jones, Watts and Doulton. After a long and eventful history, the company is known today as the Royal Doulton Fine China Co. In 1972, Royal Doulton established itself as one of the world's largest manufacturers of fine bone china, and as a result of a merger with Allied English Potteries, brought Royal Crown Derby, Royal Albert, and many other smaller companies into the Royal Doulton group. Some of the well-known names of its dinnerware patterns are Westminster, Cambridge, and Tapestry.

FOLEY CHINA WORKS

The E. Brain & Co. Ltd. (Foley China Works) was established in Fenton in 1903. Throughout the company's history, it has specialized in bone china tea and breakfast ware of high quality and good design. Foley is one of a few factories where young boys are trained in the old art of flower painting. To celebrate the company's centennial year, it adopted a pattern honoring a century rose; the pattern was an exact reproduction of a very old and beautiful design. Other popular patterns are Ming Rose and Cornflower, both of which are extremely popular and in great demand.

HAMMERSLEY & CO.

The first potter associated with this manufactory is probably George Harris Hammersley, who worked with a partner, Harvey Adams, in 1885. The company became Hammersley & Co. in 1887. The company produced many lovely dinnerware sets, and one of its popular patterns is Michaelmas. The company is part of the Royal Worcester Spode Ltd. Group today.

GEORGE JONES

The Jones family had no history or knowledge of the pottery business. George Jones, who was born in 1823, became an orphan when he was ten years old. He started his career in the ceramic business at the age of 14, when he started a seven year pottery apprenticeship with Minton. When the apprenticeship was completed, Jones went to work as a traveling salesman, insurance agent, wholesaler, and retailer.

He started the George Jones & Sons pottery manufactory in 1861, with the production of white granite ware, and in 1865, began to manufacture earthenware. Majolica production started around 1866. In 1876, fine bone china was first produced.

At the start of the twentieth century, George Jones & Sons Ltd. was the third largest pottery manufacturer in England. It employed 1,000 workers and exported at least half of its production worldwide.

Today, there is little left of what was once a powerful pottery in Stoke-on-Trent. George Jones closed its doors in 1951.

What set George Jones apart from some of the other porcelain manufacturers in Stoke-on-Trent was his emphasis on decoration. Hand painting became the company's specialty in the mid-nineteenth century, and many talented artists joined the firm, including Charles Birbeck, who was Art Director for fifty years, and his half brother William. Many dessert and tea sets can be found today with beautiful hand-painted flowers, birds, and scenes. Popular patterns on tea ware are Bismark, Linda, Pompeii, and Rhine.

JOHNSON BROTHERS

Four Johnson brothers took over the Charles Street Works Pottery in Staffordshire, England, in 1883. They made tablewares that were successful in England and the United States. Their wares were originally earthenware and white ironstone. In 1885, the whiteware was replaced by a lighter weight ware known for its lightness and finer finish. It is this quality ironstone which has been the mainstay of the Johnson Bros. tableware business. In 1968, the company became part of the Wedgwood Group. Desirable patterns are Old Britain Castles, Strawberry Fair, Wild Turkeys, Millstream, and Friendly Village.

MINTON

Thomas Minton founded his factory in 1793, in Stoke-on-Trent. He made the popular Willow pattern in the 1820s, and it became the most popular pattern ever made. In 1883, the modern company was established, and in 1885, it became one of England's leading porcelain producers. In 1968, Minton became a member of the Royal Doulton Tableware Group, and the firm continues to produce beautiful porcelain dinnerware. Popular patterns include Haddon Hall, Bellemeade, Lady Clare, and Rose Garland.

PARAGON

Paragon started operating first as the Star China Company in 1900, in Longton, England, and used the trade name Paragon. The named changed to Paragon China Ltd. in 1920. The company is part of the Royal Doul-

ton Tableware Group today.

When Queen Mary visited the Star China Co. in 1913, the Queen Mary pattern was introduced. The company made cups and saucers in Derby Imari-style patterns, as well as a large range of lusterware, introduced in 1925. Iceland Poppy was one of the most popular patterns made by Paragon in the early 1930s. Also produced was a fine hand-painted Art Deco-style pattern called Toronto. Other popular patterns include The Tree of Kashmir and Corinthian.

ROYAL ALBERT

Royal Albert was the trade name of the firm founded by Thomas Clark Wild about 1894. It has always been known for its fine quality bone china. Today, Royal Albert is produced under the Royal Doulton Tableware Group. Some popular dinnerware patterns are Old English Rose, American Beauty, Serena, Heirloom, and Christmas Magic.

ROYAL STAFFORD

Royal Stafford China was formed in 1952, in Longton, England. It was formerly the Thomas Poole Company, which had begun operation in 1952. In March 1992, it joined partnership with Barratts of Staffordshire, another well-known pottery. Cups and saucers produced by Royal Stafford are of excellent quality, and many have lavish gilt decoration. Well-known patterns are Hedgerow, Portsmouth, Sunflower, Woodland, and Country Cottage.

SHELLEY

The Shelley company began operation in 1872, when Joseph Shelley became a partner with James Wileman, owner of the Foley China Works in Longton. The company was called Wileman, and was renamed Shelley in 1925. In 1966, Allied English Potteries acquired the Shelley Company, and in 1971, Allied became part of the Royal Doulton Tableware Group.

Shelley cups and saucers remain highly collectible. The cups and saucers in the Dainty shapes are perhaps Shelley's best known. The original Dainty shape was a six-flute design. Twelve and fourteen-flute styles were also produced. The Queen Anne shape was designed in 1926, and it remains one of Shelley's most popular shapes.

There are over 160 patterns that include florals, landscapes, chintz, and solid ground colors. The National Shelley Collectors Club was founded in 1990, and has over 500 members today. The club publishes a quarterly newsletter and holds an annual conference. Information about the club can be found on its web site:

http://www.nationalshelleychinaclub.com/home.asp

WEDGWOOD

The Wedgwood pottery was established in 1759, by Josiah Wedgwood, in Stoke-on-Trent. He was born into a family with a long tradition as potters. Wedgwood produced a highly durable cream colored earthenware that so pleased Queen Charlotte that in 1762, she appointed him the royal supplier of dinnerware. Wedgwood also developed revolutionary ceramic materials, such as basalt and jasperware. Josiah Wedgwood is credited with being "The father of English potters."

During the 1960s and 1970s, Wedgwood acquired a number of English potteries, and today it is one of the largest earthenware and fine china manufacturers in the world. Teacup collectors look for early jasperware, basalt, and bone china. Popular bone china patterns are Appledore, Charnwood, Columbia, Wild Strawberry, and the Florentine patterns, which have a border of mythological griffins and winged lions. The Florentine pattern was designed for Wedgwood's creamware in 1865. In 1924, it was used for bone china, and the turquoise and cobalt variations are favorites today.

ROYAL WORCESTER

Royal Worcester fine bone china has a unique silky feel and a fine even texture that makes it stand apart from other English bone china. During the twentieth century, Royal Worcester produced high quality bone china with colorful floral patterns and blue and white transfer prints. Popular patterns are Astley, Evesham, Lavina, and Patricia.

Postcard showing a blue and white English bone china cup and saucer, B.B. London, series E45.

Postcard showing a fluted tea set.

Teacup and saucer.

Adams, Titian Ware,
c. 1896 – 1920s.

Ribbed rims, loop handle;
colorful hand-painted flowers.

$25.00 – 30.00.

Teacup and saucer.

Adams, Titian Ware,
c. 1896 – 1920s.

Footed cup, loop handle;
Della Monte border, hand-painted flowers, molded
Cupids.

$30.00 – 35.00.

Demitasse cup and saucer.

Adams, Titian Ware,
c. 1896 – 1920s.

Slightly tapered cup, loop
handle; hand-painted leaves.

$25.00 – 30.00.

Teacup and saucer.

Adderleys Ltd.,
c. 1950 – 1962.

Swirled cup with kicked loop handle; Thistle pattern.

$40.00 – 45.00.

Covered bouillon cup and saucer.

Arkenstall & Sons,
c. 1904 – 1924.

Colorful Imari-type decoration.

$100.00 – 125.00.

Teacup and saucer.

Aynsley, c. 1930 – 1950s.

Footed cup with loop handle with thumb rest; fortune telling cup.

$60.00 – 75.00.

Teacup and saucer.

Aynsley, c. 1950s – present.

Scalloped waisted cup with coiled loop handle; unusual scenic design.

$40.00 – 50.00.

Teacup and saucer.

Aynsley, c. 1950s.

Athens shape; sailing ship, turquoise ground.

$80.00 – 100.00.

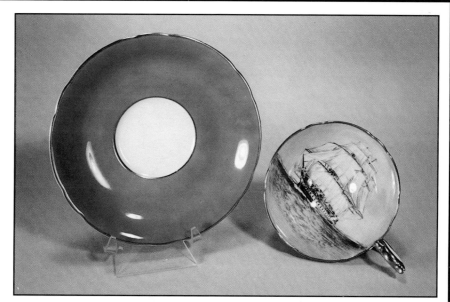

Demitasse cup and saucer.

Aynsley, c. 1930s, signed D. Jones.

Can cup 2¼", saucer 4¾"; fruit decoration. (See mark #2.)

$75.00 – 90.00.

Teacup and saucer.

Aynsley, c. 1930s, signed H. Brunt.

Footed cup with gilt interior, kicked loop handle; fruit decoration.

$100.00 – 125.00.

Teacup and saucer.

Aynsley, c. 1930s, signed J. A. Bailey.

Cup with gilt handle and foot; pink rose and spring flowers inside cup; rich turquoise ground.

$78.00 – 100.00.

Same set with red ground.

Teacup and saucer.

Aynsley, c. 1950s.

Footed slightly fluted cup, unusual handle; vivid turquoise with dramatic gold flowers.

$50.00 – 65.00.

Teacup and saucer.

Aynsley, c. 1930s.

Footed cup, ribbed at bottom, ornate handle; rose inside cup and saucer well, border of cobalt with gold decoration.

$60.00 – 75.00.

Teacup and saucer.

Aynsley, c. 1920s.

Embossed mold, cup with yellow flower handle; medallions of yellow flowers.

$200.00 – 225.00.

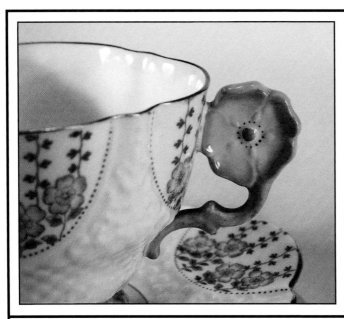

Close-up of flower handle.

Teacup and saucer.

Aynsley, c. 1920s.

Cup with blue butterfly handle; lovely Venetian scenic design with lady in fancy dress.

$250.00 – 275.00.

Teacup and saucer.

Aynsley, c. 1920s.

Embossed mold, cup with pink flower handle; colorful flowers and castle scene.

$200.00 – 250.00.

Close-up of scene on saucer.

Teacup and saucer.

Aynsley, c. 1930s.

Footed cup; rare Windsor Castle design on cobalt blue.

$150.00 – 175.00.

Demitasse cup and saucer.

Aynsley, c. 1910 – 1920s.

Can cup 2", saucer 4¼"; lovely Oriental pattern.

$55.00 – 65.00.

Teacup and saucer.

Aynsley, c. 1930 – 1950s.

Cup with D-shaped handle; pink and white border with gold fleur-de-lis, floral transfer inside cup and saucer well.

$40.00 – 55.00.

Teacup and saucer.

Aynsley cup and Shelley saucer, c. 1930s.

Footed cup with broken loop handle, molded saucer; fortune telling cup.

$40.00 – 50.00.

Teacup and saucer.

Aynsley, c. 1930 – 1950s.

Cup with kidney-shaped handle; bird and flowers inside cup, bird on saucer well, pink ground with gilt.

$45.00 – 60.00.

Teacup and saucer.

Aynsley, c. 1930 – 1950s.

Footed flared cup with D-shaped handle; blue flower petal design inside cup and around saucer well, lacy design on border.

$40.00 – 50.00.

Demitasse cup and saucer.

Aynsley, c. 1930s.

Footed cup with blue butterfly handle; ivory and blue decoration.

$175.00 – 200.00+.

Teacup and saucer.

Aynsley, present mark.

Ribbed cup with ornate handle; contemporary fruit design.

$40.00 – 50.00.

Demitasse cup and saucer.

Bodley, E. J. D., c. 1875 – 1892.

Cup with heart-shaped saucer; interior of cup and saucer well is pink, outside ground is cream.

$35.00 – 45.00.

Demitasse cup and saucer.

Bodley, c. 1875 – 1892.

Straight-sided cup with loop handle; gilt Oriental-style flowers, gold etched border on rims.

$60.00 – 75.00.

Demitasse cup and saucer.

Booths Ltd., c. 1930s, specially for Bailey, Banks & Biddle, Philadelphia.

Can cup 2¼"w x 2¼"h, saucer 4⅞"; hand-painted birds and floral cartouches on cobalt blue with hand-painted gilt flowers.

$75.00 – 95.00.

Close-up of decoration.

Demitasse cup and saucer.

Booths Ltd., c. 1930s.

Can cup with loop handle; Rajah pattern. (See mark #5.)

$60.00 – 75.00.

Teacup and saucer.

Brownfield, c. 1860 – 1891.

Twenty-four-fluted cup; cobalt and gilt border on rims, heavy gold paste flowers.

$125.00 – 150.00.

Teacup and saucer.

Burgess & Leigh, c. 1930s.

Earthenware flared cup with square handle; Calico chintz pattern.

$100.00 – 125.00.

Demitasse set.

Carlton Ware, c. 1920s.

Set includes pot, creamer, sugar, and six cups and saucers in quatre-foil shape; Rouge Royal.

$500.00 – 550.00.

Same in cobalt blue luster.

Demitasse cup and saucer.

Carlton Ware, c. 1920s.

Quatrefoil cup with ear handle, gold interior; pale yellow luster.

$60.00 – 70.00.

Teacup and saucer.

Cauldon, c. 1905 – 1920.

Footed cup with ring handle; pink saucer and cup interior, gilt rims.

$35.00 – 45.00.

Demitasse cup and saucer.

Cauldon, c. 1930s.

Flared cup with ring handle; cobalt border with gilt scrolls, rose transfer.

$60.00 – 90.00.

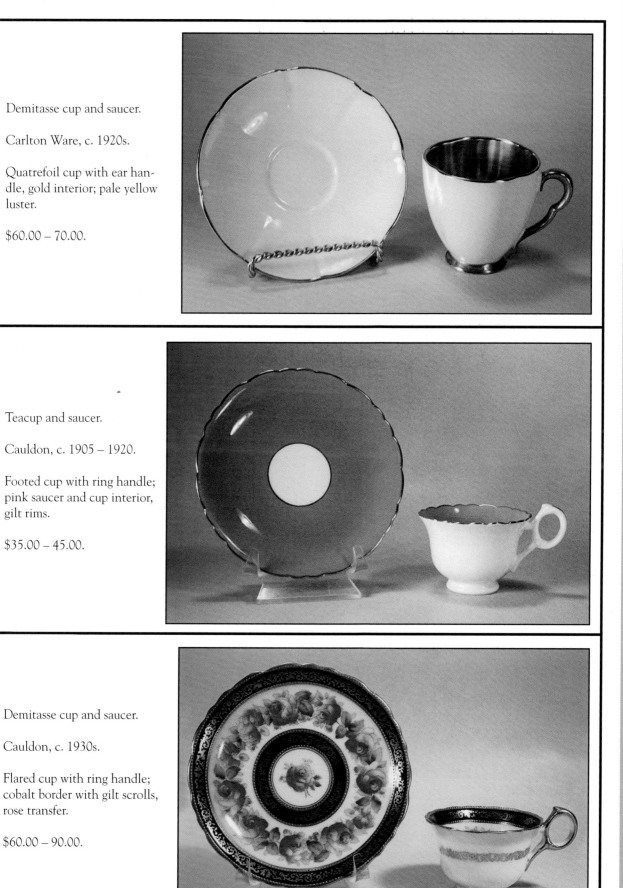

Close-up of decoration on saucer.

Demitasse cup and saucer.

Cauldon Potteries Ltd.,
c. 1950 – 1962.

Scalloped tapered cup with
wonderful red, green, and blue
handle; Victoria pattern.

$45.00 – 60.00.

Teacup, saucer, and dessert plate.

Cauldon, c. 1930s.

Straight-sided cup with loop handle; blue floral chintz design.

$100.00 – 125.00.

Teacup, saucer, and dessert plate.

David Chapman & Sons, c. 1889 – 1906.

Fluted cup with angular handle; underglaze blue flowers with gilt.

$100.00 – 115.00.

Teacup and saucer.

Coalport, c. 1960+.

Gold band on rim of cup, on foot, and on saucer; decorated with vivid peonies. (See mark #16.)

$55.00 – 65.00.

Teacup and saucer.

Coalport, c. 1949 – 1959.

Scalloped cup; coral with flowers inside. (See mark #15.)

$35.00 – 45.00.

Teacup and saucer.

Unmarked except for #837, attributed to Coalport, c. 1840 – 1950s.

Hand decorated in Imari style, with flowers and cobalt blue medallions with lavish gilt.

$150.00 – 175.00.

Teacup and saucer.

Coalport, c. 1891 – 1920.

Gadrooned gilt rim, angular handle; floral cartouches on cobalt blue, gilt hand decoration.

$100.00 – 125.00.

Teacup, saucer, and dessert plate.

Coalport, c. 1881 – 1890.

Straight cup with fat loop handle; underglaze blue floral design, pearl jeweling, and gilt on rim.

$175.00 – 200.00.

Teacup and saucer.

Coalport, c. 1950s.

Footed cup with broken loop handle; Montrose Blue pattern.

$35.00 – 45.00.

Teacup and saucer.

Colclough China Ltd., c. 1945 – 1948.

Tapered cup with broken loop handle; pastel florals on light aqua.

$30.00 – 40.00.

Teacup and saucer.

Colclough, c. 1945 – 1948.

Tapered and slightly scalloped cup with loop handle; scattered roses, overlay of gilt flowers. (See mark #17.)

$40.00 – 45.00.

Teacup and saucer.

Colclough, c. 1950s.

Tapered footed cup with pointed loop handle; floral transfer.

$35.00 – 40.00.

Teacup, saucer, and plate.

Copeland Spode, c. 1891 – 1920.

Cup 4"w x 2"h, saucer 5½", plate 7¾"; basket of fruit in center of cup and plates, with two bands of cobalt blue, beaded band of gilt leaves on white along rims.

$175.00 – 200.00.

Coffee cup and saucer.

Copeland Spode, c. 1950 – 1960s.

Can cup 2½", saucer 5"; Regency pattern. (See mark #20.)

$75.00 – 95.00.

Demitasse cup and saucer.

Copeland Spode,
c. 1950 – 1960s.

Ribbed cup, 2¼"w x 2"h,
saucer 4½"; Colonel pattern.

$40.00 – 55.00.

Demitasse cup and saucer.

Copeland Spode, c. 1950s.

Ribbed cup, 2⅛"w x 2¼"h,
saucer 4½"; gold flowers on
white ground.

$45.00 – 60.00.

Pair of teacups and saucers.

Spode, c. 1850s.

Footed paneled cups with
square handle; heavy gold
band inside cups, hand-
painted flowers. (See mark
#157.)

$125.00 – 150.00 each.

Tea set.

Copeland Spode,
c. 1891 – 1920.

Set includes teapot, creamer, open sugar, round scalloped tray, and four ribbed cups and saucers; blue chintz pattern.

$800.00 – 1000.00.

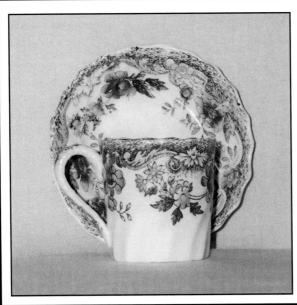

Demitasse cup and saucer.

Copeland Spode, c. 1894 – 1910.

Swirled cup with loop handle, deep saucer; floral transfer.

$45.00 – 60.00.

Demitasse cup and saucer.

Copeland Spode, c. 1950s.

Swirled and ribbed can-shaped cup with loop handle; paisley design.

$45.00 – 60.00.

Teacup and saucer.

Royal Crown Derby, c. 1900.

Slightly flared cup with decorated loop handle; hand-painted roses and gilt. (See mark #21.)

$100.00 – 125.00.

Demitasse cup and saucer.

Royal Crown Derby, c. 1940, made for Tiffany & Co., New York.

Cup with gadrooned rim and unusual handle, slightly puffed out at bottom; gilt flowers and leaves over cobalt and red. (See mark #23.)

$60.00 – 75.00.

Demitasse cup and saucer.

Royal Crown Derby, c. 1929.

Can cup 2", saucer 4⅛", unusual Imari pattern with gilt.

$75.00 – 90.00.

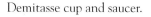

Coffee cup and saucer.

Royal Crown Derby, c. 1930s.

Quatrefoil cup, 3"w x 2½"h, saucer 5½"; Mikado pattern.

$45.00 – 55.00.

Teacup and saucer.

Royal Crown Derby, c. 1930s.

Footed cup with question mark handle; Derby Posies pattern.

$45.00 – 60.00.

Teacup and saucer.

Royal Crown Derby, c. 1913.

Pedestal cup with unusual handle with feathered thumb rest; lovely gilded beaded pattern on cobalt blue. (See mark #22.)

$125.00 – 150.00.

Teacup and saucer.

Royal Crown Derby,
c. 1891 – 1920.

Quatrefoil cup; gold beads and
flowers on a red and white
ground.

$125.00 – 150.00.

Teacup, saucer, and dessert
plate.

Royal Crown Derby, c. 1926,
made for Tiffany & Co.,
New York.

Vivid and striking Imari
pattern.

$200.00 – 250.00.

Demitasse cup and saucer.

Royal Crown Derby, c. 1911.

Cup 2¾"w x 1¾"h, saucer
4½"; Imari pattern #9698.

$90.00 – 115.00.

Teacup and saucer.

Crown Dorset Pottery, c. 1920 – 1937.

Squarish cup with four feet, unusual handle; purple pansies, gilt. (See mark #25.)

$40.00 – 45.00.

Teacup and saucer.

Crown Ducal (A. G. Richardson Co.), c. 1930 – present.

Cup and saucer with molded design, unusual double indentation in saucer, broken loop handle on cup; floral transfer on inside of cup.

$45.00 – 60.00.

Demitasse cup and saucer.

Crown Ducal, c. 1930 – present.

Tapered cup with angular handle; Colonial Times.

$40.00 – 55.00.

Teacup and saucer.

Crown Ducal, c. 1930+.

Tapered cup with angular handle; Florentine pattern. (See mark #27.)

$30.00 – 35.00.

Demitasse cup and saucer.

Crown Staffordshire, c. 1930s.

Can cup, 2"w x 2¼"h, saucer 4¾"; gorgeous hand-painted Imari decoration.

$125.00 – 150.00.

Teacup and saucer.

Crown Staffordshire, c. 1950s.

Footed cup with broken loop handle; turquoise band, white border with gilt swirls. (See mark #29.)

$35.00 – 45.00.

Demitasse cup and saucer.

Crown Staffordshire, c. 1930s.

Can cup with loop handle; colorfully enameled hunting scene.

$40.00 – 50.00.

Teacup and saucer.

Delphine China Co., c. 1930s.

Tapered cup with blue flower handle; blue forget-me-nots.

$75.00 – 100.00.

Teacup, saucer, and bread and butter plate.

Delphine China Company, c. 1933.

Cup with square base and yellow flower handle, 3¼"w x 2¾"h, saucer 5½", plate 6⅓"; cream with colorful pansies and butterflies.

$150.00 – 175.00.

Teacup and saucer.

Delphine China Co.,
c. 1950s.

Waisted swirled cup with
angular handle; floral transfer.

$30.00 – 35.00.

Teacup and saucer.

Royal Doulton,
c. 1902 – 1956.

Cup with gadrooned border,
square handle; Imari colors
and designs, trimmed with
gilt.

$45.00 – 60.00.

Teacup, saucer, and dessert plate.

Royal Doulton, c. 1895.

Octagonal cup with square handle; Norfolk
pattern.

$75.00 – 100.00.

Demitasse cup and saucer.

Royal Doulton, c. 1930s.

Cup with loop handle; The Coppice.

$40.00 – 50.00.

Teacup and saucer.

Elizabethan Fine Bone China, c. 1964 – present.

Footed and waisted cup, question-mark handle; gilt flowers and leaves on cobalt.

$40.00 – 55.00.

Teacup and saucer.

Elizabethan Fine Bone China, c. 1964 – present.

Slightly flared cup with curled handle; pink and yellow roses.

$35.00 – 45.00.

Teacup and saucer.

Embassy Ware, Fondeville, England, c. 1950s.

Gold ground with colorful flowers. (See mark #43.)

$70.00 – 90.00.

Teacup and saucer.

Embassy Ware, c. 1950s.

Cup with angular handle with gilt line; blue and white windmill scene.

$35.00 – 45.00.

Teacup and saucer.

Foley, (Wileman & Co.), c. 1948 – 1963.

Cup 3¾"w x 2¼"h, saucer 5½"; yellow with flowers inside, trimmed in gilt. (See mark #44.)

$40.00 – 50.00.

Demitasse cup and saucer.

Foley, c. 1890 – 1910.

Daisy shape; Ivy border.

$45.00 – 65.00.

Teacup, saucer, and dessert plate.

Foley, c. 1892.

Fluted cup with angular handle; blue flowers.

$125.00 – 150.00.

Teacup and saucer.

Foley, c. 1930s.

Waisted cup with kicked loop handle; Montrose pattern.

$40.00 – 55.00.

Teacup and saucer.

Grosvenor Bone China,
c. 1961 – 1969.

Footed waisted cup with
question-mark handle;
daisies inside cup and on
saucer, gilt decoration.

$35.00 – 45.00.

Teacup and saucer.

Grosvenor Bone China,
c. 1961 – 1969.

Tapered cup with broken
loop handle; bouquets of
lilies-of-the-valley.

$30.00 – 40.00.

Coffee cup and saucer.

George Jones & Sons,
c. 1920s, made for Ovington
Bros.

Footed cup, 3¾"w x 2"h,
saucer 5"; roses, band of gold
beads on rims. (See mark
#67.)

$60.00 – 75.00.

Demitasse cup and saucer.

George Jones & Sons, c. 1930s.

Cup with green rustic handle, 2¼"w, saucer 4¼"; band of flowers on white, pink ground.

$40.00 – 45.00.

Teacup and saucer.

George Jones & Sons, c. 1889.

Small earthenware cup, 2¾"w x 2"h, saucer 4¾"; red-orange peonies, heavy gilt on cobalt blue. (See mark #66.)

$75.00 – 80.00.

Demitasse cup and saucer.

George Jones & Sons, c. 1920s, made for J. E. Caldwell & Co., Philadelphia.

Cup 2½"w x 2¼"h, saucer 4½"; garland of roses, with turquoise enameled dots.

$75.00 – 95.00.

Bouillon cup and saucer.

George Jones & Sons,
c. 1891 – 1924, made for
Tiffany & Co., New York.

Slightly flared cup; turquoise
and gilt swirled design.

$50.00 – 75.00.

Teacup and saucer.

George Jones & Sons,
c. 1920s, made for Ovington
Bros., New York.

Footed cup with reinforced
ring handle; roses and gilt.

$40.00 – 55.00.

Teacup and saucer.

Hammersley, c. 1939 – 1950s.

Footed cup; transfer of grapes,
nuts, and autumn leaves.

$60.00 – 75.00.

Teacup, saucer, and dessert plate.

Hammersley, c. 1912 – 1939.

Cup 4¼"w x 2"h, saucer 5½", plate 7"; cozy chintz look.

$80.00 – 100.00.

Demitasse cup and saucer.

Hammersley, c. 1939 – 1950s.

Scalloped cup, 3"w x 1¾"h, saucer 4½"; Lady Patricia pattern.

$60.00 – 75.00.

Teacup and saucer.

Hammersley, c. 1939 – 1950s.

Fluted cup with violet handle; floral transfer. (See mark #53.)

$35.00 – 40.00.

Teacup and saucer.

Hammersley,
c. 1939 – 1950s.

Footed cup with wonderful gilt handle of nude lady, 3¾"w x 2"h, saucer 5¾"; cream ground.

$150.00 – 175.00.

Close-up of handle.

Teacup and saucer.

Hammersley, c. 1960s.

Black ground with pink and orange orchids with green leaves; dramatic colors!

$50.00 – 65.00.

Covered teacup and saucer.

Hammersley, c. 1912.

Slightly waisted cup with broken loop handle; transfer of violets. (See mark #52.)

$100.00 – 150.00.

Teacup and saucer.

Hammersley, c. 1939 – 1950s.

Slightly fluted cup with squarish kicked handle; colorful blue and purple flowers, gilt.

$40.00 – 50.00.

Breakfast cup and saucer.

Hammersley, c. 1939 – 1950s.

Cup with loop handle; transfer of fishing scene.

$35.00 – 45.00.

Teacup and saucer.

Johnson Bros.,
c. 1913 – 1930s.

Footed cup with angular pointed handle; floral transfer.

$30.00 – 40.00.

Teacup and saucer.

Melba China Company,
c. 1933.

Eight-paneled cup with full flower handle; colorful flowers. (See mark #103.)

$150.00 – 175.00.

Same cup with pink and yellow flowers, pink floral handle.

Teacup, saucer, and dessert plate.

Melba China Company, c. 1948 – 1951.

Fluted cup with angular handle; cobalt blue flowers with gilt.

$80.00 – 100.00.

Demitasse cup and saucer.

W. R. Midwinter Ltd., c. 1932 – 1941.

Bute cup with loop handle; Rural England. (See mark #104.)

$35.00 – 45.00.

Teacup and saucer.

Minton, c. 1912 – 1950.

Cup with hand-painted rose inside; cobalt ground with gilt band. (See mark #107.)

$45.00 – 60.00.

Teacup and saucer.

Minton, c. 1891 – 1902, made for Higgins & Seiter, New York.

Cup 3¼"w x 2¼"h, saucer 5½"; etched gold band and heavy gold paste flowers on green. (See mark #106.)

$75.00 – 100.00.

Demitasse cup and saucer.

Minton, c. 1902 – 1911, made for Tiffany & Co., New York.

Cup 2⅛"w x 2"h, saucer 4⅓"; cobalt blue and gold.

$90.00 – 115.00.

Demitasse cup and saucer.

Minton, c. 1902 – 1911, made for Tiffany & Co., New York.

Cup 2¼", saucer 4¾"; cobalt border with ornate gilt design.

$125.00 – 150.00.

Teacup and saucer.

Minton, c. 1869.

Cup with Monarch butterfly handle; pale green, decorated with hand-painted butterflies and flowers.

$200.00 – 250.00.

Demitasse cup and saucer.

Minton, c. 1902 – 1911, made for Tiffany & Co., New York.

Scalloped cup 2½", saucer 4⅔"; dark red and cream ground, with lovely gilt.

$80.00 – 95.00.

Demitasse cup and saucer.

Minton, c.1863 – 1872, made for Phillips & Pierce, London.

Can cup with loop handle, 2"w x 2¼"h, saucer 4¾"; heavy gilt flowers and butterflies in Japanese style. (See mark #105.)

$80.00 – 100.00.

Teacup and saucer.

Myott Sons & Co., c. 1930s.

Rounded cup, copper luster.

$45.00 – 65.00.

Cup and saucer trio.

Unmarked except for #1865, attributed to New Hall, c. 1815 – 1825.

London-shaped cup; band of hand enameled roses on cobalt border.

$200.00 – 250.00.

Teacup and saucer.

Old Royal Bone China (Sampson Smith), c. 1945 – 1963.

Tapered cup with square handle; colorful ferns. (See mark #113.)

$35.00 – 45.00.

Teacup and saucer.

Old Royal Bone China, c. 1945 – 1963.

Footed cup with reinforced D-shaped handle; roses and gilt.

$35.00 – 45.00.

Teacup and saucer.

Paragon, c. 1932 – 1939.

Slightly fluted cup with flower bud handle; yellow and red flowers on pale yellow. (See mark #114.)

$150.00 – 175.00.

Close-up of handle.

Teacup and saucer.

Paragon, c. 1939 – 1949.

Cup with scalloped foot and colorful butterfly handle; rose inside cup. (See mark #115.)

$175.00 – 195.00.

Teacup and saucer.

Paragon, c. 1939 – 1949.

Corset-shaped cup with loop handle; Minuet pattern.

$35.00 – 45.00.

Teacup and saucer.

Paragon, c. 1930s.

Cup in Art Deco shape, three flowers on handle.

$175.00 – 200.00.

Teacup and saucer.

Paragon, c. 1957+.

Chintz design inside cup and saucer well, pink ground.

$45.00 – 60.00.

Teacup and saucer.

Paragon, c. 1939 – 1949.

Rose in center of cup and saucer well, etched gold band on rim of cup and saucer.

$55.00 – 75.00.

Teacup and saucer.

Paragon, c. 1960s.

Tapered cup with loop handle; mint green sponge effect.

$40.00 – 45.00.

Teacup and saucer.

Paragon, c. 1939 – 1949.

Flared cup, with ribs at bottom, with gilt foot and broken loop handle; center cartouche of flowers framed by gilt, cobalt border with white flowers.

$45.00 – 65.00.

Teacup and saucer.

Paragon, c. 1939 – 1949.

Footed cup with feathered handle; large white flowers on pink, chintz style.

$40.00 – 55.00.

Teacup and saucer.

Paragon, c. 1930s.

Tapered cup with rings, rose handle; flowers inside cup and on saucer well.

$125.00 – 150.00.

Teacup and saucer.

Queen Anne (Shore & Coggins),
c. 1959 – 1966.

Footed cup with broken loop handle; green ivy
design. (See mark #121.)

$35.00 – 40.00.

Teacup and saucer.

Queen Anne, c. 1959 – 1966.

Footed cup with broken loop
handle; paisley-type design.

$40.00 – 45.00.

Teacup and saucer.

Queen Anne, c. 1950s.

Slightly fluted footed cup with
high loop handle with spur
and thumb rest; purple plums,
gilt border.

$40.00 – 50.00.

Teacup and saucer.

Radford, Samuel,
c. 1938 – 1957.

Three-tiered cup with wisteria
flower handle; hand-painted
with purple wisteria flowers.
(See mark #122.)

$150.00 – 175.00.

Teacup and saucer.

Regency China Ltd.,
c. 1953 – present.

Tapered foot with coiled
broken loop handle; large
orange flowers, gilt. (See
mark #123.)

$35.00 – 45.00.

Teacup and saucer.

Rosina China Co.,
c. 1948 – 1952.

Tapered cup with angular
handle, scalloped saucer;
chintz pattern. (See mark
#134.)

$60.00 – 90.00.

Teacup and saucer.

Rosina China Co.,
c. 1948 – 1952.

Tapered cup with angular
handle; chintz pastel flowers.

$60.00 – 75.00.

Teacup and saucer.

Rosina China Co., c. 1950s.

Waisted cup with gilt foot and
handle; vivid paisley-style
design.

$45.00 – 65.00.

Small teacup and saucer.

Royal Albert, c. 1945+.

Footed cup with eight puffy
flutes, feathered broken loop
handle; Regal series. (See
mark #136.)

$30.00 – 40.00.

Teacup and saucer.

Royal Albert, c. 1917.

Footed cup with broken loop handle; Flow Blue flower decoration. (See mark #135.)

$35.00 – 45.00.

Snack set.

Royal Albert, c. 1950s.

American Beauty pattern.

$60.00 – 75.00.

Teacup, saucer, and dessert plate.

Royal Albert, c. 1945+.

Scalloped saucer and plate; chintz pattern.

$75.00 – 95.00.

Teacup and saucer.

Royal Albert, c. 1945+.

Small cup 2¼"w x 2½"h, saucer 4¾"; lovely mill scenic pattern.

$40.00 – 45.00.

Close-up of scene.

Teacup and saucer.

Royal Albert, c. 1935 – 1944.

Footed puffy cup; Chelsea Bird pattern.

$40.00 – 55.00.

Teacup and saucer.

Royal Albert,
c. 1935 – 1944.

Footed cup with elongated
pinched loop handle; colorful hand-painted flowers.

$40.00 – 55.00.

Teacup and saucer.

Royal Albert,
c. 1930 – 1950s.

Cup slightly puffed,
question-mark handle;
chintz design.

$60.00 – 75.00.

Teacup and saucer.

Royal Albert,
c. 1930 – 1950s.

Cup slightly flared and
puffed at bottom; Moonlight
Roses pattern.

$40.00 – 55.00.

Teacup, saucer, and dessert plate.

Royal Albert, c. 1927 – 1934.

Cup with angular handle; cobalt blue in Oriental style, with gilt.

$125.00 – 150.00.

Teacup, saucer, and dessert plate.

Royal Albert, c. 1960 – 1970s.

Footed puffy cup with broken loop angular handle; "Flower of the Month" series, March.

$50.00 – 60.00.

Teacup and saucer.

Royal Chelsea, c. 1950s.

Footed cup with broken loop handle; orchid transfer. (See mark #139.)

$35.00 – 40.00.

Teacup and saucer.

Royal Chelsea, c. 1950s.

Ribbed cup; cobalt and gold decoration.

$45.00 – 65.00.

Teacup and saucer.

Royal Chelsea,
c. 1950 – 1960s.

Scalloped cup and saucer;
gilt flowers on cobalt border,
flowers inside cup and on
saucer well.

$40.00 – 55.00.

Teacup and saucer.

Royal Grafton (A. B. Jones
& Sons), c. 1957 – 1960.

Scalloped cup; cobalt border
with gilt, colorful flowers
inside the cup and saucer
well. (See mark #141.)

$40.00 – 55.00.

Teacup and saucer.

Royal Grafton, c. 1957 – 1960.

Slightly fluted cup with broken loop handle with thumb rest; panels of coral flowers alternating with yellow panels, separated by gilt flowers.

$35.00 – 45.00.

Teacup and saucer.

Royal Stafford China, c. 1950s.

Cobalt bands with gilt flowers and heavily etched gilt band. (See mark #142.)

$45.00 – 55.00.

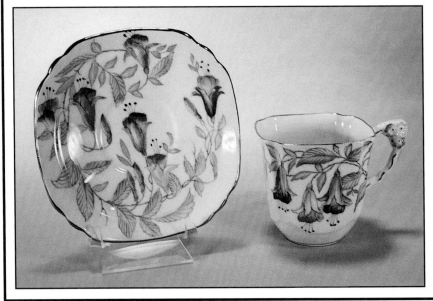

Teacup and saucer.

Royal Stafford China, c. 1950s.

Cup with three flowers on the handle; Fuchsia pattern. (See mark #143.)

$100.00 – 125.00.

Teacup and saucer.

Royal Stafford China,
c. 1950s.

Pedestal cup with reinforced
gilt loop handle; black matte
ground, purple flowers inside
cup and saucer well.

$40.00 – 55.00.

Teacup and saucer.

Royal Stafford China,
c. 1950s.

Delicately fluted cup with
coiled loop handle, scal-
loped saucer; scattered roses,
gilt.

$35.00 – 45.00.

Teacup and saucer.

Royal Stafford China,
c. 1930s.

Cup with three-flower handle;
Primrose Dell pattern.

$100.00 – 125.00.

Teacup and saucer.

Royal Standard, c. 1950s.

Virginia Stock chintz pattern. (See mark #144.)

$60.00 – 75.00.

Teacup and saucer.

Royal Standard, c. 1950s.

Footed cup with angular broken loop handle; floral transfer.

$40.00 – 55.00.

Teacup and saucer.

Royal Stuart, c. 1950s.

Fluted cup with green flower handle, 3⅓"w x 2¼"h, saucer 5½"; pale green and white, with flowers. (See mark #145.)

$60.00 – 75.00.

Same cup in yellow.

Teacup and saucer.

Royal Winton, c. 1951+.

Footed cup with unusual ring handle; all gilt.

$30.00 – 35.00.

Demitasse cup and saucer.

Shelley, c. 1945-1966.

Dainty shape with pale green loop handle; Rosebud. (See mark #156.)

$50.00 – 65.00.

Teacup and saucer.

Shelley, c. 1945 – 1966.

Dainty shape, Shamrock pattern.

$85.00 – 100.00.

Teacup and saucer.

Shelley, c. 1945 – 1966.

Dainty shape, Lily-of-the-Valley pattern.

$75.00 – 95.00.

Teacup and saucer.

Shelley, c. 1945 – 1966.

Dainty shape, Morning Glory pattern.

$75.00 – 95.00.

Teacup and saucer.

Shelley, c. 1945-1966.

Flared molded cup with light blue loop handle; Harebell pattern.

$65.00 – 75.00.

Teacup and saucer.

Shelley, c. 1945 – 1966.

Colorful chintz pattern inside cup and saucer well; dark red ground with gilt, some paint wear spots on saucer.

$100.00 – 125.00.

Teacup and saucer.

Shelley, c. 1945 – 1966.

Scalloped and footed cup with curled handle; light blue ground with chintz decoration inside cup.

$125.00 – 150.00.

Demitasse cup and saucer.

Shelley, c. 1945 – 1966.

Fourteen flutes; Rose Spray pattern.

$50.00 – 65.00.

Teacup and saucer.

Shelley, c. 1945 – 1966.

Oleander shape; variation of Rose Pansy and Forget-me-not pattern, blue ground.

$50.00 – 75.00.

Teacup and saucer.

Shelley, c. 1945 – 1966.

Oleander shape; variation of Rose and Red Daisy pattern, pale yellow ground.

$50.00 – 75.00.

Teacup and saucer.

Shelley, c. 1945 – 1966.

Footed slightly waisted cup with loop handle; Heavenly Blue pattern.

$60.00 – 80.00.

Teacup and saucer.

Shelley, c. 1925 – 1940s.

Queen Anne shape; red flower with black leaves, orange trim on rims.

$60.00 – 85.00.

Demitasse cup and saucer.

Shelley, c. 1945 – 1966.

Fourteen flutes; Regency pattern.

$45.00 – 60.00.

Teacup and saucer.

Tuscan, c. 1950s.

Footed slightly fluted cup; black ground with dramatic pink cherry blossom chintz decoration. (See mark #161.)

$45.00 – 60.00.

Teacup, saucer, and dessert plate.

Tuscan, c. 1960s.

Pedestal cup, 3⅓"w x 3"h, saucer 5½", dessert plate 8"; Golden Blossom pattern.

$60.00 – 90.00.

Teacup and saucer.

Tuscan, c. 1930 – 1950s.

Footed and flared cup with curled handle; yellow flowers in chintz.

$45.00 – 60.00.

Teacup, saucer, and dessert plate.

Tuscan, c. 1898+.

Scalloped cup with pinched loop handle; cobalt floral border.

$75.00 – 100.00.

Breakfast cup and saucer.

Wedgwood, c. 1901 – 1920.

Cup 4"w x 2¼"h, saucer 6¼"; band of blue and white flowers on rim with a village scene and deer on saucer, trimmed with gilt. (See mark #165.)

$45.00 – 60.00.

Demitasse cup and saucer.

Wedgwood, c. 1930s.

Can cup with loop handle; heavily enameled design.

$40.00 – 50.00.

Demitasse cup and saucer.

Wileman & Co., c. 1884.

Cup 2⅛"w x 2⅛"h, saucer 4⅞"; vivid Imari pattern.

$40.00 – 55.00.

Teacup and saucer.

Windsor (Cooperative Whole-salers Society, Ltd.), c. 1950 – 1960s.

Footed cup; Dogwood pattern.

$30.00 – 40.00.

Demitasse cup and saucer.

Royal Worcester, c. 1910.

Straight cup with loop handle with inner spur; hand gilded flowers on green.

$55.00 – 70.00.

Covered bouillon cup and saucer.

Royal Worcester for J. E. Caldwell, Philadelphia, c. 1887.

Footed cup with reinforced ring handle, cover with gilt ring finial; brown floral transfer. (See mark #168.)

$75.00 – 100.00.

Teacup and saucer.

Royal Worcester, c. 1939.

Persian motif.

$35.00 – 45.00.

Teacup and saucer.

Royal Worcester, c. 1944 – 1955.

Patricia pattern.

$35.00 – 45.00.

Breakfast cup and saucer.

Royal Worcester, c. 1904.

Straight cup with ring handle; hand-painted elves at work.

$150.00 – 200.00.

Teacup and saucer.

Royal Worcester, c. 1950s.

Swirled cup with loop handle; Lavina pattern.

$40.00 – 50.00.

Breakfast cup and saucer.

Unmarked, c. 1860 – 1870s.

Cup 3¾"w x 2½"h, saucer 6¼"; gold Greek Key border with gilt leaves.

$50.00 – 75.00.

Gaelic coffee cup and saucer.

Irish Belleek,
c. 1956 – 1965.

Shamrock design.

$100.00 – 125.00.

Coffee cup and saucer.

Irish Belleek,
c. 1927 – 1941.

Shamrock design. (See mark
#3.)

$95.00 – 100.00.

Teacup and saucer.

Irish Belleek,
c. 1891 – 1926.

Tridacna design.

$100.00 – 125.00.

Teacup and saucer.

Royal Tara, Ireland, c. 1942 – present.

Fluted cup with question-mark handle; green shamrocks and gilt. (See mark #146.)

$35.00 – 45.00.

JAPANESE TABLEWARES

IMPORTANCE OF TEA

The earliest record of tea drinking in Japan was in 729 A.D. when Emperor Shomu invited one hundred Buddhist monks to take tea in his palace. About one hundred years later, upon his return from China, the monk Eichu made tea for the Emperor Saga. It was so well received that an official tea garden was opened in the Imperial Palace, and tea drinking began to take hold in the court and in temples.

The first tea seeds were brought to Japan in the twelfth century by the returning Buddhist priest Yeisei, who had observed the value of tea in China for enhancing religious meditation. Yeisei wrote a book, *Kissa-yojo-ki* (Tea Drinking for the Cultivation of Life). As a result, he became known as the "Father of Tea" in Japan.

Sen-no-Rikyu (1522 – 1591) was known as "The Great Tea Master." He was born in Kyoto and studied the tea ceremony and Zen. He perfected the tea ceremony as a highly formalized ritual of preparing tea for guests

Lovely lady in an embroidered Japanese kimono drinking tea, 1905 French postcard.

JAPANESE TEA CEREMONY (CHA-NO-YU)

Cha-no-yu involves much more than enjoying a cup of tea in a formal manner. Influenced by Zen Buddhism, the purpose is to purify the soul by becoming one with nature. The basic idea is expressed by four Chinese characters: wa, kei, sei, and jaku. Wa means harmony, kei means respect, sei means purity, and jaku means tranquillity.

The tea ceremony requires years of training and practice. The act must be performed in the most polite, most graceful, and most charming manner possible. The artistic hostesses of Japan, the Geishi, began to specialize in the presentation of the tea ceremony.

The tea ceremony takes place in the chashitsu, a special room designated for tea. It is usually within the tea house, which is located in a garden away from the residence. (A special form of architecture developed for tea houses, based on the replication of a forest cottage.)

The guests are shown into a waiting room.

Japanese Tea House, postcard from Tokyo, Japan.

Here the hanto, the host's assistant, offers them the hot water that will be used to make tea. The guests choose one of their group (four is the preferred number) to act as the guesto (main guest).

The hanto then leads the main guest, followed by the others, to a water sprinkled garden without flowers, called a roji (dew ground). Here the guests rid themselves of the dust of the world.

The guests sit on a bench, waiting for the host, who has the official title of teishu (house master). Before receiving the guests, the teishu takes a ladle of water from a stone basin to purify his hands and mouth. He then goes through the chumon (middle gate) to meet his guests. No words are spoken.

The teishu leads the hanto, main guest, and others through the chumon, which symbolizes the door between the coarse physical world and the spiritual world of tea. The guests and hanto purify themselves at the stone basis and enter the teahouse. All who enter must bow their heads and crouch, as the sliding door is only 36" high. This symbolizes that all are equal in tea.

The only decoration in the room is a kakemono (scroll painting) hanging in the alcove. It has been carefully chosen by the hosts and reveals the theme of the ceremony. Each guest admires the scroll and is seated.

The host enters with the chawan (tea bowl), which holds the tea whisk, the tea cloth, and the tea scoop, a slender bamboo scoop used to dispense the matcha (finely powdered green tea). The chawan, representing the moon, or yin, is placed by the water jar, which represents the sun, or yong.

The host purifies the tea container and scoop with a fukusa (a fine silk cloth that symbolizes his spirit). The host's careful inspection, folding, and handling of the fukusa has special significance. Hot water is ladled into the tea bowl, the whisk is rinsed, and the tea bowl is emptied and wiped.

The host then places three scoops of tea per guest into the tea bowl. Enough hot water is added to make a thin paste with the whisk. Additional water is added.

The host passes the tea bowl to the main guest, who bows when accepting it. The bowl is raised and turned in the hand, to be admired. The guest then drinks some of the tea, wipes the rim, and passes the bowl to the next guest.

All utensils are then rinsed and cleaned, and usa cha, or thin tea, is served. This rinses the palate and prepares the guest for leaving the spiritual world of tea and re-entering the physical world.

At the end of the ceremony, the guests express their appreciation for the tea and for the art of the host. They leave as the host watches from the door of the teahouse.

Cha-no-yu plays an important role in the artistic life as well as the spiritual life of the Japanese people. The tea ceremony involves the aesthetic appreciation of the room in which it is held, the garden attached to the room, the utensils for preparing and serving the tea, and the hanging scroll.

The tea bowl, or chawan, is the most significant of all the tea utensils. Its primary role is to serve as the direct connection between the host and guest. As these tea bowls are used over time, they mature and improve. Chawan are the most popular and commonly collected of all the various tea utensils, with some treasured bowls over 400 years old and still in use today.

Japanese Geisha performing tea ceremony, postcard from Japan.

DEVELOPMENT OF JAPANESE CERAMICS

The earliest ceramic art in Japan was a black coiled pottery known as Joman ware made over 2,000 years ago. In the early thirteenth century, Kato Shirozayemon went to China to study the art of pottery, especially the technique of producing black-glazed tea bowls (temmoku) valued by the Japanese for use in their tea ceremony. Upon his return, Shirozayemon started to make similar bowls.

In the sixteenth century, the victorious master Hideyoshi returned to Japan from Korea, bringing potters with him. These potters settled in a number of areas like Kyoto, Karatsu, and Satsuma and started to produce ware in current Korean styles.

A Korean potter named Ameya developed a popular type of tea bowl around 1525. He was awarded a gold seal from Hideyoshi engraved with the word raku, which means enjoyment. The manufacture of rakuware, this earthenware fired on a hearth at low temperature and covered with a treacle-type glaze, spread widely.

The art of porcelain making was brought to Japan from China in the first half of the sixteenth century, by Shonsui. The first kilns were established in the early decades of the seventeenth century, at Arita. The first wares were produced in underglaze blue. Soon large quantities were shipped to Holland.

Ceramic techniques continued to develop during the next three centuries in Japan. Entire families worked in the pottery centers, passing their skills down to their children.

Following the reopening of trade with Japan by Commodore Perry of the United States in 1853, Japanese pottery and porcelain became extremely popular, attracting the attention of collectors. During the last quarter of the nineteenth century, Japanese influence played an important part in the Art Nouveau movement.

MAKERS

IMARI

Imari is the most famous name in Japanese porcelain. It was first produced in the seventeenth century, in the secluded mountain villages of the Arita district of the southern Japanese island of Kyushu, and was guarded by samurai warriors to protect the secret ingredients. The earliest Imari was the blue and white ware known as Arita. The clay had a high iron content that made it good for firing at high temperatures. The finished products from the Arita district were often shipped through the port of Imari, from which the company took its name.

At the end of the seventeenth century, overglaze red was introduced, and it rapidly grew in popularity. During the nineteenth century, enamel decoration in multiple colors was popular among the wealthy Japanese who were the main buyers of expensive porcelain. Five colors dominated: cobalt blue, pale blue, iron red, green, and gold. Complexity of design increased during the nineteenth century, and the ware became known as nishiki Imari, or brocade.

KUTANI

The kilns at Kutani, in the Kaga province, were established in 1664. Kutani is distinguished by the use of five bold colors, in particular red, deep blue, deep yellow, purple, and green. The entire surface of the item is covered with colorful decoration. Themes include birds and flowers, landscapes, and geometric patterns.

Pretty lady drinking from a Japanese tea cup, 1913 postcard, D & C., Berlin series 2391.

There is rarely a seal on the base of Kutani wares; nevertheless, the characters for Kutani, as well as those for the name of the artist, often appear.

Kutani ware was unknown in the West until a group of the pieces were displayed at the Paris Exhibition of 1867. Here the red, gold, and soft white tones were greatly admired. Soon a wide variety of decorated items, such as tea, coffee, and chocolate sets were produced for both domestic and foreign markets with white backgrounds and eggshell-thin bodies. Kutani kilns are still producing porcelain for export.

SATSUMA

Satsuma is a type of earthenware made in Japan as early as the seventeenth century. The earliest wares were enameled with simple flowers. By the late eighteenth century, a floral brocade (nishikide design) was frequently used. Gold and silver enamels were used as accents by the late nineteenth century. Human forms such as samurai warriors and geisha girls were used to appeal to Western tastes in the twentieth century.

Some cabinet cups and saucers can be found that have exquisite miniature paintings that one has to look at under a magnifying glass to appreciate fully. They are covered with intricate diapering and are overlaid with gilt. These pieces are rare, and command high prices today.

In the mid-twentieth century, a tremendous amount of Satsuma-type ware was produced for export to the United States. Much is poor quality, with rather crude paintings.

Satsuma is still being produced today.

NIPPON

Nippon cups and saucers are among the most sought after in the marketplace today. Nippon is not the name of a single manufacturer, but rather the area of origin. Nippon is porcelain made in Japan between 1891 and 1921, for export.

At least 300 kilns operated in Honshu, Kyushu, Skikoku, and other Japanese provinces in the late nineteenth century. Whole villages made and decorated porcelain. Children were often used to help decorate Nippon.

A tremendous amount of Nippon was exported to the United States, and there is a significant difference in quality. In a 1908 Sears catalog, Nippon cups and saucers are priced as low as $1.49 a dozen. One Nippon cup and saucer might be priced as high as $150.00 today.

There are many types of decoration on Nippon. Gold was used quite lavishly on pieces exported before 1912. Gold overlay pieces are very desirable and bring the highest prices. Some top quality Nippon cups and saucers have heavy gold on a cobalt blue ground, on white porcelain, or on floral or scenic designs. The gold was not very durable, and today a number of these pieces have considerable gilt wear.

Cobalt items were made with oxidized cobalt blue coloring. Originally, gosu – a pebble found in Japanese river beds – was used for cobalt coloring. Gosu became too scarce and expensive, and in the 1860s, oxidized cobalt was imported into Japan and used in its place. Nippon with cobalt and gold is extremely desirable with collectors.

Beading is another decorative technique used on many pieces of Nippon. Beading consists of a series of dots of clay slip that have been painted; a number of colors were used for this, especially gold and brown. Beading was used on rims and around floral and scenic cartouches.

Another interesting decoration on Nippon is moriage, applied clay or slip. The most available and popular moriage design is the jewel-eyed, slip-tailed dragon. This motif was used extensively after the first half of the Nippon period.

NORITAKE

After the reopening of trade between Japan and the United States in the late nineteenth century, many Japanese business executives realized the potential for export of porcelain to the United States. Baron Ichizaemon Morimura was one of these businessmen. He established the Morimura-Kumi Company to ship china and gift items to the United States through a New York wholesaler.

Morimura soon realized that America was eager for fine china dinnerware made in Japan. To insure that exports were of the highest quality, he decided to build his own factory. It was called Nippon Toki Gomei Kaisha, and was established in the village of Noritake, near Nagoya, on January 1, 1904. Since then, Noritake has steadily built its reputation as one of the world's premier manufacturers of tabletop products. From the beginning, the china itself was given the name of the town where the factory was built, and the name of the company was officially changed to the Noritake Company in 1981.

Today, Noritake china and crystal are manufactured in factories located around the world and exported to over one hundred countries. Collectors especially look for early Art Nouveau and Art Deco pieces.

Noritake's goal is "to create exceptional pieces, each of which serves as a reflection of our commitment to superior quality and craftsmanship."

OCCUPIED JAPAN

After World War II, the mark "Made in Occupied Japan" was used on all items for export in an effort to bolster Japan's economy. This mark was used from February 1947 until the end of the occupation in 1952. Occupied Japan pieces have caught on with collectors, and prices continue to rise. Companies that produced excellent quality Occupied Japan cups and saucers were Ardalt, Maruyama, and SKG.

Occupied Japan cups and saucers provide a lot of variety for the collector. The Japanese had a reputation for copying and reproducing European designs, and collectors can find interesting copies of Royal Dux, Meissen, Royal Bayreuth, and Capodimonte on Occupied Japan ware.

Occupied Japan Imari-style cups and saucers offer the collector an opportunity to upgrade their collection. The Imari pieces have deep blue, red, and orange overglaze with much gold decoration. The Hokutosha mark is found most often on these Imari-style pieces. They are as elegant as their early ancestors.

OKURA CHINA

Okura China is one of Japan's top dinnerware companies. In 1919, Okura split from the Noritake Company (Nippon Toki Gomei Kaisha). Okura Sonbeé and his son Kazuchika created the company with the goal of making fine quality porcelain that would equal porcelain from Meissen and Sevres in Europe.

Okura started receiving international orders in the late 1920s. It also made a series of dinnerware for the Embassy of Japan in the United States, as well as receiving commissions from Japan's royal family. In particular, 36 sets of gold-embossed dinnerware were made for the wedding of a princess in 1943, and the result was praised as a masterpiece of the highest quality. A set of dinnerware with white birch leaves and fruit designs was created especially for Empress Michiko in 1959.

Okura china is known for its elegance. Its whiteness, smoothness, and durability make Okura China one of Japan's highest quality tableware companies. Okura's painting of roses is exceptional, and their most popular pattern is the Blue Rose.

LEFTON

The Lefton Company was established in Chicago in 1940, by George Zoltan, a Hungarian immigrant. He had always admired the quality and workmanship in finer Japanese porcelain, and after the end of World War II, he established business relationships in postwar Occupied Japan to export Japanese porcelain to American.

Early Lefton china was imported into the United States with an Occupied Japan mark. The porcelain was of excellent quality and was affordable to middle-class Americans in post war years. Today, Lefton Occupied Japan cups and saucers are beginning to attract the attention of collectors.

LIPPER INTERNATIONAL

This company originated as Lipper & Mann in 1946, as importers of fine glass and ceramic items. Many tea and dinnerware sets were imported from Japan. Its most famous pattern, Blue Danube, was produced in 1951, and is still distributed in better department and specialty stores today. The border was designed by Mr. Lipper himself and was copied from Meissen's famous Blue Onion pattern. The flowers in the Blue Danube pattern portray the ancient Chinese symbols of good fortune and happiness.

MIKASA

Mikasa, which in Japanese means three umbrellas, was started in 1936 by Setsuo Aratani, a Japanese-American, as an import-export company specializing in trade with Japan. The firm ceased operation during World War II, but in the 1950s, his son George Aratani reopened it. In 1976, Alfred Blake was made president, and he extended the company's line and added crystal stemware. A showroom was opened in mid-Manhattan, and an outlet store in Secaucas, New Jersey.

Mikasa owns no factories. It contracts out designs to manufacturers in 17 countries. This not only keeps costs down, but also gives Mikasa the flexibility to sell many new patterns and phase out old ones. Mikasa is best known for bold colors and big fruit designs. It now claims the number one position in the United States for casual china. In the higher ranges of the market, Mikasa ranks fifth, after Lenox, Noritake, Wedgwood, and Royal Doulton.

NARUMI BONE CHINA

The forerunner of the Narumi porcelain manufacturer was Nagoya Potteries, established in the late nineteenth century. Narumi is the name of a town in the Aichi Prefecture. The company developed its own version of tableware after British bone china. In 1970, it exported a set of Japanese bone china tableware to the United States for the first time,

and it was well received. Today, Narumi is known worldwide for its durable bone china and its unique patterns, such as alpine plants drawn from the *Red Data Books,* and illustrations from *The Little Prince* by Antoine de Saint-Exupuy.

JAPANESE LUSTERWARES

Japanese lusterware was imported to the United States in large quantities between the World Wars. It was sold in dime stores, given as prizes, and was available through mail order. Today lusterware offers the collector a wide variety of interesting pieces at remarkably low prices. Even the high end of lusterware, the tea sets, are reasonably priced, considering every piece is hand painted. Many pieces are just marked "Japan" or "Made in Japan." One known manufacturer of lusterware was Takito, a Japanese firm operating between 1880 and 1948.

OTHER FIRMS

It has been impossible to find any information about a number of Japanese firms, such as Royal Sealy, Ucagco China, Maruta, Cherry, and Hira China. Royal Sealy produced a number of lovely cups and saucers. Cups are often footed, with ornate handles, and saucers are reticulated, with gilt trim. They are decorated with colorful flower and fruit transfers and are reasonably priced.

Many Japanese cups and saucers in the marketplace today are unmarked and date c. 1950 – 1970s. They often appeal to collectors because of their unusual shapes and handles and low prices.

Two Japanese girls having tea, 1908 postcard, the "Popular" series, New Zealand.

Teacup and saucer.

Castle China,
c. 1930 – 1950s.

Five-sided footed and paneled cup, unusual handle;
pink and gilt, with floral
design on saucer well.

$30.00 – 35.00.

Teacup and saucer.

Charles Roberts, contemporary.

Can cup with fat loop handle; tar-
tan ware print.

$30.00 – 40.00.

Three teacups and saucers.

Double Phoenix Company,
Japan, c. 1960s.

Flared cups with pinched
loop handles; Blue Willow
pattern, trimmed with gilt.
(See mark #30.)

$25.00 – 30.00 each.

Teacup and saucer.

Fine China, Japan, c. 1960s.

Footed cup with broken loop handle; violets inside cup and out, gold floral border on rim of cup.

$35.00 – 40.00.

Teacup and saucer.

Fukagawa, Arita, c. 1920s.

Rounded cup with loop handle; cobalt and white floral design.

$40.00 – 55.00.

Teacup and saucer.

Grantcrest China.

Footed waisted cup with elongated loop handle; violets.

$35.00 – 40.00.

Teacup and saucer.

Imari, c. 1920 – 1930s.

Translucent cup and saucer; orange cartouches with screens and cherry blossoms, rich cobalt, red, green, and gold colors. (See mark #62.)

$50.00 – 75.00.

Demitasse cup and saucer.

Kasuga Fine China, c. 1930 – 1950s.

Tapered cup with wide loop handle; chintz design.

$30.00 – 35.00.

Teacup and saucer.

Kutani, c. 1880s.

Quatrefoil cup, 3¼"w x 1¼"h, saucer 5" x 4½"; eggshell-thin porcelain, hand-painted butterflies and gilt. (See mark #63.)

$200.00 – 225.00.

Demitasse cup and saucer.

Kutani, c. 1890s.

Cup with scalloped foot and rim, 2½"w x 2¼"h, saucer 4¾"; heavy enameled cranes, extensive diapering with much gold. (See mark #64.)

$125.00 – 150.00.

Close-up of saucer design.

Teacup and saucer.

Kutani, c. 1920s.

Low cup with loop handle; Thousand Faces design.

$125.00 – 150.00.

Demitasse cup and saucer.

Kyokuto China,
c. 1920 – 1930s.

Six-sided cup on four feet,
angular handle; floral decoration.

$30.00 – 35.00.

Breakfast cup and saucer.

Lipper & Mann, Japan,
c. 1930 – 1950s.

Cup with loop handle; floral
chintz design.

$50.00 – 75.00.

Demitasse cup and saucer.

Unmarked, lithophane,
c. 1930s.

Rounded cup, 1¾"w x 2"h,
saucer 3¾"; eggshell fine,
hand-painted village and
lake scene.

$60.00 – 75.00.

Demitasse cup and saucer.

Unmarked, lithophane, c. 1950s.

Rounded cup, eggshell thin; white flowers with green and gold centers.

$60.00 – 75.00.

Teacup and saucer.

Marked Japan, Satsuma-style lithophane, c. 1930 – 1940s.

Cup 3¾"w x 2"h, saucer 5½"; heavy gold and enameling of Gods of Good Fortune.

$60.00 – 90.00.

Close-up of lithophane.

Demitasse cup and saucer.

Satsuma-style lithophane, c. 1930s.

Bute cup with loop handle; rakans and gods. (See mark #65.)

$60.00 – 90.00.

Demitasse cup and saucer.

Unmarked, lithophane, c. 1950s.

Cup 2"w x 2"h, saucer 3¾"; matte green with gold flowers and white enameled centers.

$40.00 – 55.00.

Teacup and saucer.

Unmarked, Nippon type, c. 1880s.

Pedestal cup, 3½"w x 2½"h, saucer 5½"; cobalt blue with medallions of hand-painted roses surrounded by gold beading.

$75.00 – 100.00.

Teacup and saucer.

Unmarked, Nippon type, c. 1930s.

Cup scalloped at bottom, 2½"w x 2½"h, saucer 5¼"; hand-painted pink flowers on cobalt, heavy gilt trim.

$150.00 – 200.00.

Teacup and saucer.

Nippon, blue maple leaf mark, c. 1891 – 1921.

Cup with unusual handle, 3¼"w x 2½"h, saucer 5¼"; cobalt blue ground, with heavy gold paste flowers and scrolls and a beaded rim.

$175.00 – 225.00.

Teacup and saucer.

Gold Japanese mark, Nippon type, c. 1880s.

Cup with three curved gold feet, angular handle, 3¾"w x 2¼"h, saucer 5½"; hand-painted roses and heavy gilt and beading.

$80.00 – 100.00.

Chocolate cup and saucer.

Nippon, blue maple leaf mark, c. 1891 – 1921.

Fluted cup with ornate handle; heavy gilt flowers on cream.

$75.00 – 100.00.

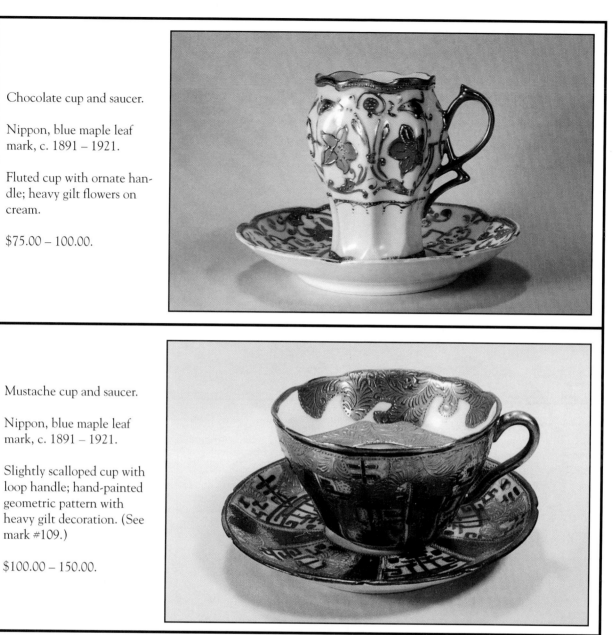

Mustache cup and saucer.

Nippon, blue maple leaf mark, c. 1891 – 1921.

Slightly scalloped cup with loop handle; hand-painted geometric pattern with heavy gilt decoration. (See mark #109.)

$100.00 – 150.00.

Teacup and saucer.

Nippon, c. 1891 – 1921.

Cup with loop handle; hand-painted roses.

$45.00 – 60.00.

Demitasse cup and saucer.

Nippon, c. 1891 – 1921.

Can cup with gilt interior, 1¾"w x 2"h, saucer 4"; Cobalt with gilt floral decoration. (See mark #110.)

$125.00 – 150.00.

Teacup and saucer.

Japanese mark, Nippon type, c. 1880s.

Cup 3¾"w x 1¾"h, saucer 5¼"; heavy gold and hand-painted roses.

$75.00 – 90.00.

Teacup and saucer.

Nippon, c. 1891 – 1921.

Pedestal cup, 2¼"w x 4"h, saucer 5⅔"; floral cartouches and heavy gold beads.

$75.00 – 100.00.

Close-up of beading.

Teacup and saucer.

Unmarked, Nippon type, c. 1880s.

Pedestal cup with gilt curled handle, 3¼"w x 2½"h, saucer 5"; cobalt blue with heavy gilt flowers, scrolls, and beading.

$175.00 – 200.00.

Teacup and saucer.

Nippon, c. 1891 – 1921.

Cup with angular handle; cartouches of hand-painted flowers framed by beading on gilt, black and gilt ground with jewels.

$100.00 – 125.00.

Teacup and saucer.

Nippon type, c. 1920s.

Pedestal cup with ornate handle; hand-painted pansies, mountain scene, enameled flowers.

$75.00 – 100.00.

Snack set.

Noritake, c. 1911.

Kidney-shaped tray with gilt handle; hand-painted flowers and gilt.

$80.00 – 100.00.

Snack set.

Noritake, c. 1911.

Kidney-shaped tray with gilt handle; hand-painted flowers and gilt.

$75.00 – 90.00.

Teacup and saucer.

Noritake, c. 1920 – 1930s.

Low cup with gilt loop handle; black and gilt camel scene on orange.

$40.00 – 50.00.

Teacup and saucer.

Noritake, c. 1917 – 1929.

Footed cup with loop handle; Crandon pattern.

$35.00 – 40.00.

Demitasse cup and saucer.

Noritake, c. 1917 – 1929.

Footed cup with loop handle; Crandon pattern.

$35.00 – 40.00.

Teacup and saucer.

Occupied Japan,
c. 1945 – 1952.

Pedestal cup, 3½"w x 2½"h,
saucer 5½"; lovely fruit decoration with gilt.

$100.00 – 125.00.

Pair of demitasse cups and
saucers.

Occupied Japan, Ardalt,
c. 1945 – 1952.

Quatrefoil cups; pink and
green panels, gilt flowers. (See
mark #112.)

$30.00 – 35.00 each.

Demitasse cup and saucer.

Occupied Japan, c. 1945 – 1952.

Melon-shaped quatrefoil cup and saucer; turquoise band, floral decoration.

$45.00 – 60.00.

Demitasse cup and saucer.

Occupied Japan, Maruka China, c. 1945 – 1952.

Swirled cup with rope handle; red and blue design on luster.

$30.00 – 35.00.

Demitasse cup and saucer.

Occupied Japan, Cherry China, c. 1945 – 1952.

Footed cup with loop handle; floral transfer.

$30.00 – 35.00.

Teacup and saucer.

Occupied Japan, Maruta Co., c. 1945 – 1952.

Footed cup with loop handle; decoration is Blue Willow style.

$30.00 – 35.00.

Teacup and saucer.

Occupied Japan, Hira China,
c. 1945 – 1952.

Footed cup with curled loop
handle; pansy decoration, gilt.

$30.00 – 35.00.

Teacup and saucer.

Occupied Japan, Maruta Co., c. 1945 – 1952.

Round cup with loop handle; Phoenix Bird pattern.

$30.00 – 35.00.

Demitasse cup and saucer.

Richard, Japan,
c. 1950 – 1960s.

Fluted tapered cup with ornate
gilt handle; violet transfer.

$40.00 – 50.00.

Demitasse cup and saucer.

Royal Ainsley,
c. 1940 – 1950s.

Fluted cup with three curved
gilt feet, curled gilt handle;
flowers, pink luster.

$35.00 – 45.00.

Teacup and saucer.

Royal Sealy, c. 1950s.

Cup on three curved feet,
reinforced loop handle;
white and pink roses on
shades of green.

$40.00 – 50.00.

Teacup and saucer.

Royal Sealy, c. 1950s.

Cup on three curved feet,
reinforced loop handle; pink
roses.

$40.00 – 50.00.

Teacup and saucer.

Royal Sealy, c. 1950s.

Pedestal melon-shaped cup with unusual handle; purple luster.

$40.00 – 45.00.

Teacup and saucer.

Royal Sealy, c. 1950 – 1960s.

Round shallow cup with ornate gilt feet and unusual handle, reticulated saucer framed with leaves; colorful fruit transfer.

$40.00 – 50.00.

Demitasse cup and saucer.

Royal Sealy, c. 1950 – 1960s.

Unusually shaped cup on ornate foot, with dove handle, saucer has well on side; gilt floral cartouches on pink and white.

$60.00 – 75.00.

Demitasse cup and saucer.

Royal Sealy, c. 1950 – 1960s.

Straight-sided cup on four curved feet, square handle; black border with gilt flowers.

$30.00 – 40.00.

Teacup and saucer.

Royal Sealy, c. 1950 – 1960s.

Can cup with four gold feet, triangular handle; medallions of transfer courting scenes, handkerchief motif on saucer.

$40.00 – 50.00.

Teacup and saucer.

Royal Sealy, c. 1970 – 1980s.

Pedestal cup with unusual handle; transfer of yellow roses.

$40.00 – 50.00.

Teacup and saucer.

Royal Sealy, c. 1950 – 1960s.

Pedestal cup with ring handle; transfer border of courting scenes.

$40.00 – 50.00.

Teacup and saucer.

Royal Sealy, c. 1950s.

Melon-shaped cup on three gilt feet, gilt broken loop handle with inner spur and thumb rest; pink luster with gilt flowers in saucer well and inside cup.

$35.00 – 45.00.

Teacup and saucer.

Sealy China, c. 1970 – 1980s.

Footed waisted cup, broken loop handle; Moss Rose pattern.

$30.00 – 35.00.

Demitasse cup and saucer.

Satsuma, c. 1900 – 1910.

Cup 1¾"w x 2"h, saucer 4"; fine quality, decorated with cartouches of painted figures, heavy gold.

$275.00 – 300.00.

Close-up of designs on saucer.

Demitasse cup and saucer.

Satsuma, c. 1920s.

Cup 2¼"w x 1½"h, saucer 4¼"; cobalt blue ground, hand-painted flowers outlined in gold, uniform crazing throughout. (See mark #149.)

$80.00 – 100.00.

Teacup and saucer.

Satsuma, c. 1920s.

Cup 3½"w x 2"h, saucer 5¼", eggshell thin; two figures inside cup, hand-painted with Rakens and warriors, gilt.

$80.00 – 100.00.

Demitasse cup and saucer.

Satsuma, c. 1920 – 1930.

Can cup 2⅛"w x 2"h, saucer 4¾"; hand-painted Lohans and heavily enameled dragon, usual crazing.

$60.00 – 75.00.

Demitasse cup and saucer.

Seckin Limoges mark, unidentified but possibly Japanese, c. 1930s.

Cup with ring handle and ruffled gilt foot, gold interior; black ground, ornate hand-painted Oriental motif with exotic bird.

$50.00 – 75.00.

Demitasse cup and saucer.

Shafford, c. 1950s.

Footed cup, handle with thumb rest and spur; hand-painted roses.

$45.00 – 60.00.

Child's cup and saucer.

Takito, c. 1880 – 1948.

Can cup with triangle-shaped handle; Thousand Faces pattern.

$60.00 – 75.00.

Demitasse cup and saucer.

Voagco Ceramics of Japan, c. 1950 – 1970s.

Tapered cup on three curved gilt feet, ornate handle, reticulated saucer; black rose on white.

$35.00 – 45.00.

Teacup and saucer.

Unmarked, made in Japan, c. 1950s.

Cup with unusual handle and three curved gilt feet, 3¾"w x 2½"h, reticulated saucer 5"; violets and gilt.

$35.00 – 40.00.

Demitasse cup and saucer.

Unmarked, unidentified impressed mark, c. 1900.

Brown stoneware cup with ring hanging from handle, 2½"w x 2½"h, saucer 4¾"; heavily enameled pink flowers and daisies.

$40.00 – 60.00.

Close-up of handle.

Demitasse cup and saucer.

Unmarked, c. 1900.

Flower form cup 2"w x 2"h, petal form saucer 3¾"; rose shaded to yellow, with gilt accents.

$40.00 – 50.00.

Demitasse cup and saucer.

Unmarked, c. 1900.

Cup 2"w x 1⅞"h, saucer 4"; black ground with violet chintz decoration.

$35.00 – 45.00.

Sake set.

Japanese mark, c. 1920s.

Flared can cups without handle, pot; gilt dragon on turquoise.

$100.00 – 125.00.

Mismatched teacup and saucer.

Unmarked, c. 1920 – 1930s.

Cup on four curved feet; Geisha Girl pattern.

$20.00 – 25.00.

Mismatched teacup and saucer.

Unmarked, c. 1920 – 1930s.

Shallow cup with red kicked loop handle; Geisha Girl pattern.

$20.00 – 25.00.

Teacup and saucer.

N in wreath mark, Japan, c. 1930s.

Cup with three curled feet, reinforced ring handle with thumb rest; yellow luster with sunburst design.

$30.00 – 40.00.

Teacup and saucer.

Unidentified mark with crossed flags, c. 1880s.

Round cup with loop handle; beaded and heavily enameled design.

$40.00 – 50.00.

Teacup and saucer.

Unidentified mark with crossed flags, c. 1880s.

Footed cup with broken loop handle; beading and enamel decoration on pastels.

$45.00 – 55.00.

Chocolate cup and saucer.

Unidentified mark with crossed flags, c. 1880s.

Fluted cup with loop handle; beading and enamel decoration, gilt.

$45.00 – 55.00.

Demitasse cup and saucer.

Unmarked, c. 1930s.

Straight cup with heavy diamond-shaped handle; blue and white Oriental figures and flags.

$30.00 – 35.00.

Teacup and saucer.

Unmarked, c. 1950 – 1960s.

Pedestal cup with unusual ornate handle, reticulated saucer; rose transfer on cup, verse commemorating Mother on saucer.

$30.00 – 35.00.

Teacup and saucer.

Unmarked, c. 1950 – 1960s.

Footed cup with reinforced ring handle; gilt decoration, magenta band.

$25.00 – 30.00.

Teacup and saucer.

Unmarked, c. 1950s.

Pedestal cup with ornate gilt handle; roses on pearl luster.

$30.00 – 35.00.

Demitasse cup and saucer.

Unidentified wreath mark, c. 1960 – 1970s.

Can with gold loop handle; chintz floral transfer.

$25.00 – 30.00.

Demitasse cup and saucer.

Unmarked #102.

Unusually shaped all gold cup with square handle, white saucer with gold scroll decoration.

$20.00 – 25.00.

Teacup and saucer.

Marked Japan, c. 1960 – 1970s.

Footed cup with loop handle; yellow flower transfer.

$20.00 – 25.00.

Teacup and saucer.

Unmarked, c. 1950 – 1960s.

Footed cup with broken loop handle, reticulated saucer; pearlized luster, yellow roses.

$35.00 – 45.00.

Teacup and saucer.

Unidentified mark with wings, c. 1920 – 1930s.

Rounded cup with unusual double ring handle; black cartouches with gilt flowers on pearlized white.

$35.00 – 45.00.

Teacup and saucer.

Unidentified banner mark, c. 1920 – 1930s.

Fluted cup with angular handle; floral cartouches, intricate design on white ground.

$50.00 – 75.00.

Demitasse cup and saucer.

Marked Japan, c. 1950s.

Quatrefoil cup with high heart-shaped handle; three flowered panels alternating with orange panels.

$25.00 – 30.00.

MINIATURES

Miniature collecting is one of the world's leading hobbies, and many cup and saucer collectors are miniature ware enthusiasts. People collect miniatures for a variety of reasons. Some want to recapture something from their childhood. Others enjoy it because miniatures don't take up much room and are easy to display. Beverly Foss Stoughton, writer of the article "The Art of Miniature Display," *Hobbies*, 1981, explains, "It is the continuation, passionately renewed, of the love humans always have had for small things."

Two little girls having a picnic with a miniature tea set, postcard from Germany, series 448.

TYPES

DOLLHOUSE SIZE

The first documented dollhouse was ordered by Duke Albrect V of Bavaria for his daughter in 1558. The house was four stories high and contained many rooms that were beautifully decorated with woven tapestries. It was filled with lovely pottery tableware, as well as other furnishings. The dollhouse was so elegant that the Duke decided to include it with his art collection rather than give it to his daughter.

In Nuremberg, Germany, pottery dinnerware for dollhouses was produced in the middle 1500s. Many items were decorated with vivid colored flowers, fruit, and birds. Examples are on display in the Nuremberg Baby House Museum.

Dollhouses were also called baby houses in England. A very famous early house was given by Queen Anne of England to her goddaughter, Ann Sharp, in the 1690s. The house had nine completely furnished rooms.

Queen Mary, grandmother of Britain's present Queen Elizabeth, had a spectacular dollhouse presented to her in 1924 by her loyal subjects. Several famous English porcelain factories made dinner and tea sets for it.

The 1920s silent film star Colleen Moore was always fascinated with dolls, dollhouses, and miniatures. Her father suggested she indulge her fancy for miniatures by building the "dollhouse of her dreams."

In 1928, she did just that. The famed Fairy Castle was conceived, and by 1935 it was built, with the help of over 700 experts. The palace is approximately nine feet square and contains over 2,000 miniatures, including a set of Royal Doulton tableware displayed in the kitchen. This remarkable example of the art of the miniature created a widespread interest in dollhouses and miniatures that has continued to the present day. The Fairy Castle can be seen at the Museum of Science and Industry, in Chicago, Illinois.

On display in the Yesteryear's Museum, in Sandwich, Massachusetts, are individual miniature rooms. The dining rooms are furnished with the finest Limoges, Wedgwood, and Meissen tea wares.

CHILD'S SIZE

In the second half of the nineteenth century, a nursery system was normal for the children of affluent households. Children often ate in the nurseries, overseen by nannies, and children's sized china was used to educate them.

A series of Staffordshire ware was made especially for the nursery. It usually had transfer-printed decoration. Themes were religious texts and scenes from children's books. These early sets are eagerly sought by collectors.

Charles Allerton & Sons, Longton, manufactured many children's sets for export to the United States. They had at least five basic molds, and many different transfers. Most of these came in monochromatic designs of brown, red, or blue and had a border design. Some sets had mixed decoration, with hand painting over the transfers. Popular patterns were Stag and Punch, after the famous Punch and Judy puppets.

Children's sets made in Germany are choice items for the collector. Often these sets were made in the late nineteenth century and were charmingly decorated with scenes of children and pets. Some sets contained a motto, such as "Youthful pleasures — what a boy does not learn, a man does not know."

Very few children's dishes were made in the United States before the 1880s. The Buffalo Pottery Company, of Buffalo, New York, began production in 1903. They offered children's sets from 1904 to 1918. The Larkin Company produced dishes for premiums to be given with their soap. Baby Bunting was produced from 1906 – 1910 and includes decals of children's nursery rhymes. After 1914, it was cheaper to import children's ware from Japan.

Japanese children's sets, hand painted in bright colors, have considerable collector appeal. Many were exported to the United States, and these sets were played with by children during the 1930s and 1940s. Japanese children's sets are increasing in value.

"A Little Hostess, Granny's Darling," Raphael Tuck &Sons, "Oilette" postcard 9542, England.

SALESMEN SAMPLES

Tiny miniature tea and dinnerware sets were made by porcelain companies in England and Europe and were given to their traveling salesmen. It was much easier to help the customer visualize the line through a miniature set of the original than it would have been through the display of a few full-sized pieces. Salesmen samples can be found in the marketplace, but it is rare to find a complete set. Often the piece is marked to indicate it is a sample and is not to be sold.

TOY SIZE

Chinese porcelain miniatures were collected in Holland as early as the seventeenth century. However, not enough of the Chinese blue and white porcelain could be obtained to meet growing demand, and by the mid-1650s, the Dutch factories at Delft began to produce tin-glazed earthenwares with blue and white chinoiserie or floral patterns in imitation of the more expensive Chinese porcelain. Both full and toy size sets were made.

For at least 200 years, English potters have produced toy or miniature tea and dinner services as children's playthings or for adults to display. The early examples in salt glaze stoneware, tortoiseshell glazed ware, or early porcelain are extremely rare and costly today. These toy services are true miniatures of their full-size counterparts, both in form and pattern.

By the 1760s, Wedgwood was producing many of its creamware items as miniatures. Queen Charlotte, wife of George III, ordered two toy tea sets. It is amazing that some late-eighteenth-century creamware toy dishes are still found today in complete and mint condition. Wedgwood Jasperware miniatures began to be made in the eighteenth century, and because of their popularity with collectors, they have remained in production up to the present.

Spode became one of the most prolific miniature porcelain makers. Popular patterns with flowers and birds are readily available in the marketplace today. Most date from the 1960s to the present.

In 1904, Royal Crown Derby introduced toy shapes that became well-known to collectors of miniatures. These pieces were made entirely for ornamentation. Cups measuring less than two inches and saucers less than three, these miniatures were decorated in the company's famous Imari patterns 198, 1128, 2451, and 6299. Standard tableware patterns were also made. "What makes these tiny pieces so desirable and expensive is the fact that the decoration is a perfect miniaturism of the whole pattern, with not a stroke missed." (Margaret Sargent, Royal Crown Derby) Production of miniatures largely ceased by 1940, but a new range of miniatures was introduced by Royal Crown Derby in 1996.

Coalport produced some wonderful examples of miniatures in the late nineteenth century. Highly treasured by collectors is the hand-painted scenic ware, richly embellished with gold. In the 1960s, Coalport began to produce a large variety of toy tea sets in the Willow, Indian Tree, and Ming Rose patterns.

Chinese export porcelain was made in miniature and full-size, and was very popular in the United States in the late eighteenth century. A cup and saucer decorated with a portrait of a woman with a bonnet, with a border of gold stars against a blue background, is on display at the Winterthur Museum. In the early nineteenth century, Staffordshire potters exported many toy and dinner services to the United States. In the 1816 – 1818 period, a blue printed toy tea set was sold in Boston for $1.10 a set. Today it would be worth over $500.00.

As travel became practical for American businessmen for the first time, in the late nineteenth century, miniatures made ideal souvenirs to be packed in a trunk and brought home. Many miniature cups and saucers and mugs bear the names of places and events, and are quite reasonably priced today.

Two girls playing dress-up and taking tea in miniature cups and saucers, Raphael Tuck & Sons, Christmas series 1761, England.

A FEW WORDS FROM A COLLECTOR

Mia Alphenaar, who resides in the Netherlands with her husband, Hans, has a magnificent collection of miniature cups and saucers. Mia is a discriminating collector and has examples of the very best of the English and European manufacturers, as well as some extremely rare early Chinese examples. We appreciate Mia's generosity in sharing photographs of her collection to include in this book.

When asked why she started collecting miniatures, Mia says she learned to appreciate beautiful objects from her mother. She remembers admiring a lovely small service in an expensive shop as a child, and believes her love for miniatures began then. In 1975, she saw a miniature service in a catalog from a butter company. One could buy that service with stamps from butter packages. Mia saved enough stamps to buy a Healacraft miniature service.

Soon after, she saw a collection of Coalport miniatures. "I was completely hooked," she exclaims. "There were about eight or ten different decorations, and my plan was to buy them all. But because they were quite expensive for such small cups and saucers, I only bought two of them. A few months later they were all gone, and I have never seen them again in any porcelain shop."

"It's difficult to find good miniatures in Holland, and they can be very expensive," Mia explains. She enjoys traveling to England with Hans to look for miniatures. They visit Harrods, the NEC Antiques for Everyone Fair in

Birmingham (at the National Exhibition Centre), the Ardingly Antiques Fair, antique shops, auctions, and all kinds of small fairs and "car boot" sales.

Mia has about 100 miniatures in her collection, which consists of three categories. Category I follows these rules:

1. It is an example of a full-size service or cup and saucer.
2. It is marked (not always the case with early examples).
3. The height of the cup is between ¾" and 1¼", and diameter of the saucer is between 2" and 3⅛"
4. It is fine quality porcelain.

Category II miniatures are cups and saucers that aren't examples of a full service or full-size cup and saucer, and category III are tourist cups and saucers that are usually unmarked and of fair to poor quality.

Some of Mia's favorite pieces are a beautifully hand-painted Coalport, a Meissen Deutsche Blumen, and a wonderful hand-painted fruit set from Royal Worcester. "It's also my most expensive buy," explains Mia. "Royal Worcester made it in commission for me. I had to wait months, because I was told that the painting and gilding were very difficult to do. There was a 70% probability of a mistake."

"It's not only collecting, but it's also searching for information that I enjoy," Mia says enthusiastically. "I like talking to people, writing to factories, meeting fellow collectors or English dealers specializing in miniatures." Mia even found a job as an assistant curator in the communal museum in her hometown because of her general knowledge of antiques. "When you start a collection, you fall in love with it."

When asked if she had any advice for beginning collectors, Mia recommends starting with category II or I, even if you have to save money. "Always go for quality, not quantity."

A SHORT NOTE FROM HANS:
"As Mia's husband, I was not particularly thrilled by these little cups and saucers at first. I found it too much money for something as small as that. But through the years I have changed my mind (with a little persuasion by Mia, of course), and now I'm fascinated by them also. Mia does the actual gathering of information (she has more time to read all those books…). I myself do a great deal of supporting: chauffeur, cash register, computer wizard (my job is teaching computer skills…), photographer, translator, etc., etc. We've a profound love of England, and combined with the searching for the little devils, that makes a nice vacation! It made me take up collecting too, and so I collect slide rules and mechanical adding machines. They're becoming rarer and more expensive too. So we happily collect, tour the south of England (we've been to places no tourist has ever heard of), look around Holland, and sell some stuff at a couple of fairs to get some revenues, which are put into new buys. So the circle continues…."

Teacup and saucer.

Dresden, Helena Wolfsohn, c. 1843 – 1883.

Round cup, 1⅝"w x 1"h, saucer 2½"; hand-painted purple roses and other flowers, trimmed in gilt. (See mark #41.)

$200.00 – 225.00.

Teacup and saucer.

Dresden, illegible mark, c. 1891.

Quatrefoil cup with Dresden handle; hand-painted flowers on black alternating with courting scenes, gold embell-ishments.

$200.00 – 250.00.

Coffee cup and saucer.

Dresden, Helena Wolfsohn, c. 1843 – 1883.

Can cup, 1¼"w x 1¼"h, saucer 2¾"; hand-painted courting scenes alternat-ing with flowers on black.

$250.00 – 275.00.

Coffee cup and saucer.

Dresden, Helena Wolfsohn, c. 1843 – 1883.

Can cup, 1½"w x 1½"h, saucer 3"; hand-painted flowers on gold.

$275.00 – 300.00.

Coffee cup and saucer.

Dresden, Helena Wolfsohn, c. 1890.

Can cup with decorated loop handle, 1⅓"w x 1⅛"h, deep saucer without well; courting scenes and flowers.

$200.00 – 250.00.

Teacup and saucer.

Dresden, Helena Wolfsohn, c. 1843 – 1883.

Rounded cup with loop handle, 1⅓"w x 1"h, saucer 2⅔"; courting scene medallion.

$225.00 – 275.00.

Teacup and saucer.

Hutschenreuther, c. 1998.

Cup in Royal Flute style; Blue Onion transfer.

$40.00 – 45.00.

Teacup and saucer.

Lindner, Germany, c.1997.

Cup in Royal Flute shape, ornate broken loop handle; 1¾"w x 1⅓"h, saucer 2⅔"; style of Meissen Purple Indian pattern.

$30.00 – 45.00.

Teacup and saucer.

Meissen, c. 1820 – 1860.

Round cup with loop handle, 1⅔"w x 1¼"h, saucer 2⅔"; hand-painted applied flowers.

$600.00 – 700.00.

Teacup and saucer.

Meissen, c. 1850 – 1870, outside painting.

Round cup with loop handle, 1⅔"w x 1⅛"h, saucer 2⅔"; hand-painted Cupid in reserve, in purple camaieu style on yellow ground.

$350.00 – 400.00.

Coffee cup and saucer.

Meissen, c. 1850 – 1900.

Can cup with loop handle, 1⅛"w x 1"h, deep saucer without well, 2½"; hand-painted strewn flowers, gilt.

$300.00 – 350.00.

Teacup and saucer.

Josef Schachtel, Charlottenbrun, c 1866 – 1919.

Round cup with loop handle; Dresden-style hand-painted courting scene medallion.

$175.00 – 200.00.

Teacup and saucer.

Volkstedt, c. 1884 – 1894.

Low cup with fat angular handle; Imari colors.

$100.00 – 125.00.

Child's tea set.

Marked Germany, c.1900 – 1920.

Paneled set, service for six; slightly pearlized on the rim, decals of children playing.

$250.00 – 300.00.

Child's cup and saucer.

Unmarked, German, c. 1900.

Flower form cup with branch handle; pale pink and blue shading.

$50.00 – 75.00.

Coffee cup and saucer.

Unmarked, R. S. Prussia style, c. 1900.

Paneled cup with squarish handle; hand-painted flowers in relief.

$75.00 – 100.00.

Coffee cup and saucer.

Unmarked, probably Germany, c. 1900.

Footed fluted cup with loop handle; gold decoration on white.

$40.00 – 50.00.

Teacup and saucer.

Indistinguishable mark, c. 1900.

Footed flared cup with loop handle; silhouette inside cup and on saucer well, turquoise border with gilt decoration.

$125.00 – 150.00.

Close-up of silhouette.

Teacup and saucer.

Genma, Germany, c. 1910.

Footed and scalloped cup, 1⅔"w x 1 ⅔"h, saucer 2¾"; souvenir cup made for city of Hoorn, the Netherlands.

$35.00 – 40.00.

Coffee cup and saucer.

Pirkenhammer, c. 1857 – 1875.

Swirled can cup, 1½"w x 1½"h, saucer 3"; hand-painted flowers and gilt in Dresden style.

$150.00 – 175.00.

Child's cup and saucer.

Unidentified mark, possibly Russian, c. 1890s.

Cup with rustic ring handle; Oriental motif.

$75.00 – 100.00.

Two coffee cups and saucers.

Haas & Czjzek, Czech Republic, c. 1996.

Ornate cups and handles, 1⅓"w x 1½"h, saucer 2⅔"; pink with gold decoration.

$35.00 – 40.00 each.

Coffee cup and saucer.

Armando Grave, Portugal, c. 1980.

Can cup with narrow loop handle, 1½"w x 1⅛"h, saucer 2⅞"; hand-painted flowers.

$30.00 – 35.00.

Pair teacups and saucers.

The Netherlands,
c. 1960 – 1980s.

Delftware cups and saucers
made for the tourist industry,
hand-painted design under the
glaze.

$25.00 – 30.00 each.

Teacup and saucer.

Limoges, Bawo & Dotter,
c. 1896 – 1900.

Cup attached to saucer, 1¼",
saucer 1¾"; heavy gold flowers.

$75.00 – 100.00.

Teacup and saucer.

Limoges, marked Limoges, France; c. 1950s.

Dollhouse size; decorated with pastel flowers
and gilt trim.

$75.00 – 100.00.

Teacup and saucer.

Caughley, c. 1780.

Bute cup with loop handle; 1⅛"w x 1¼"h, flat saucer without well, 2¾"; rare underglaze Island pattern.

$550.00 – 660.00.

Coffee cup and saucer.

Coalport, c. 1881 – 1890.

Can cup with ring handle, 1⅛"w x 1½"h, deep saucer 2¼"; all gold, with bird and bamboo in underglaze blue painting.

$350.00 – 400.00.

Teacup and saucer.

Coalport, c. 1960 – 1970.

Round cup with loop handle; Indian Tree pattern.

$75.00 – 100.00.

Teacup and saucer.

Coalport, c. 1960 – 1970.

Round cup with white and gilt handle; Green Willow pattern.

$75.00 – 100.00.

Teacup and saucer.

Coalport, Coalbrookdale, c. 1830.

Flared and footed cup, loop handle with thumb rest, 1⅛"w x 1⅛"h, saucer without well, 2⅔"; hand-painted applied flowers.

$400.00 – 450.00.

Coffee cup and saucer.

Coalport, c. 1881 – 1890.

Can with ring handle, 1"w x 1¼"h, saucer 2⅓"; lovely hand-painted castle scenes on gold ground, gilt wear on saucer well.

$450.00 – 500.00.

Coffee cup and saucer.

Coalport, c. 1881 – 1890.

Can cup with ring handle, 1⅛"w x 1¼"h, saucer 2⅓"; hand-painted scene on gold ground.

$350.00 – 400.00.

Three teacups and saucers.

Coalport, c. 1960 – 1980s.

Round cups with loop handles, 1⅓"w x ¾"h, saucers 2⅓"; Red, Green, and Blue Willow patterns.

$60.00 – 90.00 each.

Pair teacups and saucers.

Coalport, c. 1960 – 1980s.

Round cups and saucers; Pageant and Brown Indian Tree patterns.

$60.00 – 90.00 each.

Coffee cup and saucer.

Coalport, c. 1891 – 1920.

Bute cup with loop handle, gold interior, 1¼"w x 1"h, saucer 2¼"; heavy paste gold decoration on green.

$350.00 – 400.00.

Pair teacups and saucers.

Coalport, c. 1960 – 1980s.

Round cups with loop handles, 1⅓"w x ¾"h, saucer 2⅓"; Red Indian Tree and Ming Rose patterns.

$60.00 – 90.00 each.

Teacup and saucer.

Spode/Copeland, c. 1891 – 1910.

Bute cup with loop handle, 1⅔"w x 1½"h, saucer 3"; over-painted birds and flowers.

$175.00 – 200.00.

Teacup and saucer.

Spode, c. 1955 – 1970.

Waisted cup with fat loop handle, 1⅔"w x ⅞"h, saucer 2½"; Gloucester pattern.

$75.00 – 100.00.

Teacup and saucer.

Spode, c. 1970s.

Slightly flared cup with loop handle, 1½"w x ⅞"h, saucer 2¼"; bird transfer.

$75.00 – 100.00.

Teacup and saucer.

Royal Crown Derby, c. 1907.

London-style cup, 1½"w x ¾"h, saucer 2¼"; exquisite Imari pattern.

$300.00 – 350.00.

Teacup and saucer.

Royal Crown Derby, c. 1910.

London-style cup; beaded medallion of hand-painted flowers on a cobalt ground, gilt.

$300.00 – 350.00.

Teacup and saucer.

Royal Crown Derby, c. 1905.

London-style cup, 1½"w x ¾"h, saucer 2¼"; Imari pattern #383.

$300.00 – 350.00.

Teacup and saucer.

Royal Crown Derby, c. 1905.

London-style cup, 1½"w x ¾"h, saucer 2¼"; Imari Scissors pattern #2649.

$300.00 – 350.00.

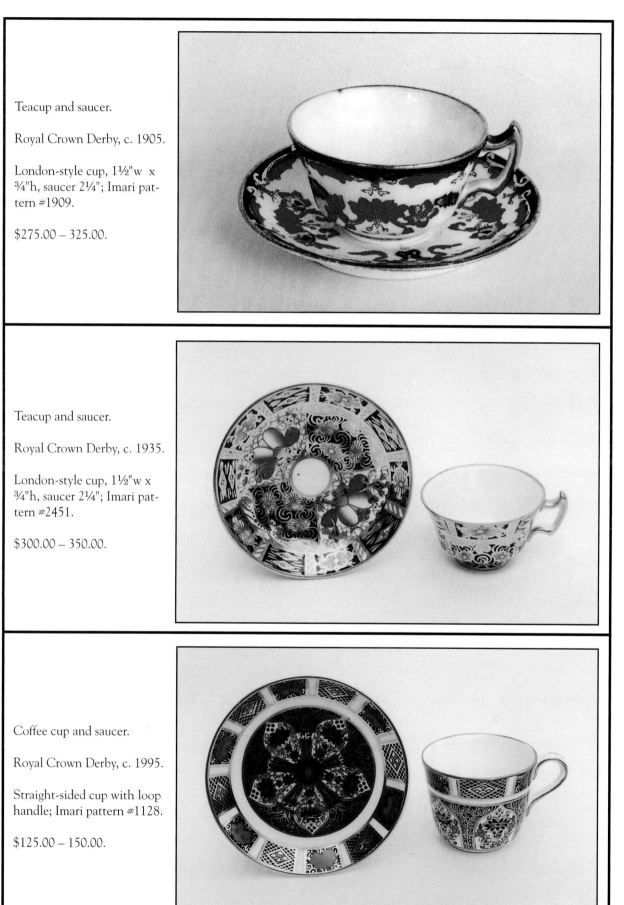

Teacup and saucer.

Royal Crown Derby, c. 1905.

London-style cup, 1½"w x ¾"h, saucer 2¼"; Imari pattern #1909.

$275.00 – 325.00.

Teacup and saucer.

Royal Crown Derby, c. 1935.

London-style cup, 1½"w x ¾"h, saucer 2¼"; Imari pattern #2451.

$300.00 – 350.00.

Coffee cup and saucer.

Royal Crown Derby, c. 1995.

Straight-sided cup with loop handle; Imari pattern #1128.

$125.00 – 150.00.

Coffee cup and saucer.

Royal Crown Derby, c. 1995.

Fluted cup, handle with gold bands, 1⅔"w x 1¼"h, saucer 2⅔"; Derby Posies pattern.

$50.00 – 75.00.

Teacup and saucer.

Crown Staffordshire, c. 1950s.

Cup 1½"w x 1"h, saucer 2⅓"; turquoise and gilt, with rose inside cup.

$60.00 – 75.00.

Teacup and saucer.

Crown Staffordshire, c. 1920s.

Cup 1½"w x ¾"h, saucer 2¼"; Oriental bird design.

$100.00 – 125.00.

Teacup and saucer.

Crown Staffordshire,
c. 1920 – 1930s.

Flared cup with pinched
loop handle, very thin
porcelain, cup 1½"w x ¾"h,
saucer 2¼"; underglaze
cobalt blue with gilt cross-
hatching, overglaze florals.

$150.00 – 175.00.

Pair teacups and saucers.

Crown Staffordshire,
c. 1960s.

Flared cups with pinched
loop handles, 1½"w x ⅞"h,
saucer 2⅓"; floral transfers.

$100.00 – 125.00 each.

Teacup and saucer.

Davenport, unmarked,
c. 1830.

Cup 2⅔"w x 1¾"h, saucer
without well 2⅔"; poly-
chrome Imari decoration.

$450.00 – 500.00.

Teacup and saucer.

Royal Doulton, c. 1990.

Footed cup with ornate handle, cup 1⅞"w x 1½"h, saucer 3"; Autumn pattern from Brambly Hedge series.

$35.00 – 45.00.

Same as above.

Winter pattern.

$35.00 – 45.00.

Same as above.

The Wedding.

$35.00 – 45.00.

Teacup and saucer.

Fenton, c. 1910.

Cup with fat loop handle, 1½"w x 1¼"h, saucer 2¾"; blue and white printed landscape.

$125.00 – 150.00.

Teacup and saucer.

Foley (E. Brain & Co., Ltd.), c. 1930 – 1940.

Slightly flared cup with loop handle; hand-painted floral design.

$100.00 – 125.00.

Teacup and saucer.

Green, T. A. & S. G., c. 1876 – 1889.

Flared cup with loop handle, 2⅞"w x 1"h, saucer 2⅔"; polychrome Imari decoration.

$200.00 – 250.00.

Teacup and saucer.

Grosvenor, c. 1920s.

Cup 1¾"w x 1¼"h, saucer 2¾"; floral transfer. (See mark #50.)

$60.00 – 75.00.

Teacup and saucer.

Hammersley, c. 1939 – 1940s.

Ribbed cup with squarish handle; floral transfer, gilt.

$75.00 – 100.00.

Teacup and saucer.

Healacraft, c. 1985.

Footed cup with ornate handle; printed floral decoration.

$40.00 – 45.00.

Two teacups and saucers.

Jones, J. B., c. 1985.

Rounded cup with narrow loop handle; printed floral decoration.

$40.00 – 50.00.

Teacup and saucer.

Lymes China, c. 1995.

Footed waisted cup with gilt broken loop handle, cup 1⅔"w x 1½"h, saucer 2¾"; scenic transfer design, artist signed.

$40.00 – 50.00.

Coffee cup and saucer.

Masons, c. 1970.

Cup with angular handle, 1⅓"w x 1"h, saucer 2⅓"; Mandalay pattern.

$50.00 – 75.00.

Teacup and saucer.

Minton, c. 1891 – 1902.

Flared cup with kicked loop handle, 1½"w x ¾"h; Posies pattern.

$200.00 – 250.00.

Teacup and saucer.

Queens China, c. 1994.

Footed cup with puffy waist; part of Zodiac sign series.

$30.00 – 35.00.

Miniature and regular teacup and saucer.

Royal Albert, c. 1990s.

Puffy flutes with broken loop handle; popular Old Country Rose pattern.

$35.00 – 40.00 miniature.

$35.00 – 45.00 full size.

Teacup and saucer.

Royal Albert, c. 1990, second quality.

Puffy flutes with broken loop handle, cup 1¾"w x 1½"h, saucer 3"; "Flower of the Month" series, December.

$35.00 – 45.00.

Teacup and saucer.

Shelley, c. 1945 – 1966.

Straight-sided cup with pink loop handle; Rose Spray pattern.

$150.00 – 175.00.

Teacup and saucer.

Shelley, c. 1945 – 1966.

Dainty shape, floral pattern.

$175.00 – 200.00.

Coffee can cup and teacup, no saucers.

Shelley, c. 1945 – 1966.

Floral pattern.

$100.00 – 125.00 each.

Teacup and saucer.

Shelley, c. 1930s.

Cup with pink loop handle; floral design.

$150.00 – 200.00.

Teacup and saucer.

Shelley, c. 1935.

Westminster-style cup, 1½"w x 1¼"h, saucer 2⅓"; purple flower decoration.

$200.00 – 250.00.

Pair teacups and saucers.

Wedgwood, c. 1980s.

Bute cup and saucer, loop handles; blue Jasperware and Kutani Crane.

$75.00 – 100.00 each.

Three teacups and saucers.

Wedgwood, c. 1980s.

Bute cups with loop handles; Mirabelle, Peter Rabbit, and Wild Strawberry patterns.

$60.00 – 90.00 each.

Child's cup and saucer.

Royal Worcester, c. 1885.

Can with question-mark handle; blue and white design.

$75.00 – 100.00.

Teacup and saucer.

Royal Worcester, present mark.

Footed cup with question-mark handle; reproduction of early Sevres design.

$100.00 – 125.00.

Coffee cup and saucer.

Royal Worcester, c. 1983.

Straight-sided cup with loop handle, 1⅓"w x 1¼"h, saucer 2¼"; Christmas, 1983.

$50.00 – 75.00.

Coffee cup and saucer.

Royal Worcester, c. 1994, signed Russell.

Straight-sided cup with backwards C-shaped handle, gold interior; special edition made for a London antique shop (Russell was gold painter at Royal Worcester).

$200.00 – 300.00.

Coffee cup and saucer.

Royal Worcester, c. 1995, artist signed S. Wood.

Straight-sided cup, backwards C-shaped handle, 1½"w x 1⅛"h, saucer 2¼"; "Hand-Painted Fruit."

$600.00 – 650.00.

Coffee can and saucer.

Palissy (part of Royal Worcester Factory 1946 – 1982), c. 1960.

Can cup with square handle; floral transfer.

$50.00 – 60.00.

Teacup and saucer.

Unmarked English, c. 1890s.

Cup with French Loop handle, 1½"w x 1"h, saucer 2½"; polychrome flowers, hand molded.

$75.00 – 100.00.

Teacup and saucer.

Gort, United States, c. 1950s.

Round cup, 1¾"w x 1"h, saucer 2½"; green flowers and gilt. (See mark #49.)

$90.00 – 125.00.

Same cup with red flowers.

Teacup and saucer.

Leneige, United States, c. 1930.

Flared cup with loop handle; gilt leaves on black.

$60.00 – 90.00.

Teacup and saucer.

Blue Bird Co., Canada, c. 1960s.

Slightly fluted cup with pinched loop handle; Christmas holly with gilt.

$50.00 – 75.00.

Tea bowl, no saucer.

China, Jade sign on base, c. 1690.

Footed bowl, very thinly potted, 1½"w x ¾"h; rare Crab and Bass pattern, hand painted under the glaze.

$600.00 – 700.00+.

Teacup, no saucer.

China, unmarked, c. 1710.

Bute cup, 1⅓""w x 1¼"h, no saucer; one of first cups with handles for European market; hand painted under the glaze.

$350.00 – 450.00.

Tea bowl and saucer.

China, unmarked, c. 1720.

Slightly ribbed cup, 1¾"w x 1⅛"h, saucer 3⅛"; hand-painted mountain scene under the glaze.

$200.00 – 225.00.

Child's teacup and saucer.

China, unmarked, c. 1820.

Footed and scalloped cup with fat loop handle, 2"w x 1⅛"h, saucer 3⅓"; underglaze floral design.

$175.00 – 200.00.

Four of above rare early Chinese blue and white miniature cups.

Coffee cup and saucer.

Kutani, Japan, c. 1920s.

Can cup, 1¼"w x 1½"h, saucer 3¼"; hand-painted flowers and birds, much gilt.

$100.00 – 125.00.

Teacup and saucer.

Occupied Japan, c. 1945 – 1952.

Straight-sided cup with square handle; Dresden flowers.

$50.00 – 75.00.

Teacup and saucer.

Made in Japan, c. 1930s.

Cup with heavy angular handle; hand-painted flowers.

$50.00 – 75.00.

Teacup and saucer.

Noritaki, c. 1930s.

Round cup, leaf form saucer; applied flowers and gilt.

$75.00 – 100.00.

Child's cup and saucer.

Japan, c. 1950s.

Quatrefoil cup with angular handle; pink and white, with gilt flowers.

$40.00 – 45.00.

Mustache cup and saucer.

Unmarked, probably Japan, c. 1930 – 1950s.

Flared cup with gilt loop handle; mixed decoration, man with mustache portrayed on cup.

$100.00 – 125.00+.

Teacup and saucer.

China, c. 1960s.

Paneled and footed cup, angular handle, 2"w x 1⅓"h, saucer 3¼"; souvenir set.

$30.00 – 35.00.

Teacup and saucer.

China, c. 1950s.

Flared, scalloped cup with angular handle; luster border, made on commission for Holland, showing traditional costume.

$30.00 – 35.00.

Teacup and saucer.

Japan, c. 1950s.

Footed scalloped cup, 1⅞"w x 1⅓"h, saucer 3¼"; dragon-ware.

$25.00 – 30.00.

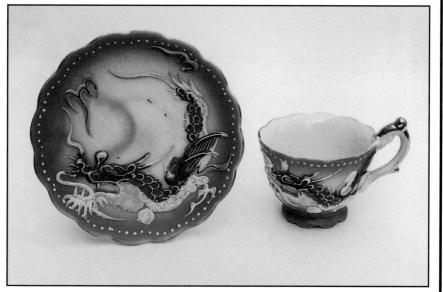

Teacup and saucer.

Japan, c. 1910.

Quatrefoil cup, angular handle, 1⅞"w x 1¼"h, saucer 3¼"; floral polychrome decoration.

$45.00 – 55.00.

ART GLASS CUPS AND SAUCERS

Highly treasured by a number of collectors are the beautiful art glass cups and saucers made by the leading glass factories in Europe and the United States. Art glass cups and saucers are not easily found in the marketplace, as they were not produced in large quantities. The hunt is exciting and the rewards are great when that elusive glass cup and saucer is found!

A BRIEF HISTORY

Since the earliest of times, glass has been admired for its delicate yet enduring beauty. Ordinary utensils made of glass, such as tumblers, goblets, pitchers, and cups and saucers, are also often works of art.

Glass is formed when sand, soda, and lime are fused together at high temperatures. The color of glass can be changed by adding specific metal oxides to a glass batch, such as cobalt for dark blue.

Glass was discovered in Mesopotamia around 2500 B.C. and was used for beads, seals, and architectural decoration. About 1000 years elapsed before glass vessels were produced. Around 1500 B.C., Syria and Mesopotamia emerged as glassmaking centers, and factories spread throughout the Mediterranean area. Glass drinking cups came in many different sizes and shapes. Conical glass vessels were used both as drinking cups and as oil lamps. Many cups were in beaker form.

The most important development in the history of glass was glass blowing, discovered by the Syrians around 50 B.C. A one-handled blown glass beaker dating from the first century A.D. was excavated in Egypt. It was made of greenish glass, with wheel cut rings and a blue applied handle and base.

Clear glass was much admired in ancient Rome, and the philosopher Pliny said, "…there is no other material nowadays that is more pliable or more adaptable, even to painting. However, the most highly valued glass is colorless and transparent…"

New centers of glass making sprung up in the Bohemian area of Europe in the eleventh century. Ash from plants (potash) was used as a raw material to make glass with a lower melting point. Bohemian glass continued to flourish in the seventeenth through the nineteenth centuries.

In Venice, glass factories were established on the island of Murano in the fifteenth century. The Venetian industry dominated the European market until 1700. In England, George Ravenscroft developed lead crystal in 1675. This new heavy glass enabled cutting, engraving, and decoration.

During the last half of the nineteenth century, beautiful art glass was made in Europe, England, and the United States. It flourished because of the Victorian preoccupation with the fussy and elaborate. During the Art Nouveau movement, the art glass of Tiffany, Gallé, and Lalique captured the attention of the world with sensuous lines, vivid colors, and iridescence. During the depression years, machine-molded glass was produced in great quantities, and inexpensive tableware was made.

DECORATIVE TECHNIQUES

Glass cups and saucers are found in a variety of shapes and decorative styles. The finest glass artists of the time decorated the elaborate art glass cups and saucers.

Enameled decoration has been used on glass since Roman times. Finely powdered colored glass is added to vegetable oil, resulting in a paint to use on glass. The glass is decorated with the enamel paint and then heated in a kiln. The powdered glass pigment fuses to the surface of the softened glass, allowing the enamels to adhere. Gilt decoration was also painted on outside surfaces, adding a richness and brilliance to the piece. Ludwig Moser of Carlsberg, Czechoslovakia, produced some of the most exquisite enameled glass cups and saucers, and they are eagerly collected today.

Engraved designs were perfected by glass makers in Germany and Bohemia in the nineteenth century. The glass cutter positioned a small stone or copper wheel on the far side of the object and looked through the glass to do his work. Once completed, an engraved design could be polished to make it transparent or left with a grayish, matte finish to make it stand out.

Overlay glass was also perfected at the Bohemian glass factories. This is a glass molding technique of placing one colored glass over another with the design cut through one layer only.

Cups and saucers made of opalescent or satin glass are favorites with collectors. Opalescent glass is a clear or colored glass with a milky white decoration that becomes fiery when held to the light. It is achieved by applying bone ash chemicals while the piece is hot and then refiring it at high heat. Satin glass was produced by most glass companies and has a dull, satiny finish resulting from a hydrofluoric acid bath.

The most highly prized art glass cups and saucers are those rarities found in cameo glass. This technique originated in Alexandra, Egypt, 100 – 200 A.D. The oldest and most famous example is the Portland vase found near Rome in 1852. It contained the ashes of Emperor Alexander Serverius, who was assassinated in 235 A.D. Cameo glass is cased glass of different colors with a design cut out of the outer layer that exposes the inner layer.

Silver overlay decoration was used during the nineteenth and early twentieth centuries. Silver overlay is a network of silver, usually sterling, which is applied to a cup and saucer by a silver craftsman after the pieces are completely finished. Many silver manufacturers were involved in this kind of decoration. Silver overlay is often engraved with floral, fruit, and rococo swirls.

MAKERS

BOHEMIAN GLASS

Bohemian glass was produced as early as the eleventh century. A complex technique involving etching, overlaying, and flashing became popular from the 1820s to the end of the nineteenth century. The colors most frequently used were ruby, amber, blue, black, and green, often combined with clear glass. Popular patterns were the deer and castle and various floral or animal patterns. A tremendous quantity of Bohemian glass was imported into the United States and the rest of Europe. A cup and saucer with an applied clear handle, ruby flashed and in an engraved castle and trees pattern, sells in the $125 – 150 range.

One of the most renown Bohemian glassmakers was Ludwig Moser. He founded a glass polishing and engraving workshop in 1857, in Carlsbad, Austria (which became Czechoslovakia after World War I). Moser employed many famous glass designers and incorporated with his sons in 1900. His work was outstanding, and includes cut colored glass with classical scenes, cameo glass, intaglio cut glass, and beautiful enameled glass. In 1922, Leo and Richard Moser bought Meyr's Neffe, their biggest Bohemian competitor; they are still in business today. Moser cups and saucers are some of the most prized in any collection. Two useful books on this subject are *Moser — Artistry in Glass 1857 – 1938* by Gary Baldwin and Lee Carno, published by Antique Publications, 1988, and *Moser Artistic Glass Edition Two* by Gary Baldwin, The Glass Press, 1997.

VENETIAN GLASS

Venetian glass dates from the thirteenth century to the present. Many glass factories were established on the island of Murano, near Venice. Venetian glass was usually colored, very thin walled fragile glass with applied flowers and fruits with embedded gold dust. A type of filigree glass was developed and widely imitated. This striated glass, called latticino, had a lace-like effect. Opaque white threads were incorporated into the glass and worked into intricate patterns.

Murano glass made in the twentieth century is popular today. A renowned glassmaker, Paola Venini, established a glassworks in 1925. He revived some old Venetian techniques, and his items bring high prices in today's marketplace. The Barovier & Toso Studios has been a popular glassworks since the 1950s. The company's wares include cordial and demitasse sets in cranberry, cobalt blue, and green, with applied enameled flowers and heavy gold embellishments.

FRENCH ART GLASS

René Lalique began as a jewelry designer around 1900, in Combs, France. He achieved his greatest success as a glass maker in the 1920s and 1930s, and elegant glass is still being produced by his factory today. Lalique glass is often a combination of clear white and frosted glass that was treated with hydrofluoric acid. Molded birds, nudes, and flowers are popular subjects. There are many reproductions on the market today.

The Baccarat-Sainte-Anne Glassworks is one of the oldest French glass companies and was established in Baccarat, France, in 1764. In the late nineteenth century, the firm achieved international renown for its cut glass table services and decorative items, as well as its famous paperweights. A lovely amberina cup and saucer in Baccarat's Rose Tiente pattern would be quite a prize!

AMERICAN ART NOUVEAU GLASS

At the turn of the century, Art Nouveau glass (originally from France) became fashionable in the United States. The most prominent glass makers were Tiffany and Steuben. Louis Comfort Tiffany created wonderful Art Nouveau art glass from 1894 to 1920. He imitated the iridescence found on ancient glass and experimented with new techniques. His most famous glass was favrile, or handmade, glass.

Gold chloride was used to achieve the gold sheen which characterizes favrile glass. Tiffany's pieces are highly sought by collectors and are being reproduced.

Lovely art glass and crystal tableware is still being made by Steuben today. The company originated in 1903, in Corning, New York. It was established by Thomas Hawkes and famous English glass designer Frederick Carder. During the period from 1903 to 1933, the company produced wonderful colored and crystal tableware and art glass, including iridescent aurene glass, calcite glass, Verre de Soir, and Rosaline glass. Rosaline glass is a pink jade-type cloudy glass that often has an alabaster trim. It was also made in England by the Stevens & Williams Company. Cups and saucers have been found in this form.

CARNIVAL GLASS

Many cups and saucers can be found today in carnival glass, a colored pressed glass with a fired-on iridescent finish. It was made in 1905, to copy the expensive iridescent Art Nouveau glass, and was very popular in the United States and abroad. Over 1,000 different patterns have been identified. The companies making carnival glass were Northwood, Fenton, Dugan, Imperial, and Millersburg. Color is the most important factor in pricing carnival glass. A green Grape & Cable cup and saucer made by Fenton is valued at $375; in purple it is $475. A marigold Kitten pattern cup and saucer is $250.

DEPRESSION GLASS

During the period from 1925 to 1940, American glassmakers produced inexpensive lines of mostly clear and pastel dinnerware. New techniques of tank molding permitted automatic pressing and pattern etching. Fancy designs were attractive and covered up defects, such as bubbles caused by the pressing process. Complete sets were used as promotion give-aways or could be ordered from Sears & Roebuck catalogs for $1.99. A higher quality glassware made by Cambridge, Fosteria, and Heisey was made c. 1930 – 1950s and sold in fine department stores. Today, depression glass cups and saucers are eagerly collected.

INFORMATION FOR THE COLLECTOR

Collectors throughout the world appreciate the unique features of glass cups and saucers, not only because of their place in history, but because they offer such a diversity of style, shape, and decoration. Various collector clubs are scattered throughout the country. Antique glass shows and auctions take place all year round.

Glass cups and saucers are easy to care for and store. Nevertheless, a glass cup will shatter not only when it is dropped, but when it is exposed to sudden changes in temperature. Never wash glassware until it reaches room temperature. It is best not to put your art glass cup and saucer in the dishwasher, as the temperatures are too severe and the water pressure too great. A gentle hand washing is the best method of cleaning.

Take care when buying an art glass cup and saucer. Examine both pieces carefully. Check the handle; it's very vulnerable. Glass can be repaired quite reasonably. Edges with chips can be ground. The value is lower, but not significantly.

Unfortunately, there are many glass reproductions on the market today. Patricia Dean, in *The Official Identification Guide to Glass Ware*, offers these wise suggestions:

1. Buy from a knowledgeable and reputable dealer.

2. Study the type of glass that interests you. Learn about it. See it in museums, antique shows, and shops.

3. Observe signs of age such as wear and random scratches.

4. Beware of too low prices. If it looks too good to be true, it probably is.

5. Learn the correct colors on the early pieces, as colors are usually different on reproductions and reissues.

Demitasse cup and saucer.

Verries de Nancy, France, for
G. C. & Co., New York,
c. 1920s.

Footed and panel cut cup with
loop handle; enameled gilt garland design.

$75.00 – 100.00.

Demitasse cup and saucer.

Unmarked, probably French,
c. 1920 – 1930s.

Cup with unusual handle;
smoky frosted body, lovely
molded leaves, style of
Lalique or Verlys.

$125.00 – 150.00.

Demitasse cup and saucer.

Unmarked, possibly Baccarat,
c. 1930s.

Fluted; garlands of gilt
enameled flowers.

$100.00 – 125.00.

Demitasse cup and saucer.

Lobmeyr, c. 1885 – 1900.

Footed panel-cut cup with fat square handle, 2⅔"w x 2"h, saucer 4⅞"; hand-painted lady holding a basket of flowers, enameled scrolls and flowers.

$400.00 – 450.00.

Close-up of portrait.

Demitasse cup and saucer.

Unmarked, probably Czechoslovakian, c. 1950s.

Straight cup with squarish handle; cobalt blue with gold leaf frieze, jeweling.

$75.00 – 100.00.

Teacup and saucer.

Bohemian, c. 1930s.

Tapered cup; cobalt blue with enameled applied flowers.

$200.00 – 225.00.

Demitasse cup and saucer.

Bohemian, c. 1930s.

Can cup, aqua with gold overlay.

$175.00 – 200.00.

Demitasse cup and saucer.

Mary Gregory type, c. 1940s.

Pedestal cup with fat loop handle; hand-painted white figure of a little boy on cup, swirls on saucer on deep green ground.

$75.00 – 100.00.

Teacup and saucer.

Unsigned, attributed to Meyr's Neffe, c. 1920s.

Footed paneled cup with fat loop handle; floral decor in the Lobmeyer style, enameled figure of man and woman.

$375.00 – 425.00.

Demitasse cup and saucer.

Moser type, c. 1920s.

Glass cup with panels of dark red alternating with clear glass, gilt decoration.

$100.00 – 125.00.

Coffee cup and saucer.

Unsigned Moser, c. 1885.

Straight cup with fat loop handle; enamel foliate decor and 24kt gold.

$375.00 – 425.00.

Teacup and saucer.

Unsigned Moser, c. 1900.

Footed cup with fat loop handle; 24kt gold in a six-pointed star form, engraved floral decor.

$300.00 – 350.00.

Demitasse cup and saucer.

Unsigned Moser, c. 1885.

Footed cup with fat loop handle; Rubina coloration with composition gold/enamel decor.

$375.00 – 425.00.

Teacup and saucer.

Signed Moser, c. 1885, deeply etched signature.

Low cup with fat loop handle, scalloped saucer; cased and engraved floral decor.

$400.00 – 450.00.

Demitasse cup and saucer.

Unsigned Moser, c. 1885.

Cup with curled feet, loop handle; alternating 24kt gold patterns with enameled foliate decor.

$400.00 – 450.00.

Teacup and saucer.

Unsigned Moser, c. 1885.

Footed cup with fat loop handle; rare applied glass acorns and enameled oak leaves on cranberry.

$1,100.00 – 1,300.00.

Teacup and saucer.

Unsigned Moser, c. 1885.

Pedestal quatrefoil cup and saucer; composite gold/enamel foliate decor, delicate cranberry shading.

$375.00 – 425.00.

Teacup and saucer.

Unsigned Moser, c. 1885.

Footed cup with fat loop handle; delicate floral composite gold/enamel decor.

$350.00 – 400.00.

Teacup and saucer.

Unsigned Moser, c. 1885.

Quatrefoil cup; Islamic and floral enameled decor, beautiful turquoise color.

$425.00 – 475.00.

Teacup and saucer.

Unsigned Moser type, c.1925.

Rounded cup with loop handle; 24kt gold leaf panels, composite gold/enamel scrollwork and high relief floral decor, six-pointed star decor on saucer.

$375.00 – 425.00.

Demitasse cup and saucer.

Unsigned Moser, c. 1885.

Wonderful tooled rim, high curled handle; clear shaded to blue, floral decor.

$425.00 – 475.00.

Teacup and saucer.

Unsigned Moser, c. 1885.

Pedestal cup with square saucer; Rubina glass with engraved and gilded decor.

$400.00 – 450.00.

Teacup and saucer.

Unsigned Moser, c. 1885.

Pedestal cup with loop handle, square saucer; lacy white enameled decor on Rubina glass.

$400.00 – 450.00.

Teacup and saucer.

Unsigned Moser, c. 1885.

Pedestal quatrefoil cup and saucer; white enamel decor on green shaded to clear, 24kt gold flower in saucer well.

$325.00 – 375.00.

Teacup and saucer.

Unsigned Moser, c. 1890.

Footed cup with wavy molding, strange handle; composition gold/enamel floral decor on green.

$325.00 – 375.00.

Demitasse cup and saucer.

Unsigned Moser, c. 1990.

Slightly flared cup with fat loop handle; enameled birds on cup, gold alternating with cranberry.

$400.00 – 450.00.

Teacup and saucer.

Unsigned Moser, c. 1885.

Pedestal cup with loop handle; alternating 24kt gold leaf swirled panels with enameled foliate and scroll decor.

$375.00 – 425.00.

Teacup and saucer.

Unmarked Moser, c. 1895 – 1905.

Flared cup with fat loop handle; cranberry shaded to clear, gold/enamel decoration.

$300.00 – 350.00.

Coffee cup and saucer.

Unsigned Moser, c. 1895 – 1905.

Pear-shaped cup with large loop handle; cranberry with gold foliage.

$200.00 – 250.00.

Demitasse cup and saucer.

Unmarked Moser,
c. 1895 – 1905.

Waisted cup with gold
angular handle; cranberry,
gold/enamel swirls.

$300.00 – 350.00.

Demitasse cup and saucer.

Signed Moser,
c. 1895 – 1905.

Quatrefoil cup and saucer;
amethyst shaded to clear,
heavy gilt scrolls and leafy
design.

$300.00 – 350.00.

Demitasse cup and saucer.

Unmarked Moser,
c. 1895 – 1900.

Slightly tapered cup with fat
C-shaped handle; cobalt
blue shaded to clear, gold
foliate decoration.

$300.00 – 350.00.

Demitasse cup and saucer.

Unmarked Moser,
c. 1895 – 1900.

Pedestal cup with fat C-shaped handle; aqua shaded to clear, enameled flowers and gold swirls.

$300.00 – 350.00.

Demitasse cup and saucer.

Venetian glass, c. 1950s.

Footed flared cup with curled loop handle, deep saucer; white latticino, green swirls.

$175.00 – 225.00.

Demitasse cup and saucer.

Venetian glass, c. 1950s.

Footed flared cup with curled loop handle, deep saucer; white swirls and aventurine.

$175.00 – 225.00.

Demitasse cup and saucer.

Venetian glass, Murano
sticker, c. 1950s.

Straight-sided cup;
enameled flowers and heavy
gold paste swirls.

$75.00 – 100.00.

Demitasse cup and saucer.

Venetian glass, Murano,
c. 1950s.

Tapered cup with fat loop
handle; cobalt blue glass
with gold overlay, applied
flowers.

$125.00 – 150.00.

Demitasse cup and saucer.

Signed Heisey,
c. 1901 – 1930.

Octagon cup with pointed
loop handle; green with rare
sterling silver overlay decoration.

$125.00 – 150.00.

Teacup and saucer.

Heisey, Newark, Ohio, c. 1945 – 1950.

Footed cup with modified ring handle; #1540 Lariat pattern.

$30.00 – 40.00.

Teacup and saucer.

Heisey, Newark, Ohio, c. 1935 – 1940.

Paneled cup with angular handle; #1503 Crystolite pattern.

$35.00 – 45.00.

Demitasse cup and saucer with Steuben insert.

J. E. Caldwell, c. 1914.

Sterling silver liner and saucer, gold aurene calcite insert.

$300.00 – 350.00.

Tea cup and saucer.

Unmarked, pressed glass, c. 1870 – 1930s.

Flared cup with low fat loop handle; Kings Crown thumbprint, gold bands.

$55.00 – 65.00.

Teacup and saucer.

Unmarked, pressed glass, c. 1910 – 1930s.

Rounded cup with fat ribbed loop handle, ruffled saucer; amber with stippled decoration.

$40.00 – 50.00.

Teacup and saucer.

Unmarked, Depression, c. 1930s.

Eight-paneled cup with squarish handle, octagon-shaped saucer; amethyst, pattern is Modern tone type.

$15.00 – 25.00.

Chocolate cup and saucer.

Unmarked pressed glass, c. 1870 – 1910.

Footed cup with squarish handle; intricate saw tooth and floral pattern, light amber.

$40.00 – 55.00.

Teacup and saucer.

Unmarked pressed glass, c. 1930s.

Rounded cup with fat angular handle; arch design with beads around the rim of the saucer and under the rim of the cup.

$25.00 – 30.00.

Teacup and saucer.

Unmarked pressed glass, c.1930s.

Slightly flared cup with angular handle; sawtooth pattern.

$40.00 – 55.00.

USEFUL INFORMATION

Some people are just born collectors, and they thrive on the hunt. It's a satisfying moment when they find the item they are collecting for a price they are willing to pay. Some buy antique cups and saucers to decorate and beautify their homes; a collection of cups and saucers can brighten up a dull area in a living room. Some buy cups and saucers to use daily or at parties. Still others collect antique cups and saucers as an investment. Whatever the reason for collecting cups and saucers, this pastime is exciting and a lot of fun!

GETTING STARTED

When asked why she started her collection, cup and saucer collector Brenda Pardee says, "I have always found cups and saucers very interesting. The shapes and hand painting to me are a masterpiece, but without the canvas."

Another cup and saucer collector, Lisa Cilli, explains, "It all started for me when I was given a bouquet of flowers in a cup and saucer that had been glued together when I was 14 years old. Well, that cup and saucer started it all. On an April Fool's day not long after the flowers had been discarded, I convinced my mom to use this cup and saucer when she had some of my aunts coming over to tea. Well, imagine the intended victim's surprise when the saucer came up with the cup when she went to drink. I started holding teas myself, and one cup led to another, but always I use the joke cup to get the conversation started."

Everyone has a story to tell about how they got started collecting. Make some decisions before you start. Decide what direction you want your collection to take. Do you want to buy durable cups and saucers to use, or beautiful cabinet cups and saucers to display? Do you want full size teacups, demitasse, or miniatures?

Visit shops, exhibits, auctions, and museums. Start by buying a good marks book. Jump right in and buy a cup and saucer from a reputable dealer, and study it. Talk to dealers at antique shows, especially dealers that specialize in cups and saucers, and sound them out. Visit a museum, and look at its collection of cups and saucers. You may find them uninteresting, or you may be hooked.

Collector Linda Gibbs inherited a wonderful collection of miniature cups and saucers from her grandmother, who started collecting them before Linda was born. "My grandmother must have been a very discriminating collector, as she had examples of the very best of English and European manufacturers. She also had a wide variety of the many different styles, such as tea bowls, coffee cans, tea and coffee cups and saucers."

Another collector, Karen Piper, started her collection when she bought some cups and saucers for her mother-in-law. "I got so attached to them and enjoyed them so, that when the time came to give them to her I found that I missed having them, so I decided to get some cups and saucers of my own."

KNOWLEDGE

Knowledge is the key that opens the door for you. You should know how to determine both the maker and how old a piece is. Know the difference between the just average and the great, even between those made from the same company. Know the difference between a decal and a hand-painted piece. The value of a hand-decorated piece is much more than that of one with a decal. It would be good to know the difference. It is a wise collector that can tell an authentic piece from a reproduction. It's helpful to know the age and rarity. Know how to examine a piece to determine its condition.

The knowledge you can gain from books on porcelain and porcelain manufacturers and antiques in general is unlimited. Each porcelain company has an interesting history of how it got started and the people responsible for it. This makes for some fascinating reading. You will be able to identify the different types of cups and saucers and their shapes. You will know why one cup and saucer costs so much more than another. With a good marks book you can tell when and where the piece was made.

When asked if she would take the same approach if she were starting her collection today, Karen Piper states, "The only thing I would do differently would be to educate myself more. Books, books, and more books. Lots of reading and lots of learning." B r e n d a Pardee says, "I would do the same thing, but learn a little more history. "

AVAILABILITY

Cups and saucers can be found in many places. Occasionally, a rare cup and saucer can be found at a garage sale, flea market, swap meet, or house sale. Collector Joyce Geeser found a rare eighteenth-century Chelsea tea bowl in an antique mall, taped together with two other cups for $6.00. It is worth $700.00 – 800.00.

You can add to your collection by buying at antique shows or shops. This is a way to talk to the dealer and ask questions about the items. It also gives you a chance to tell the dealer what you are looking for and how to get in touch with you if it is found.

Lisa Cilli tells us she finds cups and saucers at tag sales, garage sales, flea markets, and antique markets. Brenda Pardee says, "I find cups and saucers at auctions, flea markets, garage sales, antique shops, and eBay."

Auctions are also a source to use to add to your collection. You get to see and handle the item when you preview the auction items. It can help you determine the overall condition of the item. Remember, it is the buyer's responsibility to check for the condition of a piece.

INTERNET BUYING

A new method of adding to your cup and saucer collection is buying on the Internet. There are many advantages to buying on the Internet. You can shop in the comfort of your home with your reference materials handy, and you have access to a world-wide market.

It also has its down side. There is no better way to buy an antique than a hands on inspection. Buying on the Internet has altered the ability to do this. Buying from a photograph and a short description has significantly changed the way we buy and sell antiques.

One of the problems is that some sellers don't have a good knowledge of what they are selling, and therefore have a hard time describing the items. A buyer must read between the lines. Certain conditions could be missed, such as the item is sold "as is" and cannot be returned or returned only if the item is not as described. A buyer should know the return policy of the seller.

Another problem is that the seller does not always know of or fails to see a defect, such as a hairline crack or a chip. Excessive crazing is also a problem on some English cups and saucers. Some sellers don't know what crazing is, and don't mention it in their description. Also, some sellers don't mention that an item is second quality or less.

The buyer should ask questions before bidding on an item. If there is any doubt about the piece, don't buy it.

When buying on the Internet, consider the postage costs. The United States Postal Service (USPS) has increased the postage rates, and it has to be added to the buyer's winning bid price. This could be significant, especially if the piece has to travel a long distance from the seller. Insurance rates have also gone up.

PACKAGING

A tremendous problem that is often overlooked with Internet buying and selling is the packaging and shipping of the item. Proper shipping is not just the responsibility of the seller. Buyers need to know how to pack as well. Occasionally, a package may have to be returned to the seller for one reason or another, and it should be packed with care.

A shipper's first consideration is finding a good box. It's okay to reuse a cardboard box if it is in good condition. All of the old tape and tags should be removed. The box should be big enough to hold the item, yet small enough that it can be fitted into an outer box. Cups and saucers are fragile and should be double boxed. There should be space enough to encase the item completely in the box, top and bottom and on all sides. It makes little sense to put the item in a box and not cover the top and bottom, as these are the most vulnerable areas. A layer on top and bottom are just as important as the sides. Remember, the top and bottom have to be protected by more than a thin layer of cardboard.

Styrofoam peanuts are good to use, as they offer a lot of protection and are light in weight. Paper offers good protection if enough is used, but it weighs much more than the peanuts. Shredded paper is fine as long as you don't have to be the one who opens the package; it makes quite a mess. Cups and saucers should be wrapped in bubble wrap, and enough should be used to protect the item.

Many shippers think that the more tape used to encase the item, the more the item is protected. This is not the case. A small piece of scotch or masking tape is enough to keep the bubble wrap in place on the item. Sometimes there is so much clear tape on the piece, it has to be cut off. This act itself could cause some damage to the item.

Proper packing could eliminate a lot of unnecessary problems. Filing a damage claim is a hassle; it takes a long time to receive the insurance money, and it means an extra trip to the shipping facility. The goal of the shipper is to have the package arrive at its destination safely. A lost antique is a loss to the world forever.

CONDITION

The condition of a cup and saucer is a critical factor for the collector to consider. Excessive wear, cracks, chips, hairlines, or crazing can affect the value. Sometimes crazing and hairline cracks are invisible to the naked eye, but can be detected with a jeweler's loupe or by the sound. Tap the cup or saucer with your finger, and if you get a dull thud, it is probably damaged. If it rings like a bell, it should be okay.

Rosenthal cup with hairline crack.

Dresden cup and saucer with rim chip on saucer.

Carlton Ware saucer with crazing.

Make sure the cup and saucer are a matched set. Are the patterns identical? Are the colors the same? Cobalt blue is a difficult color, and shades vary from navy blue to almost black. Are the marks and pattern numbers the same? Some companies produce the same pattern for many years, and it's very possible to find a matching cup and saucer with different date marks. This doesn't bother some collectors; it's an individual decision.

Carlton Ware cup and saucer with two different patterns.

Hutschenreuther Black Knight demitasse set, two different shades of cobalt blue.

Herend large breakfast cup on regular teacup size saucer.

Pieces that have gilding sometimes show gilt wear. If it's excessive, it could take away from the appearance and value. It depends on the age and rarity of the piece.

Inside of Carlton Ware cup with gilt wear.

Carlton Ware cup and saucer, excessive wear on saucer.

Just a few words on restoring a damaged antique. Unless you are very talented in this area, you shouldn't attempt it. Nothing looks worse that a badly glued piece or one that has been "touched up" with paint. A good restorer is hard to find and is expensive. If a seller tells you it's easy to fix, ask yourself, "If it's so easy to fix, why didn't he/she fix it?" A good policy is to not buy anything that is not in near perfect condition.

KPM cup, poorly restored handle.

Most china cups and saucers were from dinner sets and were made to be used. Many are able to go right into a dishwasher, but to play it safe, hand wash them with a mild soap and hot water. It's a good idea to put a towel down in the sink. Wash, and then gently spray with a hose if available. Dry and put them away right away in a safe storage area.

If you have a cup and saucer with a glazed surface and it has an old price sticker mark, it can be removed with a glass cleaner or nail polish remover. A bisque or unglazed piece is a little harder to clean. Use only water and a mild soap.

DISPLAY

We asked our collector friends how they displayed their cup and saucer collections. Brenda Pardee tells us, "I have custom built cabinets and rails and hooks and free glass standing cabinets, and I still don't have enough room!"

Cup and saucer collection displayed in beautiful custom built cabinets, courtesy of Brenda Pardee, Bloomville, New York.

Wall cup and saucer display, courtesy of Brenda Pardee, Bloomville, New York.

Mary Davis had custom built-in cabinets made for her lovely blue and white collection. It makes a striking display in her home.

Cobalt blue and white trios attractively displayed in custom built-in cabinets, courtesy of Mary Davis, San Diego, California.

"I have a couple of cabinets, but want to add more because so many of my sets are just carefully packed in boxes. I am working on a project of photographing each and every set and putting the photos in an album to share," states Karen Piper.

Lisa Cilli explains, "I laugh with this question. It is ALL over the house…mainly in the dining room."

Linda Gibbs' grandmother displayed her lovely miniature collection in special glass-topped tables made of wood with wells just deep enough to display them. Gibbs has two of these beautiful display tables, which make an attractive decoration in her living room.

MARKS

The marks on a cup and saucer are extremely important to the collector. They tell the company's name, where and when a piece was made, often the pattern name or number, and sometimes the artist's initials. In the case of a cup and saucer, the mark is found on the bottom of each piece.

It cannot be stressed enough that if you are a collector at any level and can afford only one book, it should be a marks book. Most porcelain makers used different marks at different periods of their existence. You might wish to refer to the bibliography in this book for some of the excellent marks references available today.

PATTERN NUMBERS

There may be marks on the bottom of some cups and saucers besides the backstamp of the manufacturer. For instance, some potteries put pattern numbers on the bottom of the wares.

The first factory to mark its wares with pattern numbers was probably Derby. A Derby pattern number was referenced in correspondence written in 1784.

Pattern numbers were originally intended to help ceramics manufacturers identify the different designs and to assist with the processes of invoicing and pricing. The factory would keep a pattern book with all its patterns described and colored alongside their reference numbers. Even when a factory used such a system, there might still be some designs that remained unnumbered.

Pattern numbers should be considered as just one of several potential clues to be noted when trying to identify which factory was responsible for a particular piece, especially if it is not marked with a trademark.

TALLY MARKS

Other marks on the underside of cups and saucers are called tally marks, and were applied by the painter either as a personal mark or to represent the work of a group of employees.

Because factory workers were most often paid by the amount of pieces produced, they used to keep a tally or total of the items produced by a particular person or group.

REPRODUCTIONS

The rarer and more valuable the antique, the more likely it may have been faked or reproduced. Many unscrupulous people try to dupe the public and make a quick dollar. Many buyers have been fooled into buying an item because the marks have been either altered or reproduced. The best advice is to know the person from whom you are buying. Again, the golden rule applies — if it doesn't feel right or look right, don't buy it.

There are a number of early reproductions in the marketplace, and some of these still bring high prices because they are of excellent quality. Most Sevres cups and saucers available today were actually made or decorated by Paris shops or even by German manufacturers. The Royal Vienna beehive mark is probably one of the most reproduced marks ever. The company ceased operation in the 1860s, so there are few authentic Royal Vienna pieces turning up today.

Dresden cups and saucers have not been reproduced in any great quantities; however, a few fake pieces have recently shown up on the Internet. An example is a quatrefoil cup and saucer with alternating courting scenes and flowers. It is poorly painted and gilded, and the porcelain body is heavy and coarse. The mark is a poor rendition of a fish. Another cup and saucer in the same style has a cobalt band with gold squiggles. It is very poor quality, and the mark has illegible entwined initials.

Many cups and saucers are being sold on the Internet with fake Limoges marks. One fake mark is a fleur-de-lis with "Limoges" printed in blue or gold inside a ribbon. Another fake mark is a crown with two crossed swords and "Limoges" underneath, printed in gold.

New cups and saucers are being made in Taiwan with a gold crown and "Royal Vienna" underneath. A number of fake Nippon marks have surfaced and are included in Joan Van Patten's *Collector's Encyclopedia of Nippon Porcelain Fourth* and *Fifth Series*.

PROTECTION

As your collection gets larger and more valuable, you should think about getting some kind of insurance. It's expensive, but so would your loss be in a fire or if someone robbed you.

Look into the possibility of having a "Fine Arts" rider added to your homeowner's insurance policy. You many need an outside appraiser to determine the value of your antiques. If so, make sure you get the service of a qualified appraiser with recognized credentials. Any antique dealer may be able to recommend one, or you can find one in the telephone book in the yellow pages.

RECORD KEEPING

As your collection grows, it will be hard to remember what you paid for a given item and when you acquired it. If you have computer skills, you can list your entire inventory, and put it on a floppy disc for safekeeping.

If a computer is not your "cup of tea," another way to keep track of your collection is to photograph it. This could also be valuable for insurance purposes.

MORE OBSERVATIONS FROM COLLECTORS

WHY DO YOU ENJOY COLLECTING CUPS AND SAUCERS?

"Collecting cups and saucers is fun! I like to see what kinds I can find. The find of a rare and unusual one is a great feeling," states Brenda Pardee.

Karen Piper says, "Collecting cups and saucers is challenging and rewarding. I love the fact that some of these beautiful sets survived for one-hundred-plus years. I always wish that they could talk and tell their story of where they have been, and who they were with."

When Lisa Cilli was asked why she enjoyed collecting, she said, "It gives me pleasure. Tea has been such a part of my family; it was the one grownup thing I would do with my grandmother and mom. We would always share a cup of tea, and I was allowed to sit with the grownups, and they would let me talk, and the best part is, they listened. It made me feel like such a young lady."

Linda Gibbs collects cups and saucers for the sheer pleasure and beauty of them. She buys what is attractive to her and what she can afford. "I look forward to the day that I have time to learn a little bit about each of the companies that I have in my collection. I feel I would appreciate them that much more."

WHAT ADVICE WOULD YOU GIVE THE BEGINNING COLLECTOR?

Lisa Cilli advises, "Start really slow and get a feel for what you like…buy only what you like, and if something really jumps out at you, and you walk away and keep thinking about it, go back and get it."

"Please read and learn much about porcelain and the makers marks, and ask many questions from a long time collector," suggests Brenda Pardee.

Karen Piper says, "Collect whatever you enjoy. Don't get caught up in trendy collecting. There are many beautiful sets to be had that are not popular favorites. READ — buy books and learn; education is your greatest asset in identifying and collecting cups and saucers."

Japanese teacup and saucer with adorable teacup faeries by artist Kate Hiddleston, Bend, OR, courtesy of Karen L. Piper, Martinez, CA.

1. Aynsley, c. 1891 – 1901

2. Aynsley, c. 1930s.

3. Belleek Pottery Co. (David McBerney & Co.), c. 1927 – 1941.

4. Bloch, M. E., Paris, c. 1868 – 1887.

5. Booths Ltd., c. 1930s.

6. Brown-Westhead, Cauldon, c. 1891.

7. Capodimonte (Ginori), over-glaze blue mark, c. 1890s.

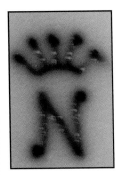

8. Capodimonte (Ginori), under-glaze blue mark, c. 1890s.

9. Carlton Ware, (Wiltshaw & Robinson), c. 1920 – 1925.

10. Carlton Ware, c. 1925+.

11. Castleton China Inc., c.1940+.

12. Cauldon, c. 1920s, made for Henry Morgan, Montreal.

13. Coalport, c. 1881-1890, made for Davis Collamore & Co., New York.

14. Coalport, c. 1891 – 1920.

15. Coalport, c. 1949 – 1959.

16. Coalport, c. 1960+.

17. Colclough China Ltd., c. 1945 – 1948.

18. Copeland, Spode, c. 1891 – 1900, made for Wigmore Daniell, London.

19. Copeland, Spode, c. 1891 – 1920s, made for Davis Collamore & Co., New York.

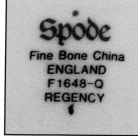
20. Copeland, Spode., c. 1950 – 1960s.

21. Royal Crown Derby, c. 1900.

22. Royal Crown Derby, c. 1913.

23. Royal Crown Derby, c.1940, made for Tiffany & Co., New York.

24. Crown Devon (S. Fielding), c. 1930 – present.

25. Crown Dorset Pottery, c. 1920 – 1937.

26. Crown Ducal (A. G. Richardson Co.), c. 1915 – 1925.

27. Crown Ducal (A. G. Richardson Co.), c. 1930 – present.

28. Crown Staffordshire, c. 1906 – 1920s.

29. Crown Staffordshire, c. 1950s.

30. Double Phoenix Co., Japan, c. 1960s.

31. Doulton & Co., Burslem, c. 1882 – 1890.

32. Doulton & Co., Burslem, c. 1891 – 1902.

33. Doulton & Co., c. 1930s.

34. Dresden, Donath & Co., c. 1893 – 1916.

35. Dresden, Hamann, c. 1883 – 1893, blank made by Silesian Porcelain Factory.

36. Dresden, Heufel & Co., c. 1900 – 1940.

37. Dresden, Hirsch, F., c. 1901 – 1930.

38. Dresden, Klemm, R., c. 1891 – 1914.

39. Dresden, Lamm, A., c. 1891 – 1914.

40. Dresden, Thieme C., c. 1901 – present.

41. Dresden, Wolfsohn, H., c. 1843 – 1883.

42. Edelstein Porcelain Factory, c. 1934 – present.

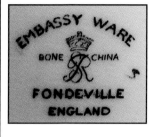

43. Embassy Ware, Fondeville, England, c. 1950s.

44. Foley China (E. Brain & Co.), c. 1948 – 1963.

45. Fraureuth Porcelain Factory, c. 1898 – 1935.

46. Furstenberg Porcelain Manufactory, c. 1950s.

47. Ginori, Firenze Ware, c. 1900 – 1920.

48. Ginori, C. 1920 – 1930s.

49. Gort, USA, c. 1950s.

50. Grosvenor, c. 1920s.

51. Hammersley, c. 1887 – 1912, made for Davis, Collamore & Co.

52. Hammersley, c. 1912.

53. Hammersley, c. 1939 – 1950s.

54. Haviland, Johann (Waldershof), c. 1939 – present.

55. Herend, c. 1900.

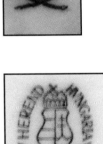

56. Herend, c. 1941.

57. Hutschenreuther, C. M., c. 1918 – 1945, made for Hahn, Berlin.

58. Hutschenreuther, C. M., c. 1950 – 1963.

59. Hutschenreuther, Black Knight, c. 1925 – 1941.

60. Hutschenreuther, L., c. 1920 – 1967.

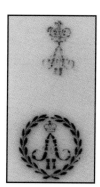

61. Imperial Russia, St. Petersburg, c. 1855 – 1881.

62. Japan, Imari mark, c. 1920 – 1930s.

63. Japan, Kutani mark, c. 1880s.

64. Japan, Kutani mark, c. 1890s.

65. Japan, Satsuma-style mark, c. 1930s.

66. Jones, George & Sons, c. 1889.

67. Jones, George & Sons, c. 1920s, made for Ovington Bros., New York.

68. KPM (Royal Porcelain Manufactory, Berlin), c. 1837 – 1844.

69. KPM (Royal Porcelain Manufactory, Berlin), c. 1849 – 1870.

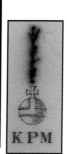

70. KPM (Royal Porcelain Manufactory, Berlin), c. 1870 – 1890.

71. KPM (Royal Porcelain Manufactory, Berlin), Iron Cross mark, c. 1915 – 1918.

77. Lenox, c. 1930 – 1940s, made for Joseph Horne Co., Pittsburgh, Pennsylvania.

72. Krister Porcelain, c. 1904 – 1927.

78. Limoges, Ahrenfeldt, C., decorated by Paris Studio CRA, c. 1900s.

73. Leart, Brazil, c. 1950s.

79. Limoges, B & F, imported by L. S. & S., c. 1890 – 1920.

74. Lenige, USA, c. 1930s.

80. Limoges, B & H (Blakeman & Henderson), c. 1890s.

75. Leningrad Factory, Russia, c. 1950 – 1960s.

81. Limoges, Barney, Rigoni & Langle, c. 1904 – 1906.

76. Lenox Belleek, c. 1906 – 1924.

82. Limoges, Bawo & Dotter, c. 1896 – 1900.

83. Limoges, Borgfeldt, G., c. 1906 – 1930.

84. Limoges, D & Co., c. 1894 – 1900.

85. Limoges, GDM (Gérard, Dufraisseix & Morel), c. 1882 – 1900.

86. Limoges, Guerin, W., c. 1890 – 1932.

87. Limoges, Haviland, c. 1876 – 1880.

88. Limoges, Haviland, c. 1894 – 1931.

89. Limoges, Haviland, c. 1904 – 1925, made for Bailey, Banks & Biddle, Philadelphia.

90. Limoges, Klingenberg, c. 1900 – 1910.

91. Limoges, Legrand, c. 1920s.

92. Limoges, Laporte, R., c. 1891 – 1897.

93. Limoges, Latrille Freres, c. 1899 – 1913.

94. Limoges, L. S. & S. (Straus, Lewis & Sons.), c. 1890 – 1925.

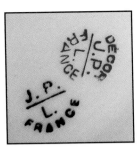

95. Limoges, Pouyat, c. 1876 – 1890.

96. Limoges, Redon, M., c. 1882 – 1890.

97. Limoges, LeTallec, Paris, c. 1950s.

98. Limoges, T & V (Tressemann & Vogt), c. 1892 – 1907.

99. Meissen, c. 1850 – 1924.

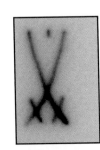

100. Meissen, c. 1924 – 1934.

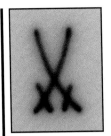

101. Meissen, c. 1930s.

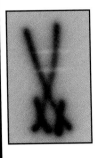

102. Meissen, second quality, c. 1930s.

103. Melba China Co., c. 1933.

104. Midwinter, W. R., c. 1932 – 1941.

105. Minton, c. 1863 – 1872, for Phillips & Pierce, London.

106. Minton, c. 1891 – 1902.

107. Minton, c. 1912 – 1950.

108. Mottahadeh, c. 1980s.

109. Nippon, blue maple leaf mark, c. 1891 – 1921.

110. Nippon, c. 1891 – 1921.

111. Nymphenburg, c. 1961 – 1968.

112. Occupied Japan, Ardalt, c. 1945 – 1952.

113. Old Royal Bone China (Sampson Smith), c. 1945 – 1963.

114. Paragon China Co., c. 1932 – 1939.

115. Paragon China Co., c. 1939 – 1949.

116. Pickard, c. 1912 – 1918.

117. Pickard, c. 1925 – 1930, Thomas blank.

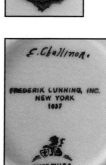

118. Pickard, c. 1935 – 1939, made for Frederick Lunning, New York.

119. Pirkenhammer, c. 1950s.

120. Prov Saxe, E.S. Germany, c. 1902 – 1938.

121. Queen Anne (Shore & Coggins), c. 1959 – 1966.

122. Radford, Samuel, c. 1938 – 1957.

123. Regency China Ltd., c. 1953 – present.

124. Retsch & Co., Wunsiedel, Germany, c. 1953 – present.

125. Rosenthal, c. 1898 – 1906.

126. Rosenthal, c. 1910.

127. Rosenthal, c. 1926.

128. Rosenthal, c. 1930.

129. Rosenthal, c. 1938.

130. Rosenthal, c. 1945 – 1949 (U. S. Zone Mark).

131. Rosenthal, c. 1946, includes silver decorator's mark.

132. Rosenthal, c. 1949 – 1954.

133. Rosenthal, c. 1960s.

134. Rosina China Co., c. 1948 – 1952.

135. Royal Albert ('Thomas C. Wild & Sons), c. 1917.

136. Royal Albert (Thomas C. Wild & Sons), c. 1945+.

137. Royal Bayreuth, c. 1887 – 1902.

138. Royal Bayreuth, c. 1916 – 1930s.

139. Royal Chelsea, c. 1950s.

140. Royal Copenhagen, c. 1920s.

141. Royal Grafton (A. B. Jones & Sons), c. 1957 – 1960.

142. Royal Stafford China, c. 1950s.

143. Royal Stafford China, c. 1950s.

149. Satsuma, Japan, c. 1920s.

144. Royal Standard (Chapmans Longton Ltd.), c. 1949 – present.

150. von Schierholz, c. 1920 – 1930s.

145. Royal Stuart (Stevenson, Spencer & Co. Ltd.), c. 1951+.

151. Schumann, Carl, c. 1918.

146. Royal Tara, Ireland, c. 1942 – present.

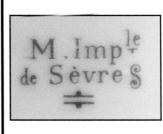

152. Sevres, First Empire, c. 1804 – 1809.

147. R.S. Germany, c. 1904 – 1920.

153. Sevres, c. 1840s.

148. R.S. Prussia, c. 1904 – 1938.

154. Sevres-type mark, possible Paris decoration, c. 1870s.

155. Sevres-type mark, probably Paris decoration, c. 1890s.

156. Shelley Potteries, Ltd., c. 1940 – 1966.

157. Spode, Josiah, c. 1850s.

158. Stouffer, c. 1930 – 1940s.

159. Thomas, F. Porcelain Factory, c. 1908 – 1953.

160. Tirschenreuth Porcelain Factory, c. 1969 – present.

161. Tuscan (R. H. & S. L. Plant Ltd.), c. 1950s.

162. Vienna-type, beehive mark, c. 1890s.

163. Vienna Porcelain Factory Augarten, c. 1923 – 1960s.

164. Wachter, R., Bavaria, c. 1930s.

165. Wedgwood, c. 1901 – 1920.

166. Willets Belleek, c. 1879 – 1912.

167. Royal Worcester, c. 1870 – 1890s, made for Goode & Co., London.

172. Worcester Grainger, c. 1870 – 1989.

168. Royal Worcester, c. 1887, made for J. E. Caldwell, Philadelphia.

173. Worcester Grainger, c. 1889.

169. Royal Worcester, c. 1898.

174. Worcester Grainger, c. 1901.

170. Royal Worcester, c. 1925, made for Hardy Bros. Ltd.

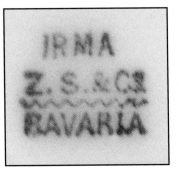

175. Zeh, Scherzer & Co., Bavaria, c. 1880 – 1900.

171. Royal Worcester, c. 1940.

BIBLIOGRAPHY

Anderson, Digby. "In My Cups." *National Review*, June 23, 1993.

Archambault, Florence. "Lots of Variety for Collectors of Occupied Japan Items." *Antiques & Auction News*, December 5, 1997.

Bagdade, Susan and Al. *Warman's American Pottery and Porcelain*. Radnor, Pennsylvania: Wallace-Homestead Book Co., 1994.

_____. *Warman's English and Continental Pottery and Porcelain*. Iola, Wisconsin: Krause Publications, 1998.

Baldwin, Gary D. *Moser Artistic Glass Edition Two*. Marietta, Ohio: The Glass Press Inc., 1997.

Battie, David. *Guide To Understanding 19th and 20th Century British Porcelain*. Wappingers' Falls, New York: Antique Collector's Club, 1994.

Bergesen, Victoria. *Bergesen's Price Guide to British Ceramics*. London, England: Barrie and Jenkins, 1992.

Bishop, Gordon, of the Star-Ledger. *Gems of New Jersey*. New York: Prentice-Hall Inc. 1985.

Bowman, Barbara. "All About Pots de crème." *Internet: http://gourmetsleuth.com/pdcinfo.htm.*

Brewer, Susan. "Lomonosov Porcelain." *Internet: http://www.worldcollectorsnet.com/lomonosov/htm.*

Cushion, John. *Continental Porcelain*. England: Reed Consumer Books Ltd., 1998.

_____. *An Illustrated Dictionary of Ceramics*. New York, New York: von Nostrand Reinhold Co., 1974.

Dean, Patricia. *The Official ID Guide to Glassware*. Orlando, Florida: The House of Collectibles, 1984.

DeLorme, Rita. "A Sampling of Children's Tea Sets," *The Antique Trader Annual of Antiques for 1976*.

Faÿ-Hallé, Antoinette and Mundt, Barbara. *Porcelain of the Nineteenth Century*. New York: Rizzoli International Publications, 1983.

Field, Rachael. *Buying Antique Pottery & Porcelain*. Radnor, Pennsylvania: Wallace-Homestead Book Co., 1987.

Fleming, Joan. "The Miniature World." *The Antique Trader Annual of Articles for 1974*.

Forrest, Tim. Consulting Editor Paul Atterbury. *The Bullfinch Anatomy of Antique China and Silver*. New York, New York: Little, Brown and Company, 1998.

Gaston, Mary Frank. *The Collector's Encyclopedia of Limoges Porcelain*. Paducah, Kentucky: Collector Books, 1980.

Godden, Geoffrey. *Encyclopedia of British Pottery and Porcelain Marks*. London, England: Barrie & Jenkins, 1986, 1991.

_____. *Godden's Guide to English Porcelains*. Radnor, Pennsylvania: Wallace-Homestead Book Co., 1978, 1992.

_____. *Godden's Guide to European Porcelains*. London, England: Cross River Press, 1993.

_____. *Antique Glass & China*. New York: Castle Books, 1966.

BIBLIOGRAPHY

Goss, Steven. *British Tea and Coffee Cups, 1745-1940*. England: Shire Publications, Ltd., 2000.

Gottschalk, Mary. "Loving Cups," *Savvy Education*, April 2000.

Grandjean, Bredo L. *Flora Danica*. Copenhagen, Denmark: Hassing Publisher, 1950.

Gura, Judith B. "The Sevres Manufactory," *Antiques & The Arts Weekly*, December 12, 1997.

Harran, Jim and Susan. *Collectible Cups and Saucers, Identification & Values*. Paducah, Kentucky: Collector Books, 1997.

_____. *Collectible Cups and Saucers, Identification & Values Book II*. Paducah, Kentucky: Collector Books, 2000.

_____. *Dresden Porcelain Studios, Identification & Value Guide*. Paducah, Kentucky: Collector Books, 2002.

Henderson, James D. "Chocolate Pots." *Antique Trader*, January 5, 2000.

Henkin, Stephen. "Porcelain Perfect Vienna Augarten Manufactory," *World and I*, November 2000.

Hertiage, Robert J. *Royal Copenhagen Porcelain Animals and Figurines*. Atglen, Pennsylvania: Schiffer Publishing, Ltd., 1997.

Hill, Susan. *Crown Devon: The History of S. Fielding & Co*. England: Jazz Publications, 1993.

Huxford, Sharon and Bob. *Schroeder's Antiques Price Guide 21st Ed*. Paducah, Kentucky: Collector Books, 2003.

Jones, Joan. *Minton*. Haverfordwest, England: C. I. T. Printing Services.

Keefe, John Webster. *Paris Porcelains*. New Orleans Museum of Art, 1998-1999.

Kirillova, Julia. "Russian Tea Ceremony." *Internet: http://cave.csuhayward.edu/CAVE/HOME/JuliaKirillova/Tea.html*.

Kovel, Ralph and Terry. *Kovels' New Dictionary of Marks*. New York, New York: Crown Publisher, Inc., 1986.

Lee, Yun. "Fit to a Tea." *Prevention*, May 1996.

Lehner, Lois. *Lehner's Encyclopedia of U. S. Marks on Pottery, Porcelain & Clay*. Paducah, Kentucky: Collector Books, 1988.

Marple, Lee. "Reinhold's Toys." *Internet: http://www.rsprussia.com/articles/reinhold's_toys.html*.

McClinton, Katharine Morrison. *Collecting American 19th Century Silver*. New York, New York: Charles Scribner's Sons, 1968.

Messenger, Michael. *Coalport 1795-1926*. Woodbridge, Suffolk, England: Antique Collectors Club, 1995.

Miller, Judith. *Miller's Antiques Encyclopedia*. London, England: Reed Consumer Books Ltd., 1998.

Potter, Lillian. "Silver Overlay Yesterday and Today." *Antique Trader*, June 7, 2000.

Punchard, Lorraine. *Playtime Pottery & Porcelain from the United Kingdom & the U. S.* Atglen, Pennsylvania: Schiffer Publishing Co., 1996.

Rainwater, Dorothy T. *Encyclopedia of American Silver Manufacturers*. West Chester, Pennsylvania: Schiffer Publishing Co., 1986.

Ramsey, L. G. G. *The Complete Color Encyclopedia of Antiques*. New York: Hawthron Books, Inc., 1962.

Reid, Michael. "Hunt is on for Quality Nostalgia." *The Australian*, November 18, 2000.

Rendall, Richard. "Samson á Paris." *Antique Trader*, May 3, 2000.

Rinker, Harry L. *Dinnerware of the 20th Century: The Top 500 Patterns*. New York: The Crown Publishing Group, 1997.

Rohrs, Kirsten. "Mottahedeh, Mildred; Mottahedeh & Co." *Classic American Home*, October/November 2000.

Röntgen, Robert E. *Marks on German, Bohemian & Austrian Porcelain*. Exton, Pennsylvania: Schiffer Publishing Ltd., 1981.

_____. *The Book of Meissen*. Exton, Pennsylvania: Schiffer Publishing Ltd., 1984.

Royal Copenhagen Ltd. *Flora Danica*. Copenhagen, Denmark: Royal Copenhagen, December, 1989.

Saks, Bill. "George Jones Master Potter." *Antique Trader*, January 20, 1999.

Sandon, John. *Antique Porcelain*. Woodbridge, Suffolk, England: Antique Collector's Club, 1997.

Sargeant, Margaret. *Royal Crown Derby*. Buckinhamshire, England: Shire Publications, 2000.

Schroy, Ellen Tischbein. *Warman's Glass*. Radnor, Pennsylvania: Wallace-Homestead Book Co., 1992.

Schwartz, Jeri. *The Official ID & Price Guide Silver and Silver Plate*. House of Collectibles, 1989.

Shoemaker, Ted. "Bavaria's 'White Gold' at 250 Years." *Antiques & Auction News*, August 7, 1998.

Snyder, Jeffrey B. "Tea Sets for the Middle Class, 1825-1945." *Antique Trader*, March 7, 2001.

Stoughton, Beverly Foss. "The Art of Miniature Display." *Hobbies*, May 1981.

Stout, Frappa. "Tea Time," *USA Weekend Lifestyle*, March 15-17, 2002.

Twitchett, John and Bailey, Betty. *Royal Crown Derby*. London, England: Antique Collectors Club Ltd., 1976.

Van Patten, Joan F. *The Collector's Encyclopedia of Nippon Porcelain*. Paducah, Kentucky: Collector Books, 1979.

Ware, George W. *German and Austrian Porcelain*. New York: Crown Publishers, 1963.

Watson, Rosamund Marriott Wilson. "The Art of the House." *Internet: http://www.burrows.com/booknotes/tea.html*.

Woodworth, William. "Tea, Heaven on Earth." *Internet: http://www.holymtn.com/tea/japanesetea.htm*.

_____. "Belleek — Irish Porcelain." *Internet: http://www.ladymarion.co.uk/book/introduction.htm*.

_____. "A Brief History of Paragon China" and "Paragon Collectibles." Paragon International Collectors Club. *Internet: http://www.btinternet.com/~paragoncollector/history/history.html*.

_____. "Carlton Ware — Potted History." *Internet: http://www.gales.co.nz/about.htm*.

_____. "CCH — Art History." *Internet: http://www.classicalhomeschooling.org/greek.html*.

BIBLIOGRAPHY

_____. "China Company Histories." China Traders Replacement Services. *Internet: http://www.chinatradeers.com/gen/companylist.htm.*

_____. "Coffee Fundamentals." *Internet: http://www.lucidcafe.com/fundamentals.html.*

_____. "Cooper-Hewitt Museum." *The Smithsonian Illustrated Library of Antiques,* 1983.

_____. "Crown Staffordshire Porcelain Co. Ltd." *Internet: http://www.metcentral.co.uk/steveb/allpotters/322a.htm.*

_____. "E. Brain & Co. Ltd." Foley China Works, Fenton. *Internet: http://www.metcentral.co.uk/steveb/features/brain.htm.*

_____. "The Elegance of Silver Overlay." *Internet: www.myantiquemall.com/silveroverlay.html.*

_____. "Flora Danica, the Dinner Set." *Internet: http://www.pictures.dnlb.dk/Homepage/info02eng.html.*

_____. "Focus on Colclough." *Internet: http://www.focusoncolclough.co.uk.html.*

_____. "Hammersley Bone China." *Internet: http://parcels-of-time.com/hammersley.html.*

_____. "The History of Coalport." *Internet: http://www.coalport.co.uk/history.htm.*

_____. "The History of Royal Worcester." *Internet: http://someonespecial.com/cgi.../worcesterhistory.html.*

_____. "Japanese Antique Porcelain—an Overview." *Internet: http://www.jexports.com/porcelainguide.html.*

_____. "Manufacturer: Bodley. Edwin Bodley, Burslem, Staffordshire Potteries, c. 1875-1892." *Internet: http://www.tbc.gov.bc.ca/culture/schoolmet/victoriana/objects/manufacturers/puanu14.html.*

_____. "My Dancing Cupboard's Tea Encyclopedia;" WNN-C Shizuoka. *Internet: http://www.shizuoka.isp.ntt-west.co.jp.*

_____. "Pot Web: Ceramic Online, Ashmolean Museum." *Internet: http://potweb.ashmol.ox.ac.uk/potchron6a.html.*

_____. "Royal Copenhagen." *Internet: http://www.royalcopenhagen.com/.*

_____. "Special Uses for Glass." *Internet: http://www.umich.edu/~kelseydb/Exhibits/WondrousGlass.html.*

_____. *Spode: The Story of the Original Fine Bone China.* Spode, Church Street, England.

_____. "Tea Facts." The Stash Tea Company. *Internet: http://www.stashtea.com.*

INDEX

377

APPENDIX

Schroeder's ANTIQUES Price Guide

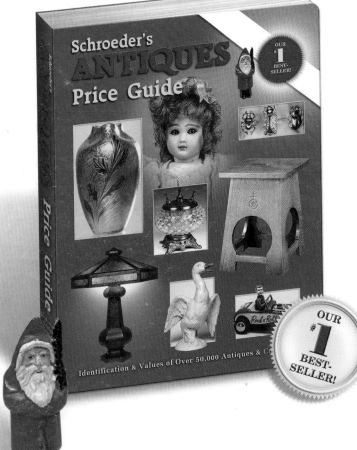

...is the #1 bestselling antiques & collectibles value guide on the market today, and here's why...

• More than 450 advisors, well-known dealers and top-notch collectors work together with ou editors to bring you accurate information regard ing pricing and identification.

• More than 45,000 items in almost 500 cate gories are listed along with hundreds of sharp orig inal photos that illustrate not only the rare and unusual, but the common, popular collectibles a well.

• Each large close-up shot shows importan details clearly. Every subject is represented with histories and background information, a feature not found in any of our competitors' publications.

• Our editors keep abreast of newly develop ing trends, often adding several new categorie a year as the need arises.

If it merits the interest of today's collector, you'll find it in *Schroeder's*. And you can feel confident that the information we publish is up-to-date and accurate. Our advisors thoroughly check each category to spot inconsistencies, listings that may not be entirely reflective of market dealings, and lines too vague to be of merit. Only the best of the lot remains for publication.

COLLECTOR BOOKS
P.O. Box 3009 • Paducah, KY 42002–3009

192-3